(Pic: Judi Dransfield)

INNER CITY SOUND

edited by
CLINTON WALKER
design by
MarjOrie McIntosh
cover artwork by
Philip Brophy

Verse Chorus Press   VCP   Portland, London, Melbourne

Back cover photo credits: The Saints' Chris Bailey and Ed Kuepper (Joe Borkowski); Rob Younger of Radio Birdman (Annette Jones); the Go-Betweens (courtesy, Rough Trade); Nick Cave (courtesy, Missing Link); the Triffids (Francine McDougall); the Hoodoo Gurus (Francine McDougall); Clinton Walker presenting 'Know Your Product' on 3RRR-FM in Melbourne, 1978 (Bruce Milne).

The editor and the publisher wish to thank all those who supplied photographs and gave permission to reproduce copyright material in this book. Every effort has been made to contact all copyright holders, and the publishers would like to hear from any copyright owners from whom permission was inadvertently not obtained. In such cases, we will be pleased to obtain appropriate permission and provide suitable acknowledgment in future printings.

The original edition of this book was published in 1982 by Wild & Woolley Pty. Ltd, Australia.
   This expanded edition was published in 2005 by Verse Chorus Press.

Printed in the USA by Thomson-Shore

♼ Printed on Fortune Matte paper, manufactured by Stora Enso with minimum 10% post-consumer recycled content and processed chlorine free.

Library of Congress Cataloging-in-Publication Data

Inner city sound / edited by Clinton Walker ;
   design by Marjorie McIntosh ; cover artwork
   by Philip Brophy.-- Expanded ed.
     p. cm.
   Discography: p.
   Includes index.
   ISBN 1-891241-18-4 (alk. paper)
   1. Punk rock music--Australia--History and
   criticism. 2. Rock groups--Australia.   I. Title:
   Subtitle on cover: Punk and post-punk in
   Australia, 1976-1985. II. Walker, Clinton.
   ML3534.I56 2005
   781.66'0994--dc22
                        2005042319

ACKNOWLEDGMENTS (1981): For all their help and encouragement the editor would like to thank:
Graham Aisthorpe, Eric Algra, Debbie A, Debbie Baer, Alan Bamford, Patrick Bingham-Hall, Vicki Bonnett, Joe Borkowski, Neil Bradbury (Vox), Philip Brophy (CHCMC, New Music, Innocent Records), David Browne, Harry Butler (DNA, Wombat Turd), Jillian Burt, Stuart Coupe, Cathy Croll, Terry Darling (Choke), Matt Dickson (Self Abuse), Judi Dransfield, Tom Ellard (Terse Tapes), Keith Glass (Missing Link), the Go-Betweens, Jim Goodwin, Lyn Gordon, Mark Green, Roger Grierson (Double-think, Green Records), Russell Handley (Doublethink, Basilisk Records), Catherine Hardy, Ian Hartley (Spurt, ICE), Laughing Clowns, Peter L and Linda, Lisa, M Squared, Marjorie, Tanya McIntyre, Andrew McMillan, Bruce Milne (Au Go Go Records, *Fast Forward*), Philip Morland Management Group of Companies, Peter Nelson, Linda Nolte, Jules Normington (Phantom Records), *RAM*, Donald Robertson *(Roadrunner), Rolling Stone*, Marie Ryan, SCAM Management, Robyn Stacey, Al Webb (Cleopatra Records), Ken West, Kim Williams, Pat Woolley, and Paul Fraser.

FOR THE 2005 EDITION: Thanks to Pat Woolley for finding a remaining mint copy that has formed the basis of this reprint; to Steve Connell of Verse Chorus Press, not only for suggesting we get the book back in print and for his scrupulous editing skills in doing that, but also for years of unstinting support and integrity. Thanks, again, to all the original contributors – many of whom remain friends, many others I've been glad to track down again – who are still so graciously making the book possible with their ongoing support and approval. Thanks especially this time around to Francine McDougall and John Foy, Francine for digging up some classic shots from the fabulous files of her previous life, and Foy for permission to reproduce some of his colour posters of the period that put a particular rock-art tradition in proper perspective: both these guys warrant books in their own right. Thanks also to Phil Brophy, Phil Turnbull, Tom Ellard, Evil Graham Lee, Jim Paton, Stuart Coupe, Iain Sheddon, Judi Dransfield Kuepper, Brett Myers, and Keith Aisthorpe. Extra thanks to Judi, again, and to Mark Louttit and Joe Borkowski, for standing up when it counted. Also to Dave Studdert, whose incidental compliment went a long way at a time when I needed it.

Dedicated to "Debbie A", and to the memory of Graham Aisthorpe, David McComb, Tracy Pew, and Ben Wallace-Crabbe.

CONTENTS

THE TRIFFIDS: David McComb rehearses in Perth, 1980, aged 18. (Pic: Kim Williams)

CHEAP THRILLS AND THE ANIMAL HOUR PRESENTS A NEW WAVE ROCK SHOW
3SW
WITH THE REALS
OBSESSIONS
+ THE BOYS NEXT DOOR
FRYDAY AUG 19th
ETHEL HALL 50c
NO ALCOHOLIC BEVERAGES
→ 8 PM
YEY HUP! YEY HUP! YEY HUP! YEY HUP! YEY HUP! YEY HUP!
→ NOT SO YEY HUP!

VOIGT/465 playing at the Darling Harbour construction site in Sydney, before they were moved on by the police, October 1978 (Pic: Peter Nelson).

PREFACE (2005)

"That's about the only advantage a man gets from growing old — he can tell the young fellows they don't know anything."

– Banjo Paterson

"Let's make some new mistakes I'm sick of all the old ones."

– The Celibate Rifles

It is with mixed feelings that I write this preface to a new edition of *Inner City Sound*.

It wasn't just because I heard it was being sold on eBay and elsewhere at collector's prices, or that bootleg copies were available at a shop in Melbourne, that I knew the book needed to get back in print. No, it was *Mojo* magazine that did it, when they put out a special issue on post-punk. It burned me up the same way the same thing used to burn me up back when: you always hear about all the English and American bands — but what about the Australian bands?! That's why I did *Inner City Sound* in the first place back in 1981.

I have always taken pride in the fact that *Inner City Sound* had an impact. For me, the book was a personal prehistory-as-it-happened of a cultural revolution, but it became something else — I have even heard it called the bible! I once met a woman who had a treasured, tattered old copy full of autographs. I like the idea of books that get passed around, *used*. It's no way to make a living, but it is tapping the passion.

My feelings are mixed, though, because *Inner City Sound* causes me as much embarrassment as pride. I cringe now at the shrillness of my prose, the sternness of my judgements, the incoherence of some of my arguments. I was such a determined iconoclast, I could barely make the link back to the Stooges, let alone the Missing Links, let alone any broader social context. A few years ago when Radio Birdman first re-formed to play the Big Day Out, I read an interview in which guitarist Deniz Tek railed: "Did Clinton Walker write that *Inner City Sound* book? . . . He has always been biased against us and for the Saints to the point of gross journalistic dishonesty. A pitiful fellow." I could hardly blame him. I had no

concept of objectivity. Although there is a solid intellectual basis to *Inner City Sound* — that punk reinvented a future for rock, and that Australia hadn't got due credit for its role in that process — I allowed my emotions, personal taste and allegiances to run all over it.

At the time I put the book together, I was living in a big share house in Woomerah Avenue, Darlinghurst. They were great days, the last sunny days, I see now, of a certain innocence in my life. *Inner City Sound* was possible because a lot of people shared my belief in it, shared a belief in the music – and we all gave to the cause. If it ever seems like propaganda, well, that's because we felt we were fighting a war. We were kids.

On delivery of Marjorie McIntosh's terrific finished artwork, I got the back half of my advance — $500, a fair whack — and I flew out for London a couple of weeks later, in early December 1981. I wasn't on hand for the launch of the book in January 1982, when Ken West put on a special Birthday Party/Hunters & Collectors/Pel Mel show at Sydney Uni that made the social pages of the *Sun-Herald*!

I returned to Australia in 1983, rite of passage completed, and resumed what I've always called my anti-career in writing. Already, *Inner City Sound* seemed light years away; now, it is half a life ago. Until recently, I had only a tattered copy belonging to my wife to refer to; I could never remember if it was 'Sound' or 'Sounds.'

It has been a bittersweet experience preparing this new edition. It is sobering to flick through it now – what a sea of faces! – and count the casualties. I don't just mean, say, Jeremy Oxley, who sadly succumbed to schizophrenia long before Sunnyboys songs were licensed for car ads. Drugs and bitterness took a far heavier toll, claiming lives in equal portions.

But I don't want to dwell only on the downside – the successes have been many. It's not just a matter of the bands that quite obviously 'made it,' either. A considerable number of the contributors to *Inner City Sound* – many of whom remain close friends – have also gone on to distinguished careers and are now

renowned artists, photographers, chefs, filmmakers, teachers, journalists, poets, novelists, editors, designers, crime writers, concert promoters and (dare I say it) record company executives. One of the biggest rewards of putting this book together again was getting back in touch with some great people I hadn't spoken to in years, and being reminded of others who have disappeared, or are gone forever.

On the recent Go-Betweens' album, *Oceans Apart*, Robert Forster begins the song "Darlinghurst Nights" (with no apologies to Kenneth Slessor): "I opened a notebook, it read 'The Darlinghurst Years' / I snapped it shut, but out jumped some tears / I didn't have to read it, it all came back . . ." He goes on to give a personal account of a brief period in history, Darlinghurst in the early 1980s. Each of us has our own version of history, but in this case Forster's correlates quite closely with my own, as he gives a roll call of friends' names: "Marjorie and Kim . . . , Debbie, Bertie" and "Joe [who] played the cello."

"People came and went," Forster goes on to say. And in many ways I consider myself lucky just to have come out of it all in one piece. Quite a few people were lost to the times. I hope that this book can at least pay tribute to their work and showcase their legacy.

Success is such a spurious concept, in any case. I can understand now why a band like Tactics, for example, hit a commercial brick wall – their sound was coarser than sandpaper! But that doesn't diminish their greatness. As long as Ian Rilen's still alive, after all, anything is possible!

And that's the thing: I was so impressed when I pulled out the old records to be reminded just how great so many of them were (and pleasantly surprised, too, to be honest, because I've never really wanted to wallow in nostalgia over the recordings of the period). It's gratifying, of course, that there is still interest in the book, but even more so given that so much of the music stands up. It was a period of extraordinary confluence, small in scale but very intense, and the music that exploded outwards had a sense of urgency and gameness that still rings irresistibly true. And it *did* change things; I can't resist the temptation to get in at least one "I told you so."

A new, final chapter has been added to this edition. The original book ended in 1981 because that's when it was compiled. But the narrative didn't actually end in 1981. It ended, I can now see with hindsight, around 1984/1985. By then, most of *Inner City Sound*'s major characters and themes had resolved themselves, whether in the way that first-generation musicians reshuffled into a third wave of bands like the Hoodoo Gurus, Died Pretty, Beasts of Bourbon and others, or second-generation bands like the Go-Betweens, Scientists and Triffids followed the Birthday Party into European exile; or in the closure of the Seaview (previously the Crystal) Ballroom, the rise of the free street press and the inception of the Australian independent charts; or in Nick Cave and Ed Kuepper going solo. "The Last Days of the Seaview" hopefully extends the spirit of what precedes it in reprinting a selection of my writing from the period (untouched by any revisionism), along with photos and graphics.

There's a famous story about Sekret Sekret. The truly wonderful Sekret were approached at one point in the early 1980s by Regular Records, a label half way between an indie and a major. The band met with head honcho Martin Fabinyi and he offered them a deal, but when they walked out of his office they weren't exchanging any high-fives — they were filled with dread, as if he'd sentenced them to death or something, and saying to one another, how are we going to get out of this? Certainly, the remnants of the band that re-emerged a decade later as the Cruel Sea were quite ready to create their own opportunities.

And so the food chain continued. Because that's what all this became, perhaps — just another show-business story. But that was later. *Inner City Sound* is about the first Australian stirrings of a cultural revolution whose DIY egalitarianism and adventurous spirit is still held up as a great pop ideal, and which has given us so much great and enduring music.

—C.W., May 2005

In the gallery to the right are brief biographies of some of the many talented people who contributed to this book. Thanks again to everyone involved, then and now.

GRAHAM AISTHORPE did more than anyone to document the early '80s scene in Brisbane. He founded the magazine *Backstage*, and was an inspiration to all who encountered him. He died in 1988 . . . **ERIC ALGRA** is an Adelaide photographer who is just as passionate as ever about his two great loves, photography and rock'n'roll . . . **JANET AUSTIN** lives in Melbourne and works for Lonely Planet publishers . . . **PATRICK BINGHAM-HALL** is one of Australia's leading architectural photographers, with extensive domestic and international publications to his credit . . . **JOE BORKOWSKI** "played the cello through those Darlinghurst nights" . . . **PHIL BROPHY** does stuff (philipbrophy.com) . . . **JILLIAN BURT** was a South Australian country girl who had to see the world before realising Melbourne is her home . . . **STUART COUPE** believes that in the right place at the right time, any band can be the greatest on the planet, and his contributions to this book reflect that. His label Laughing Outlaw Records is releasing the *Inner City Soundtrack* CD . . . **TOBY CRESWELL**, is a former member of Surfside 6, and was the publisher/editor of *Rolling Stone* and then *Juice*. The most recent of his four books is *1001 Songs* . . . **CATHERINE CROLL** lives in Newcastle and works in community cultural development and planning. Her photography was featured in the Sunnyboys' 2004 2CD retrospective and as part of Perth's 2005 Artrage festival. . . . **MATT DICKSON** produced the fanzine *Self Abuse* before founding jazz label Spiral Scratch Records . . . **JOHN FOY** made the transition from record store assistant to poster designer to Red Eye Records label founding father . . . **BRAD FRANKS** lives in the Hunter Valley where he continues to paint and love music . . . **JIM GOODWIN** doesn't take photos any more. He lives in Melbourne with his partner and two teenagers; he is a chef and still attends music events frequently . . . **LYN GORDON**, one of the original team that created *Vox* magazine, was also a musician who went on to play with Ash Wednesday's Modern Jazz and later sang with Crashland . . . **DARE JENNINGS** recently made a squillion when he sold his surf'n'streetware label Mambo . . . **ANNETTE JONES** was the Wednesday night 'door bitch' at the Sussex Hotel in Sydney ("$1.00, please"), inspired to shoot photos for a few years by the vitality of the people in the audience as much as those on stage . . . **JUDI DRANSFIELD KUEPPER** still goes to gigs and takes pics. She lives in Brisbane with Ed Kuepper and their two sons; she teaches at QUT and continues to develop her aesthetic . . . **MARK LOUTTIT** worked predominantly doing live sound production for early '80s Brisbane bands like the Go-Betweens, the 31st, Screaming Tribesmen, Pork and Zero. He also co-published *Ratsack* with Michelle McIntyre and Tex Perkins . . . **SHANE MALONEY** is one of Australia's top crime writers, with five Murray Whelan novels to his credit . . . **FRANCINE McDOUGALL** traded her still camera for filmmaking and today is perhaps the only Aussie in 'Aussiewood' that Aussieland itself is unaware of; she has directed several movies including the wonderful *Sugar & Spice* . . . **RICHARD McGREGOR**, a former member of Surfside 6, is a China-based foreign correspondent . . . **TANYA McINTYRE** married a Zambian-Australian and went to live in Botswana, where she was a volunteer youth worker and art teacher, before returning to a post at Melbourne University . . . **ANDREW McMILLAN** retired from rock journalism in 1988 and moved to Darwin. He is the author of four books, a play and award-winning poetry . . . **BRUCE MILNE** started behind the counter of Missing Link Records before founding Au-Go-Go Records. He conceived the cassette magazine *Fast Forward* and worked briefly for EMI in the 90s before founding a new label of his own, In-Fidelity . . . **PETER MILNE** published *Fish in a Barrel*, a collection of his photographs of Nick Cave and the Bad Seeds. He is now a teacher in Brisbane . . . **PHILIP MORLAND** managed the Young Charlatans and Two Way Garden . . . **PETER NELSON** retired from music writing in 1981 at the age of 23, having decided his opinions were unseemly and irrelevant. The best writer of the lot turned his back on it! . . . **LINDA NOLTE** took photographs of Darlinghurst's rock demi-monde before fulfilling a deeper ambition to see a snow leopard in the wild . . . **KATHLEEN O'BRIEN** traded her camera for the written word. She has published a Dolly novel, and her first feature film script has just completed shooting . . . **CRAIG N. PEARCE** is a music writer, now specialising in jazz . . . **DONALD ROBERTSON** was publisher/editor of *Roadrunner* from go to whoa, and then ran *Countdown* magazine, before joining the Australian Broadcasting Authority . . . **ROBYN STACEY** is an artist whose beautiful and haunting images blur the boundaries between photography, technology and dreams . . . **ED ST. JOHN** was the editor of *Rolling Stone* and subsequently Managing Director of BMG Records in Australia . . . **KEN WEST** managed Voigt/465, then became a concert promoter. He created the Big Day Out, which he still runs . . . **KIM WILLIAMS** hung up his typewriter for a guitar. He wrote the Scientists' seminal "Swampland," released a bunch of stuff as the Summer Suns, and currently works with the White Swallows, Bashful, and the Love Letters.

INTRODUCTION

For too long Australian rock, like the very fibre of the country, has been almost totally subservient to Anglo/American imperialism. Since 1976, however, there has been a distinct movement which, for perhaps the first time, has moved closer towards an Australian rock of its own invention and identity. The sad part of it is that this simply hasn't been acknowledged in its homeland — a better response has come from overseas. Mainstream Australian rock continues to kow-tow to English and mostly American demands, is unoriginal and insignificant . . .

Australian punk/post-punk music is a vital and important force that hasn't been allowed to, but could and should dominate charts and hearts around the country.

True, much of this music would seem to have been initially inspired by similar stirrings in England and America, and to a certain extent it was. But equally it proves the adage that the mark of a truly significant movement is when similar things happen at the same time yet independently. It's a fact that the Saints were pioneers in the birth of punk worldwide, and concurrently in Australia "Oz-rock's" roots were being reassessed by Radio Birdman. These two bands, regardless of what they later may have become, in turn inspired other young Australian musicians. And the Inner City Sound (because it tends to manifest itself in the inner city because of lack of support elsewhere) grew from there.

Throughout the '50s and '60s, Australia produced a mere handful of rock/pop artists who defied the laws of convention and made original music, not just a carbon copy of English and/or American music. Only the Easybeats, the Loved Ones and the young Lobby Lloyde's bands come immediately to mind — but even then their impact is lessened (in Australian terms) by the enormous part young English and European migrants played in its creation. By the early '70s, a tradition was beginning to emerge in Australian rock, or "Oz-rock" — and what a repulsive one it was — Sunbury (another imported concept), Billy Thorpe, massively loud mindless boogie and gallons of beer. Good old boys indeed! This tradition unfortunately snowballed. In the mid '70s the Skyhooks were momentary if flawed relief. Then in 1976/77 punk reared its saviour's head. In England, in America, and in Australia. But Australia, of course, was unaware of this.

Australia was content with bland pop and putrid boogie. But it was content only because it had no choice. The major record companies dictate taste in Australia, and being what they are their taste is naturally very conservative. It wasn't so much that they were scared of punk, and rejected it for that reason, it was more that they were totally unaware of it, at least in its Australian incarnation. It's a classic illustration of the ignorance and colonialism of the majors in this country that when EMI Australia signed up the Saints late in 1976 it was only because they were ordered to do so by their head office in London. So while punk/post-punk music rapidly gained recognition in England, because the majors realized its potential (and what wasn't promoted by them was served perhaps more capably by new independents), in America and Australia the music remained distinctly underground.

There was then the strange case of Suicide Records, a label formed by "Oz-rock" big-wigs (a tacky copy of the English independents) which was an attempt to exploit the "new wave" in Australia. Somehow Suicide snared some good bands. But Suicide was burned badly because it didn't know how to handle its product, and the Oz-rock establishment hasn't returned for a second bite. Only Mushroom and Regular, it must be said, have dabbled.

As in America, punk/post-punk music was forced to fend largely for itself. Bands played their own gigs, made their own records. Fans wrote fanzines. Not even the rock press was particularly moved. The only real early support — and then there was resistance — came from student, public-subscription and occasionally ABC radio, and these sources have continued their support, to varying degrees, to this day.

Slowly the influence of the new wave infiltrated the Oz-rock establishment. But the ridiculous part of it was that it didn't look in its own backyard first, to its own new wave. It looked overseas, and then tried to duplicate in Australia what it saw happening there. Never mind that there was Australian punk/post-punk music in its own right; Australian old wave bands of any persuasion dressed up as English or American new wave bands, and that was the Oz-rock new wave. And it's still like that today.

While all the time the genuine article has been begging recognition. After all, who really wants to be on the dole? The Inner City Sound is not elite; it wants success. But — and here's the rub — it wants it without compromise. Because the Inner City Sound has a vision of its own (hacks don't), which must be fulfilled.

The Inner City Sound is, at best, one of commitment and passion, intelligence, individuality and innovation — and integrity. And if it ever seems at all inaccessible that's only because it's not exactly what the Oz-rock establishment has taught is accessible.

So a minor industry sprang up as an alternative to the Oz-rock establishment and today it flourishes, providing for a small but hungry audience. Bands play gigs away from agency-controlled venues, without having anything to do with an agency themselves, and then record independently. There are many recording studios and some pressing plants accustomed if not geared to independent productions. And now more and more bands are exploiting quick and easy home recording techniques, releasing cassettes rather than records. Independent labels take risks, and distribution is available to all. Specialist stores guarantee sales.

And the media's attitude has improved. Not the electronic media's of course, excepting the aforementioned radio stations, but the press. *Roadrunner* was established in 1978 by former fanzine writers, and somehow survives to this day. It is a nationally distributed monthly which is simultaneously erratic and reliable in its support of grass-roots musical causes. Fanzines themselves have seemed less significant in recent years, with a few exceptions. Oz-rock papers like *RAM*, *Rolling Stone* and *Juke* will at least devote some space to post-punk music now, and new ones like *Vox* are right behind it. Then there's *Fast Forward*, which is perhaps a world first as a regular cassette rock magazine, and it, of course, promotes the Inner City Sound vigorously.

Despite all this though, the Inner City Sound is still a long way from being taken seriously. Many bands have been lost to time without ever receiving their due.

The Oz-rock establishment rejects the Inner City Sound, probably because to them, it is without commercial potential. Bands like Models, Riptides, and Serious

Left: The Crystal (previously the Seaview) Ballroom, run by Delores San Miguela, was home to Melbourne's Inner City Sound. (Pic: Jim Goodwin)

Young Insects may have made some inroads. And yet while the Birthday Party are applauded loudly in England and now America (and ditto the Go-Betweens in England), Australia at large remains unaware of them simply because without major support they receive little exposure. And given that exposure their music couldn't fail to connect because it's not second-hand; it's fresh and vital. Just because they're obscure is no reason to continue to ignore them. These bands, and more, are making the true Australian rock (if indeed "rock" is still an issue) of the '80s. That's all there is . . .

In so many ways, this book has grown out of *Pulp*, a punk-inspired fanzine (one of the first in Australia) conceived by Bruce Milne and me in 1977. During that year we produced four issues; a fifth was almost completed when the concept folded early in 1978. *Roadrunner* magazine had been started in Adelaide, and we got involved doing what we could for them in Melbourne. But we both harboured an ambition to put out *Pulp* 5 somehow, sooner or later. It was a matter of finding a couple of hundred dollars — which, of course, we couldn't.

As time progressed, the projected *Pulp* 5 grew into *The Best of Pulp*. After shelving the project for a year or so, I reconsidered it as something close to what you see before you now. It was a matter of making it a reality . . .

Inner City Sound was designed to provide equal parts narrative (of sorts) and reference. The narrative is comprised of five chapters: 1976/77, 1978, 1979, 1980 and 1981, of material reprinted from different places, and over 200 photographs, both classics and those never before seen. The decision to reprint material rather than to write a history now was to avoid repetition, as I have written on the subject constantly for the past five years. Also, a story written at a particular time is a better indicator of that time than one written in retrospect. Although the stories are based on specifics, they are key specifics, and the rest of the tale is told by the pictures. In covering the early years, most of the material is drawn from fanzines (most prominently *Pulp*) because they were the only source there was. Fanzines like *Pulp* were largely superseded when *Roadrunner* was born and the mainstream rock press opened up. Material from 1979 onwards was culled from these sources. The pictures came from photographers, bands, and personal collections.

With this basis, the additional graphics and discography will provide a coherent and accurate overview of the Inner City Sound. Naturally it reflects my own tastes and prejudices, for which I make no apology. It's impossible not to be subjective. But within my parameters I've told the story as fairly as I saw it.

So what are my parameters? It's hard to say; my criteria were, in a way, very much intuitive. Perhaps the best way to describe them is to say what *Inner City Sound* is not about. Obviously, mainstream "Oz-rock," from Little River Band to Cold Chisel, has no place here. Nor do acceptable rebels: a number of pub bands who emerged in the late '70s – Midnight Oil, the Angels, Icehouse, INXS, Mi-Sex – are considered 'new wave', but all they did was adopt the trappings. Midnight Oil, for example, started out as long-haired hippies who played Yes and Jethro Tull covers, while Icehouse (when they were still called Flowers) were a 'punk jukebox' – and a laughing stock. The Bleeding Hearts could have been a genuine "new wave" band, but I saw them more as part of a transitional post-hippy/pre-punk push that in some ways paralleled pub rock in the English sense (as distinct from the Cold Chisel/Midnight Oil Australian model). In common with acts like Dr. Feelgood and Elvis Costello, an Australian wave of acts from the Sports, Paul Kelly and Jo-Jo Zep in Melbourne to Mental As Anything in Sydney led a return to rootsier, more direct influences. What was unique about them was a sort of art school quirkiness and/or keen sense of kitsch Australiana, which led to so-called 'ockerbilly' — all this would be a book in its own right. (Acts like XL Capris and Dave Warner's From the Suburbs, with their satirical bent, are also closer to this tradition than they are to punk.)

In my opinion, the Mentals, the Reels and the Church are the only bands making music for the mainstream that's half-way decent, even as 'Mushroom bands' like Hunters & Collectors and the Models are shifting the boundaries of pub rock. But none of those bands, even though they've all been described as 'new wave', is in need of greater exposure. *Inner City Sound's* purpose is to expose those bands which have missed the mainstream.

Ultimately though, the Inner City Sound will speak for itself.

—C.W., August, 1981

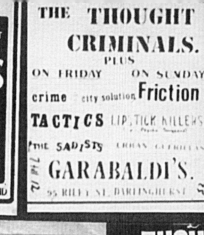

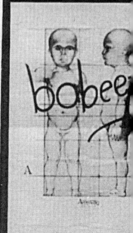
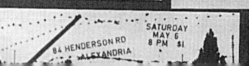

THE SAINTS VERSUS THE WORLD, PART ONE

The Saints are based on Petrie Terrace. And if you've ever been around Petrie Terrace, then you'll understand the forces behind their music.

Petrie Terrace is one of those inner city don't-go-near-there-Johnny areas. A notorious piece of turf in the midst of condemned buildings, railway yards and streets that lurk in the shadows, it is home to winos, derelicts, and vicious brawls at the Windmill Cafe. In short form matches reputation on neutral ground.

Opposite the police barracks there's a party going down. The Saints' home base has been converted into the 76 Club and every room is packed. The booze flows freely and dancing is automatic. You can't help it. In the lounge, the Saints are blasting out *Runaway*.

THE SAINTS (Pic: Joe Borkowski)

As you push the door out of your way the sound hits you, knocks you to the floor and stomps you through the boards. Without warning your brain is bombarded, shattered, trampled on and kicked, pounded and torn apart by grinding guitars and an iron-grate voice. The Saints are on.

Chris Bailey hangs onto the mike stand swigging from a bottle of Dewars, dragging on a cigarette and shouting in that voice that could fell a brick wall.

Ivor Hay's drum kit is about to fall apart. Bass player Kym Bradshaw and

THE SAINTS (above) live at Petrie Terrace. (Pic: Joe Borkowski)

This was punk? X-RAY-Z (below) were an Adelaide pub-rock band who moved to Melbourne and adopted a "poor image." They were signed by Mushroom and toured Australia supporting Lou Reed.

private label, Fatal Records. Despite the lack of rave reviews from the rock press here, it was treated favorably in the English and French rock papers.

Hundreds of copies of the single have been ordered from England, Europe and America. The reaction from overseas record companies has been nothing short of astounding.

But tonight, amidst piles of Telecom transcripts, the Saints are thrashing out *No Time* at their own party in their own house.

There are no two ways about it. The Saints are a pack of moronic punks who can't play a note, live at no fixed address and fit only into that category set aside for savage animals. That's the general concensus of opinion down at the local musicians' club where no one bothers to ask why animals turn savage in the first place.

Like son like father, the established promoters and managers of Brisbane treat the Saints like the plague, four vermin-carrying rodents with the sole aim of upsetting the status quo. And what's more, they're doing it.

"We're probably the most anarchist group around. We've got very high ideals. We could probably sell out and

guitarist Edmund Kuepper are working with the speed of a pair of well-oiled circular saws and it's down to the hot sweaty electric atmosphere of the greatest M.S.G. concert.

The freight train continues to tear down the line with *(I'm) Stranded,* their first single. It was recorded at the Window Studio and released on the band's

make a mint," says Edmund Kuepper.

But the word compromise doesn't come in the Saints' vocabulary. Consequently the band were forced to form their own record label, Fatal.

"We didn't wait for things to catch up in Brisbane. Rather than wait for trends, we've set them, in our music and our dealing."

And that doesn't go over too well with the established order. The Saints "just want to play the music. That's why we have these parties. At least this way things don't get heavy. Everyone is here because they like the band and they want to have a good time."

At present, the parties are the only times when their disciples can see the band. Defying the wishes of those who virtually have a stranglehold on the local industry can lead to only one thing: no work. Excommunication. And when a group such as the Saints actually have the nerve to get up and do something that writes the established clique off as a pack of amateurish clots, then all hell breaks loose.

In this light it's not too surprising that over the past ten months the Saints

RADIO BIRDMAN's Deniz Tek and Rob Younger. (Pic: Patrick Bingham-Hall)

have only been hired five times. Those who have dared to bypass the law of rainbow include (naturally) the university FM station, 4ZZZ, an art college, and the Communist Party. And although they're not pulling in much money, the Saints are getting their music across to those who want to listen.

(Pic: Joe Borkowski)

Despite the dedication of their fans, the Saints have gone almost unnoticed since their inception as Kid Gallahad and the Eternals some two years ago.

"We used to do the most obscure and wild stuff we could find. It's the same

Pre-BABEEZ (above) babee Gavin Quinn, aka Adam Punk, Adam Fire. The Babeez were one of Melbourne's first punkesque outfits.

↑→↑ (above right) appeared in Melbourne as early as 1975. In 1977 they were performing, among other things, a "punk set," which consisted only of covers of punk-roots material. They also organised the seminal Punk Gunk series of concerts. (Pic: Tanya McIntyre)

today really. We do some nice stuff because there is some beauty in the world. But basically we're just letting out a feeling and music is the best way of doing it.

"Rock and roll is meant to be revolutionary, aggression is always there . . . we're just opening up. We're definitely not into glorifying violence, but we are realists."

Unfortunately the realists are the only ones who bear to know what's actually going down, who can dissipate the hype from the truth, however tarnished that may be. And when the band is labelled alongside the Ramones, Iggy or Radio Birdman, then that doesn't go down too well either.

"I don't think that we're at all contrived. We don't use volume as a substitute for excitement, though we probably play twice as loud as most other local bands. It all boils down to realism. We haven't got the attitude of who-gives-a-damn-man. That's why I'd rather be a Saint than a sap."

Andrew McMillan

THE REALS were a loud, abrasive, Stooges-influenced almost pre-punk, punk band who evolved into the Negatives. (Pic: Peter Milne)

THE SURVIVORS (right) were dedicated enthusiasts and devoted craftsmen from Brisbane who recreated their fave 60's hits in a meaty, beaty, big and bouncy fashion.
(Pic: Patrick Bingham-Hall)

Radio Birdman by Janet Austin

Well, Radio Birdman's 'Rock'n'roll Soldier's' Melbourne tour is at an end. It's been a crazy week, but that's usual when Radio Birdman tour. A couple of venue cancellations and changes dampened spirits a little, but great nights like the concert at Martini's made up for most things . (except having to support TMG).

The tour co-incided with the imminent release of their album, which is now available through mail-order and import shops. Also featured on the tour was the band's most recent addition to their repertoire-'Rock'n'roll Soldiers', written by Ron Ashton and Dennis Thompson of the New Order. It summed up most of our feelings towards rock'n'roll with lines such as "Rock'n'Roll keep us alive" and "the war against the jive".

The most obvious difference in the appearance of the band was Rob's shorter hair and his lack of eye-makeup - a slight change of image.

While Birdman were in Melbourne I was fortunate enough to bore Deniz Tek (ld gtr) for a while with lots of silly questions. What do you ask one of Austalia's few guitar heroes? Well, if you have him over for tea you'd better have lots of bacon, eggs and chops covered in maple syrup around, or failing that, hot dogs and hamburgers.

Yes, Deniz is from America, Ann Arbour near Detroit to be exact. For some reason, after a visit to Australia in 1967, he decided to emigrate here in 1972. Well, I suppose the beaches and wildlands of sunny NSW are better than industrial Detroit if you like surfing. Before emigrating to this wonderful country, Deniz studied chemical engineering at Michigan University and played in fun bands like the Inducers', 'Suzy and the Pimps' and 'the Bluefront Blues Band'. He began playing the guitar (aged 13) after hearing the Stones

(common influence?), and the first riffs he learnt were 'Walk Don't Run' and 'Satisfaction'. It wasn't until Deniz became an Australian that he played paring gigs. He also began studying medecine at this time (he's now in his 5th year). So Birdman tour during his holidays and play weekends at the famous Oxford Funhouse, where they have priority in booking bands like the Hellcats' and 'the Psycho Surgeons'. In lean times Deniz has worked for a glue factory and as a computer operator, but he's never been on the dole.

In 1972, on arriving in Australia he joined a band called 'the Screaming White Hot Razor Blades' which played fun music ranging from the Bonzos to the Stones. It was together for about six months. Various line-up changes later found Deniz as lead singer in 'the Cunning Stunts', which later changed its name to 'T.V.Jones'. These bands were relatively well known around Sydney due to gigs at pubs, parties, dances and phone calls to important people (Bob Rodgers ?,John Laws?). A close friendship with a band called 'the Rats' and then the simultaneous break-up of both bands led to the

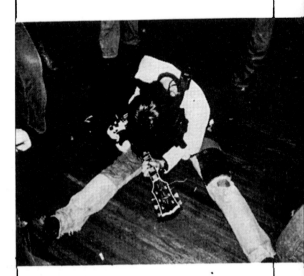

RADIO BIRDMAN

formation of a new band - yes, Radio Birdman in September '74, starring Deniz, Rob Younger (vcls), Ron Keeley (dms), Pip Hoyle (gtr& kybds) and. Carl Rorke on bass. With Carl's departure from the band, Warwick Gilbert (lead gtr in the Rats) was recruited and Chris Masuak, a friend of the band and schoolmate of MC Johnny, later replaced Pip Hoyle. The band was picked up by RAM as almost proteges after winning RAM's 'Battle of the Bands' contest. This coddling was inhibiting in some ways for the band, but useful for press coverage and publicity. To be classed as discoveries after such pasts led to inaccuracies on RAM's part. RAM over-emphasised the Detroit influence on the band, describing their music as being 'high-energy jams'. Now that the band has established itself and amassed almost a cult following in both Sydney and Melbourne, they are concerned with escaping from being labelled as 'New Wave' ('cos they're not new) and punks ('cos they're not). Such terms are writers' attempts to pigeon-hole rock'n'roll into generalizations, made particularly obvious when none of the so called 'punk' bands classify themselves as such. RAM's classification of Radio Birdman as being punk or new wave was their way of promoting them as a 'group of today' thereby making it hip to dig them (as they used to say). When the band was formed, in 1974, music was weighed down with a heavy dependence on musical expertise and resultant snobbery and boredom in music. Radio Birdman were different 'cos they weren't serious musos as such, and played good old rock'n' roll with power and effort. Their songs were short and fast without lots of boring technicalities.

That's how their music appeared then. Now, thanks to a return to rock'n'roll (new wave or otherwise), Birdman are receiving the attention they deserve. But Birdman certainly aren't simple, due to both Deniz' and Chris' amazing guitar playing and their use of off-beat rhythm. The songs involve melodies and tunes in their writing rather than solely riffs.

I'm sure most of the new album will sound familiar to those who went to see Birman. It was cut in the States to get a crisper sound, which it certainly has. There are only a few overdubs and therefore the album manages to capture the energy of the band's live performances, unlike the EP. They recorded the album on the little-known Trfalgar label because, unlike with a big company, they are allowed maximum control. Wawick designs their graphics and they are allowed to take control of advertising, the album cover etc.. Like the EP, the album was recorded, pressed and financed on Trafalgar's time, to be paid back from sales. It was recorded in four sessions of two and three days over a period of almost a year, and cost around $7000. It seems odd that just as the album is released the band are hurrying back to the studios to record their next album. However, when it is considered that they last recorded about three months ago, and it takes

a year -- well, it's not so odd after all, is it?

You'll find Deniz' all time top ten records somewhere else in the mag, Here are some of his other faves: Paul Newman is his favourite actor, and 'Performance' his favourite film (isn't it everyones?). Of course, his favourite TV show is 'Hawaii 5 O'. His favourite Australian bands are 'the Loved Ones', 'the Hell Cats' and 'the Psycho Surgeons (what about Birdman -ed.). And why hasn't Radio Birdman been on 'Countdown'? "We won't conform".

As a last thought Deniz cries "I'd do anything for a proper American-style hamburger instead of the dog-food they put on buns here!" Thank-you Deniz.

PS Wasn't New Race on Flahez great!

Last Words

by Cee Walker

LINE UP - Andy - guitar
Mick - bass
Jeff - drums
Malcolm - vocals

PHOTO BY JOE O.

MALCOLM JEFF ANDY MICK

The beginning of this story sounds like the finish. The Last Words have played publicly only a few times, earning apathetic receptions; they have no prospect of playing in the future; they have no money; and their gear is literally falling apart. In short, they seem to be on a dead-end street.

And theirony of it all is that they are quite good. Actually, I'd call them the best working (sort of) unit I've seen since the Saints or Radio Birdman, and I've seen 'em all. The reason they're good is simple: they're 1977. Unlike their Sydney compatriots, who've lodged themselves firmly in 1973, the Last Words are NOW. They've used 1976 as a springboard.

The easiest way to describe their music would be to call it mid-way between the Saints and the Ramones, if such pigeon-holing is permitted. They're fast (at last a group as fast as they should be), simple, riffy, with aggresive vocals mouthing simplistic lyrics. The Last Words are by no means revolutionary (musically speaking), they're not geniuses, they're not wildly inventive, but they are a good, solid, '77 style punk outfit. They have no trouble powering through their mostly original repertoire, and sapping a song like 'Dream Lover' in the same way the Ramones do 'Let's Dance'.

Andy, who is a better than average guitarist (but still never does solos), does most of the writing. It's apparent he's learnt a few things from Ed Kuepper, but then that's not a bad thing, is it? He is augmented by bassist Mick and singer Malcolm, and it was when these three lads from Liverpool (Western Sydney, not England!) met ex-Brisbane Jeffry that the Last Words were formed.

Jeff is a drummer who is more like Keith Moon than Keith Moon, and this causes a lot of problems for the Last Words. It seems some people are, err, 'offended' by Jeff's behavior, and it's for this reason the Last Words are 'banned' from the Oxford Funhouse. The whole affair is really very silly, on both sides, and all I can say is that I want to see the Last Words on stage, anywhere, SOON, before they self-destruct.

As it is, some of the guys are becoming discouraged, and I'd hate to see them fall apart before they're given a chance. Because they really are good, believe me. You should be demanding to see them.

Right now, the Last Words are becoming desperate. They've been considering all sorts of attention getting stunts, like; advertising themselves in RAM magazine; beating up journalists, a la Sid Vicious; playing illegally on the Sydney streets; moving to Melbourne; recording a single (even though they can't afford it); or, at worse, breaking up.

But, if they can manage to stabilise themselves, they'll most probably record a single - maybe it'll get noticed in England.

Whatever happens though, the Last Words will emerge, in maybe a new form, a stronger group.

RADIO BIRDMAN had become a big attraction in Sydney, so much so that they were able to open their own venue —the Oxford Funhouse — where they could play unhindered by the rock establishment, as well as foster young talent like the PsychoSurgeons and the Hellcats. (Pic: Patrick Bingham-Hall)

THE HELLCATS (above, pictured: Ron Doron, aka Riggy, Ronnie Pop) were symptomatic of the Funhouse — with some proficiency, they played nothing but covers, in awe of Radio Birdman. (Pic: Patrick Bingham-Hall)

THE PSYCHOSURGEONS (left) were formed by Mark Taylor, who ran White Light Import Records (then THE record store in Australia. The PsychoSurgeons played as many Stooges and Ramones songs as they did their own, or all their other covers put together. (Pic: Patrick Bingham-Hall)

SURVIVORS/HITMEN

BALMAIN, SYDNEY, NOVEMBER 5

The Hitmen are really gonna knock you out. That was one of about fifty opening sentences that I thought of to explain the concert at Balmain Town Hall.

Playing with Brisbane band, The Survivors, the Hitmen produced a finely balanced set which left a few scorched ear drums and made a number of people actually realise what sweating's all about. The hall looked like an advertisement for Aeroplane Jelly, with flesh and perspiration the order of the night.

And why shouldn't they have that effect on the audience? The nucleus of the group consisted of Radio Birdman personel. There was Chris Masuak on guitar (away from the shadow of Deniz Tek, a fine and uncomplicated metal axeman), geriatric energizer Ron Keeley on drums, Warwick Gilbert on bass and the indisputable Dark Star of the evening, Charlie (ex Hellcats) on guitar. Add Johnny Kannis, in white tux (suave, very suave), and the delicious Shauna on backing vocals and what have you got? High-energy music with subtlety.

They played Wilko Johnson's "She Does it Right" (why are my feet moving?), the simplest version of "I Don't Care" (hey, just a second, can you get any simpler than the original?) and a host of others, all with the same degree of agression and agility. Mucho favourites for the evening had to be "Sheena is a Punk Rocker" and the old Tommy James chestnut, "Hanky Panky".

Charlie on lead was a constant stream of energy throughout the evening's proceedings, with an almost morose look on his face he plugs away with some biting mindstrangle guitar. "Born to be Wild" was carried along by his slippin and slidin fuzz, and the group responded to his threat by giving their best.

The Survivors, from Brisbane, turned out to be another kettle of sweat. They are a three piece band, with leanings towards the 60s' gargantuan, like the Who and the Kinks. The set they played seemed to last two hours, and they were obviously out to please. They did.

Playing as though there was no stopping them, they pulsated through versions of "Substitute", "All Day and All of the Night" plus the rabid Damned classic "New Rose" (I gotta new rose, I got it good). Perhaps the highlight of the set was "You Really Got Me", which snapped out a few heads in the audience. And let's face facts, who isn't a sucker for that RIFF.

The kids in the hall were certainly getting off on the music, with head lubricants and other nefarious properties flowing freely to the jagged, masochistic music. The authorities announced, quite intimidatingly, that there was five minutes to go. The Survivors' bassist, Jim, wasn't amused, and he angrily reacted to the plea by saying "We've been told there's five minutes to go. Here's one for the people who wish there was three hours" as the band spat out a monolithic version of "Where Have All the Good Times Gone"

Well that was that, and after seeing the two bands, you couldn't have asked for more. After seeing some of the Birdmen back on the stage again, all I can say is when are we going to see them again? And don't forget the Survivors. You know why? Cause they're gonna survive.

Craig X.

BOYS NEXT DOOR

BANANAS, MELBOURNE, NOV. 18.

The first time I saw the Boys Next Door play live I was (to be quite frank), well...bored. But over the past few months I've seen them develop into what I consider to be the best practising rock'n'roll band in Melbourne.

I arrived at Bananas with Nick Cave (vols)2½ hrs or so before the band were due to play. On the way over in the taxi Nick had been excitedly telling me about their new songs - "Can't do it", "Maybe Zone" and "Sex Crimes" (which Nick claims to be the best and loudest song in the world). These three bring the number of songs in their standard set up to about 30.

The next couple of hours were spent thusly:
A, Dragging equipment into Bananas.
B. Trying to look important so as to be allowed in free.
And C. Indulging in the zany hi-jinx that these fun-loving fellas tend to do (sorry).

Anyway, enough of this journalist as star routine and on with the substance.

REVIEW

The Boys Next Door hit the stage around 9.00 with "I Need a Million" by the N.Y. based Laughing Dogs. Shortly after 9.00 myself and 20 or so others were informed of Iggy Pop's cancellation so we were hardly in a receptive mood.

Apart from the music the first thing you notice is Nick; black hair cut in a very Sid Vicious fashion, green shirt with large polka dots, stove pipe trousers and a highly unsuitable tie. He appears to be in a state of constant hyperactivity; dancing, shaking, straining. His voice isn't the usual new wave vocal, not falling into the Johnny Rotten shout, the Joey Ramone muted staccatto, the Joe Strummer man-on-the-street bawl or any preselected catagory.

Mick Harvey plays lead guitar and is improving all the time. He claims to be influenced by Paul Weller of the Jam, though he also delivers a few solos in the fashion of Manzanera. Phillip Calvert plays drums in a staccatto attacking style. And last, Tracey plays very good bass.

All through the first set they appeared to be having problems with the energy level. Which is a great pity because songs like "Funny isn't it" and "Big Future" are really excellent, and their version of "I'm 18" kills Alice Cooper's. It wasn't until "Sex Crimes" that they really got going. "Sex Crimes" along with "This Perfect Day" is one of Australia's new wave classics. It's simply that good.

End of first set.

During the break the place really fills up and it was dancing time. But the first song in the second set is Lou Reed's "Caroline Says pt2", so you just had to wait. Most Berlin lovers would cringe at the idea of the Boys Next Door doing "Caroline" but

NICK - BOYS NEXT DOOR (VCLS)

they did it well. Next up was "Show me a Sign"; great to dance to and instantly memorable, a hit. Then it was Mick Harvey's "Who Needs You", their surf song "World Panic", "Joyride" (another great No1 with rave backup vocals), "All this Fuss", "Masturbation Generation", "Success Story", the excellent "Secret Life" with it's wonderful spanish guitar break and (the song Nick once introduced with "I wrote this song...with Nancy Sinatra) "These Boots are Made for Walking". Great. There were no two ways about it, the audience wanted MORE. "This is "Sex Crime pt 2" said Nick, and they kicked into that song again.

'Sex crimes on the lawn
 and all the children that are
  born
 are committing crimes and doing
  things
 with aerials and piano strings'

MORE LIVE →

THE SAINTS moved to Sydney on signing with EMI, and found more work (pictured taping a performance at the ABC) if only slightly less hostile reaction. They were soon to leave for England. (Pic: Patrick Bingham-Hall)

JOHNNY KANNIS (above), Radio Birdman alumnus as Glutonic harmony singer, did a number of gigs (pictured at Balmain Town Hall) with pick-up bands always known as the Hitmen (and usually comprising most parts Birdman). (Pic: Patrick Bingham-Hall)

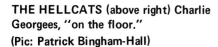

THE HELLCATS (above right) Charlie Georgees, "on the floor." (Pic: Patrick Bingham-Hall)

X (Pic: Patrick Bingham-Hall)

BLACKRUNNER (above) at the Paris Theatre, a short-lived punk venue. (Pic: Matt Dickson)

SHOCK TREATMENT (left)

JOHNNY DOLE & THE SCABS (left) (Pic: Patrick Bingham-Hall)

sydney rundown

What we've got in Sydney at the moment is about ten new wave bands playing more or less regularly (some more than others), but an audience that isn't really growing with the number of bands. Probably because there aren't enough venues, but people just don't seem to want to get actively involved. A disco freak said to me the other day that she really likes "Peaches" (getting airplay on 2SM) and she was bored with discos. That seems a good sign for the future, but while the big companies and radio and TV are flogging disco to death, new wave doesn't stand much of a chance – mainly because the majority are a bunch of sheep who only like what they're told to like (same old problem).

Just a quick run down on the Sydney bands and what's happening. The Scabs are still the best known (and most prolific giggers), but their audience is different to everyone else's. Mostly surfies, sharpies, kids and curious people off the street who've read about them in the Mirror. Most of the "original" (if you go in for that sort of cliquiness) new wave crowd have disassociated themselves from the Scabs. They've got a record coming out soon, probably "Lucky Country", or maybe "Aggro", and it <u>might</u> open the door for other bands.

Most bands play a lot more originals than they used to, Blackrunner and World War IV in particular, although X are nearly all original (and good too). Society Blitz are all original but have only played two gigs as far as I know. Rocks are one of the most energetic bands in Sydney, and Shock Treatment haven't played for a while. Subversion have disappeared from the scene too. There are a couple of bands I've heard about but haven't seen yet, Frenzy and the Only Ones I think. Psycho Surgeons still get the biggest crowd at the Grand, but still don't gig all that often. Dipsticks play occassionally, but only as support band, which is a pity because they always suffer from having no audience feedback.

The fans are still divided into the basic new wave styles – London and New York, although there is a definite hybrid peculiar to Sydney. You can see it mainly in their dress – a few wear Ramones style street clothes, T-shirts and jeans, and a few have short hair, sometimes spikey haircuts, that sort of thing. Lots are just dressed in Hawaiian shirts, longish hair.

Musically there's a split too. The Scabs are very English influenced – they even do Satisfaction and some old Beatles, and originals like "Living Like an Animal", "Psycho-Analyst" and "Stuff Your Rules" are obviously English in feel. Shock Treatment, (last time they were seen anway) do a few American sixties things, Beach Boys and Monkees in particular, and their originals are a cross between Ramones and English energy blasts. "Fall in Love" is English but "Lizzie Went Chop" and "Pure and Simple" are more American. Their guitarist, Bom Leed, is probably the best guitarist of the lot in Sydney (but it's what you do with it that counts). Apparently they've got a lot of originals together in their layoff. Blackrunner are very Stooges-influenced, as you can tell from their originals, (like the Psycos), but they aim to be all original within about 6 weeks. World War IV write a lot of their own things too, like "Hermit in a Riot", "Facist Gun in the West", "Doctor Daze" and "Lovers Leap", but they also do Saints (Wild about you), Birdman (New Race), Pistols (God Save) and Stranglers (Down in the Sewer). Singer, Cory Ruption, is probably the best front-man in Sydney at the moment.

Psycho Surgeons are like the old guard of the scene, having played at the Funhouse in the early days. They're an ideas band (with songs like "Rot in Love", "Meathook" and "Head Off") and are probably more aware than most of what it means to be playing new wave music in 1978.

So that's it. Still not great, and sometimes disappointing (like when four bands played at the Grand on Xmas Eve and the place wasn't even full), but getting better. What it needs is another venue (or two). There's more to new wave than the Ramones but it's not been realized by enough people yet.

Miles.

Reprinted from *PULP*

THE BOYS NEXT DOOR (above) came from Melbourne's exclusive Caulfield Grammar and added a dash of individuality and savvy to their punk precepts, which were steadily growing more sophisticated. Or, they admitted to being influenced by Bowie and Roxy Music. (Pic: Peter Milne)

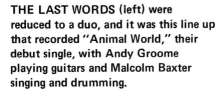

THE LAST WORDS (left) were reduced to a duo, and it was this line up that recorded "Animal World," their debut single, with Andy Groome playing guitars and Malcolm Baxter singing and drumming.

THE LEFTOVERS (left) were probably Brisbane and Australia's first punks in the real Sex Pistols mould — obnoxious, anarchic, original, powerful, violent and with a strong self-destructive bent. (Pic: Scott Bolland)

WILD WEST
- A LOOK AT WHAT'S ON IN WESTERN AUST.

CHEAP NASTIES: KEN, ROBERT, NEIL.

PUNK
ANDREW SAW

A T the risk of being instantly conscripted by Buzz Kennedy's Philistine Liberation Organisation, I must report a certain mystification over a new art form in Perth, conceptual punk.

Conceptual punk, you'll understand, is not the same as ordinary punk. It is, according to its practitioners, a fine arts version of punk.

Conceptual punk is being performed in Perth by a group of young artists who call themselves the Cheap Nasties. ... lead singer is

Robert Porritt, a recen graduate from the W Australian Institute o Technology, and the winner of several major painting prizes in Perth.

Before going any further, I should perhap point out that r stewardship concern conceptual art has n been what it should h A year or so ago with about 30

The Cheap Nasties are making an impact, as the story from the 'Australian'

pe ho te gu T fe v

...eren't ...stood in semi-circle ...received a torrent of abuse from Mr Porritt and the band through a couple of thousand watts of amplification.

The beat had a certain toe-tapping quality about it and s began d jumping.

rock ... down gorously ...ed it for ...began to get the prospect brain thumping ...st the roof of my

...ull. During a lull in the roar I asked Porritt, a normally articulate young man, what he was trying to achieve with his new art form.

I half expected to get another earful of abuse for being obviously bourgeois, but what I got was a moderately sensible explanation.

"The problem is," he said, "is that most art doesn't relate to people, ... cially young ones.

"I want to express myself, I don't believe many kids really relate to painting, so I try to reach them through rock 'n' roll."

The rest of the band didn't seem interested in being introduced, let alone giving an explanation of their motives, so I left it there.

It is hard to imagine conceptual punk becoming a hit in the Perth gallery circuit, but at least the Cheap Nasties will liven up a few of the stultifying arty parties that abound at this time of year.

By the way, has anybody thought to ask Johnny Rotten if he ever went to art school?

*

As it turned out she could have been involved with Mr Rotten himself, but there was no way she could have told anybody because of the shattering din made by the Cheap Nasties.

CHEAP NASTIES AT UNI OF W.A.
Below: A jam at 'Victim Manor' (a popular hangout) with Neil (C.Nasties), Flick (Victims), Jhonho and Ken (C.Nasties)

Above: The Victims, WA's other top group, Rudolph (bass), James (drm.) + Flick (gtr, voc.) at Kewdale Hotel.

thanx to Ian Henderson and 'Remote Control' for info and pix.

Reprinted from *PULP*

JAB

SYNTHETIC SHOCK ROCK

Bohdan - gtr/vcls
Ash Wednesday - bss/tapes
Johny Crash - drms

Things are happening very fast at the moment. Shortly after PULP#1 came out I started hearing rumours of a band that had come over from Adelaide, called JAB. By now, JAB are well know around Melbourne (perhaps bacause of their very extensive graffiti campaign) and have a number of gigs lined up.

The first time I met the band was when they invited me to a rehearsal. Boris (bss/gtr) picked me up and took me. The group's building was perfect. To get to it we had to drive down three one-way streets, up an alley, into the back of a factory and up the fire escape. The rehearsal was in a loft above the factory. Inside I met Bodhan, Ash, Johny and Chris (the band's right-hand man).

The group went straight into their stuff. It was a bit of a shock to discover JAB use two synthesisers (both played by Ash). I'm pretty dubious about synthesisers - I tend to equate them with boredom, but Ash's use of them was a neat surprise. JAB played nearly all original material, so I was interested right from the beginning. The songs were fast and catchy. The group was very tight and it was obvious that they were ready to play to an audience straight-away. The synthesiser didn't detract from the sound, it added a fullness and density to it. The songs that I remember were: 'Too Tough too Care', 'Rip Out Her Hair', '$20 Dude', 'Stuka Love' and Lou's 'Waitin' for the Man'.

For an hour they played and it was great. Then they started arguing over the intro to one of Boris' songs. This eventually led to Boris making a dramatic (and expensive) departure. A few days later they settled their differences, but Boris decided not to return to the band. Ash took over bass and the group was back to a three-piece (this was the original line-up in Adelaide before Boris joined). The synthesiser parts were put on tape.

The group lined up a few gigs. The first was supporting the Keith Glass Band at the Tiger Room on a Wednesday night. For the occasion they recorded video films of themselves(to use whilst they were playing) and covered Melbourne in posters and spray-paint.

The Tiger Room was very crowded for the first Melbourne performance of JAB. The group appeared in some pretty sharp clothes and went straight into 'Too Tough too Care'. They kept going for over an hour, one song after another. The videos were placed on the side. There were three screens: two showing the pre-recorded footage and one 'live' (a guy was walking around with a hand-held camera). The synthesiser tapes were clear and a success. The band's stage presence was too narcissistic for my tastes, but that's minor, it was still a terrific night and probably the most imposing debut I've seen.

JAB will be appearing at the Kingston and the Station in early November as well as the Melb. Uni. GAYSOC dance on Nov. 18th. Check 'em out.

Bruce.

Saints

After a successful tour of the UK, with their then-new single, 'Perfect Day', charting at #31, and recruiting Al Ward to replace bassist Kym Bradshaw, the Saints returned to Australia shortly. Ivor Hay, at least, spoke to PULP.

PULP: The Saints headlined a tour of the UK. That would be the first time you'd even played in big halls.

Ivor: Yeah, this was the first time we'd played in big halls, to packed audiences.

PULP: What sort of audience did you get? Did you attract the same kind of punk that might be a Sex Pistols fan, the real hard core?

Ivor: Yeah.

PULP: Were any of them snotty about you, not being political etc?

Ivor: I dunno. We're political, it's just that we don't express it.

PULP: Did you get any more mainstream audience?

Ivor: You get a lot of people just checking it out.

PULP: Curiousity?

Ivor: Yeah, both the audience and the band, 'cos I s'pose the Saints are more novel, in this field, we're more a novelty than other bands, like the Jam or the Clash perhaps, y'know, because, well .....we're Australian.

PULP: How did the audience, the punks, react to you?

Ivor: They used to go totally besrk. They'd pogo so high, right up in the air, and leap on the audience below. One time we were playing at the Croydon Greyhound, which holds about 600. It was packed with about 400 and about 30 or so punks jumped on stage and started pogoing around, almost took over, but we kept playing. It coulda turned into an ugly scene, but we took contol again.

PULP: Your first UK date was at the Roundhouse, with the Ramones and the Talking Heads. Phil McNeill's review in NME said you looked like you'd just wandered in from the outback. Others said you were like a poor copy of the Ramones, with none of the charms of that group.

Ivor: I dunno. I dunno how much charm the Ramones have got. I think the Ramones have got charm because thay're a famous

pop group, and therefore people tend to read into what they want, because they're not a theatrical band.

PULP: But they have got that collective image.

Ivor: I suppose...but Dee Dee's the only one who moves, and Ed sometimes moves when he feels like it.

PULP: That was another common criticism, that the Saints performed this high-energy music, but with a laid-back presentation.

Ivor: That's to do with theatrics, and we're not a theatrical band, but a lota people wanna see that.

PULP: But when you were in Australia, you'd sometimes move. Chris used to go beserk sometimes.

Ivor: Well, it's cos sometimes Chris has a funny reaction. If he sees a theatrical band, he'll go out of his way to be un-theatrical. When his aud-

ience is being theatrical, he'll go the opposite and be sorta bored. Sometimes he'll go crazy. Chris is in a quandry as to whether he should become a show-man, a theatrical person.

PULP: So it depends on how he feels, how drunk he is......

Ivor: How drunk he is, if he's having a good night or a bad night. Chris can be inconsistant.

PULP: I think it's all part of the Saints own charm anyhow.

Ivor: The whole thing is that we are a personality band, we're not just robots, which means you gotta go on stage, and go up there and put on a show because we're on stage. We're just people, and people are subject to moods.

PULP: Going to England hasn't changed the Saints at all. You retain your identity, you're still very much your own.

Ivor: We're not gonna turn punky.

PULP: The Saints are unique in England. You look and sound different, do diff-

erent style songs, you're Australian.
Ivor: Well, it has to be unique bec-

ause we were stuck in Brisbane, totally
alienated from any sort of contemporary music, so there is this uniqueness.
PULP: You've been going since, say,
the first NY Dolls album.

Ivor: The first time we heard the Dolls
album was the first time we heard a
band that sounded anything like us.
PULP: So you've been growing ever since
then.
Ivor: We had the band going already, we
had the sound.
PULP: I tend to see the Saints as being
slightly out of their time, like
they're the missing link between the NY
Dolls and the new wave. You're stylist-
ically mid-way between the Dolls and,

say, the Ramones or the UK punks, in
every respect - musically, thematically,
image-wise, presentation. And, ironic-
ally enough, neither American or English,
but Australian.
Ivor: Oh yeah, could be. The way I see
it, we're independant of anything, we're
away from everything. There's us, and
there's them.
PULP: When you recorded 'Stranded' you
had no idea what was going on in England, you were still developing as
the next step after the Dolls, and the
Ramones album had no influence whatsoever on you.
Ivor: No, certainly bloody didn't, it
kinda shitted us that this New York
band was doing the same stuff as we
were.
PULP: But 'Stranded' was one of the
first real New Wave records in the UK
anyhow, so you're trend-setters.
Ivor: That's right, it came out before
anything, the Damned, 'Anarchy'.
PULP: And since going to England, you
haven't bent to fit in. It even came
as a bit of a surprise to me that you
still include those oldies in your set,
numbers like 'Runaway','Lipstick on
your Collar' and 'River Deep, Mountain
High'. Does doing them put you in a
different league?
Ivor: Well, the Jam do sorta 60's
stuff.....even the Cortinas do 'Gloria',
the Boys do Beatles sorta songs.
PULP: So they like you doing these
oldies?
Ivor: We got a good response from 'Runaway', cos it's a good break. It's at
a slower tempo, so it gives them a br-
eather. We do it after 'Nights in Ven-
ice'.
PULP: Any new stuff then? What about
the song we've all heard about, called

'Orstralia'? Is that a more political-
type thing?
Ivor: Socialogical, about Australia,
it's more like a sarcastic thing, the
same way 'Perfect Day' was. Sorta like,
things are far from perfect, same
thing as like, Australia's far from
great. Australia's supposed to be the
land where you don't need anything,
and yet you need a lot of things, and
yet a lot of people thenk that Australia's great.
PULP: Any more songs like that one?
Ivor: On the new album? I can't think
of any.
PULP: That song will be on the new
album then.
Ivor: Yeah, it might even be released
as a single.
PULP: What else will be on the second
album?

Ivor: 'Misunderstood'......and there's
that ballad which was supposed to be
on the first album but was taken off.
Totally original - I can't remember
the titles, Ed knows them.
PULP: Who's producing it?
Ivor: Ed and Chris, with our engineer,
who worked with the Sex Pistols.
PULP: One of the criticisms of the
first album was that the ballads upset
the momentum, and I always felt that
a ballad like 'Messin' with the Kid'
was old-fashioned, and out of context
with the rest of the album.
Ivor: I dunno......there will be another ballad on the new album, it's
shorter, it'll be different to 'Messin' with the Kid' - it was sorta like
a ballad in its own right, it's just
one of those individual ballads. The
new ballad will be similar, I suppose,
to the 'Ballad in F Minor'. I think
it's called 'A MINOR Affair'. It was
called 'A Private Affair', but we
changed it, because we rearranged it,
and now it's in the key of A Minor,
so......
PULP: And the songs will have a similar approach as those on the first
album. I mean, your first album was
pretty traditional, compared to say
the Ramones or the Clash. You're
putting a new, 70's interpretation
on traditional rock'n'roll themes.
Ivor: I suppose so.....we're just a
70's band.
PULP: How do you think your singles,
like 'Perfect Day', would go without
the gimmickry of the 12" release?
Would it still have made the charts?
Ivor: I mean it sold 70,000, and only
12,000 of those were 12", so it would
have got into the chart anyway.

PULP: So we can expect that '1.2.3.4-The Saints' will do the same thing?
Ivor: Oh yeah, it'll get into the charts, probably get even higher, because it'll be a better production.
PULP: How do the Saints go, working in the studio?
Ivor: Kym was a bit hard towards the end...
PULP: What about Kym, he just wasn't measuring up, as a bassist?
Ivor: Musical differences. We had to someone so we could work when we started off a year ago with him, but now, we can get someone who we can get on with. We can pick and choose now......when we didn't use him

things worked out. I had a bit of trouble with one song. The rest went pretty easy.
PULP: The Saints seem to be able to play energetically in the studio, it's just a matter of capturing it, which is up to the producer.
Ivor: Even this new EP, it'll sound better. Well, for a start, I'm playing better, the bass is better, the guitar clearer, therefore you just get a better produced sound. Everything's being played better.
PULP: You don't play 'live' in the studio, using the first take, like the Buzzcocks or Dr. Feelgood?
Ivor: The first album was more or less like that, with the guitar overdubbed, and the vocals overdubbed, but now, with the new EP, we're working in stages, drums and guitar first, then bass, then guitar overdubs and vocal overdubs.
PULP: Who did you see in England that you liked?
Ivor: I liked the Boys and I liked the Jam. I met Captain Sensible and I

liked him. I met Joe Strummer - I didn't like him. I met a band in Scotland called the Jolt, who supported us one night, and they're a very good band. They're one of the honest bands around. They're a good pop group, they're good musicians, and they do good pop tunes.

PULP: Just recently, Sid Vicious and Johnny Rotten said a lot of people are taking to the Sex Pistols, and buying their records, because it's the groovy thing.
Ivor: At the moment it is the groovy thing, that's why it went to No1.
PULP: But surely there's a lot who buy it because they like it, because it's good rock'n'roll.
Ivor: True too.
PULP: To get to No1, they'd have to be selling to more than just the punk-audience.
Ivor: Yeah, a lot of people bought it to show support to a banned band. To prove a point.
PULP: It's a kick in the face to everyone.
Ivor: So they went out of their way to prove it.
PULP: The only real criticism the detractors of the new wave can come up with is that you can't be a successful pop group and a revolutionary at the same time. It's the weakest link..
Ivor: Well, for myself, and I suppose the rest of the band, you can use that, take them for whatever they've got. And I suppose that's the way the Pistols and the Clash look at it. Take 'em for everything they've got. But y'know, it's hard to draw the line, like Chris said, it's a thin line you walk when you're working with a big industry. Eventually you fall one way or the other, either fall out

of it totally or into it totally.
PULP: So what's happening with the Saints right now, and then in the future?
Ivor: Chris is still in England, he's supposed to be recording (the EP) and I'm putting out a single called 'Hay Fever'. I dunno exactly what it's gonna be like. I've got some ideas and Ed's got some ideas. After we've recorded the new album, with the new bass player, we'll do another tour of England, and a more extensive tour of Europe. The real test will be when we go back this time and do a tour.
PULP: Whether or not people will come to see you again.
Ivor: Yeah.

                                    Cee Walker

JAB (above left) alongside Black Chrome, were Adelaide's first real "new wave" band. Initially an experimental outfit in the Eno mould, JAB moved to Melbourne and adopted a brasher, punkier stance. (Pic: Tanya McIntyre)

RADIO BIRDMAN (left) not long before leaving Australia for England. (Pic: Patrick Bingham-Hall)

THE VICTIMS (below) three-chord thrashing was well received in the eastern states through their debut single, "Television Addict."

JOHNNY & THE HITMEN in one of their innumerable incarnations . Spot the stars. (Pic: Patrick Bingham-Hall)

THE YOUNG CHARLATANS had near
"super group" status almost right from
the outset, what with the Ian "Ollie"
Olsen / Rowland Howard / Janine Hall /
Jeffrey Wegener line-up. The band
pioneered post-punk rock in Australia.
(Pic: Philip Morland)

Here come the NEWS, punks

by SHANE MALONEY

FOR WEEKS, a four-letter word spray-painted on apparently every available space in the inner city has puzzled pedestrians, motorists and, of course, the police.

Speculation about its meaning was rumored to have even the spooks at ASIO scratching their heads.

Now the NEWS has broken.

NEWS are a new punk band who claim to know nothing about the paint-ups of their name that have spread the word from bus shelter to factory wall all over town.

"We have quite a few fans," they explain, "and we must have a particularly avid unknown admirer."

Whatever, the improvised advertising campaign has made their name a household puzzle.

NEWS made their public debut at midnight last Saturday before a largely word-of-mouth audience at the Pram Factory, the Australian Performing Group's Carlton fortress headquarters.

Observed with cool disdain by some of our cultural arbiters, they won a grudging and eventually enthusiastic response from the 200-strong audience jammed into the back theatre of the Pram Factory.

NEWS are young, brash and refreshingly anti-professional. The way they tune up on stage, shout instructions to the sound mixer between numbers and count into their songs with a chanted "1, 2, 3, 4" would horrify any band with pretence to slick commercialism. But it cuts away the false veneer of competence that surround those bands that depend on electronic fakery to hold their acts together.

There is no pretence here.

NEWS are about the sound and rebellious instincts of punk, not the fashion.

They disdain the commercialisation of the punk fad exported from England. They are doing their own thing, playing about their own experiences on the dole and in dead-end jobs.

"Those trendy 'punks' from South Yarra with tie-dyed haircuts and bones through their noses are as remote from us as we are from the establishment superstars," says NEWS' solidly-assertive bass player Joy Relentless.

Joy Relentless, 20, is the most arresting feature of the band's stage act as she strides into the Pram Factory with her instrument slung over her shoulder like a machine-gun.

On stage, she becomes an urban guerilla, her feet aggressively planted and her brows knit as she thumps out the repetitive pulsations that form the basis of punk rhythm.

Eighteen-year-old drummer Jonh-Smith-from-the-Suburbs, and lead singer Adam Five, hurl out a high-speed, high-pressure musical invective that underpins the lead guitar of Jaryl Circus.

The total effect is a sort of rhythmic electric scud with barked and angry lyrics blurred into a barely intelligible but rivetting musical assault.

"You could call it bubble gum punk," says Mr. Circus, who chose his nom-de-punk because of a family tradition of unusual performances.

Parodies of sickly sweet commercial love songs are an essential part of their act.

As well as their own compositions with titles such as Dirty Lies, Hate and Don't Care, Adam Five sneers his way through old 1910 Fruitgum Company hits injecting a self-mockery and inventiveness into punk, which the band fear is already becoming moribund overseas.

"Johnny Rotten and the Sex Pistols are already Establishment," says Joy; and adds, with a shrug, "I suppose we could be, one day".

Formed last year as the Babeez, the band has already released a single, packaged in a brown paper bag with four-letter lyrics crudely mis-typed on the outside.

"We recorded it in the lounge room, then paid for it to be pressed. We sold 500," says anti-tycoon Jonh-Smith-from-the-Suburbs.

"We have a lot of trouble getting gigs," they complain, "because once it is known that we are a punk band we are immediately excluded.

"People seem to think we are violent, but we've never been in a fight in our lives and don't want to be.

"We just want to play our kind of music, and we keep getting hassled about it."

NEWS will be playing at a punk rock extravaganza titled **Punk Gunk** along with other local punks, Teenage Radio Stars and JAB, at Bailey Hall in Richmond on Tuesday, February 28, and at the Kingston Hotel on March 4.

NEWS relax between bouts. . . blasting out more decibels than the F-19 at peak hour. Jonh-Smith-from-the-Suburbs is the missing member.

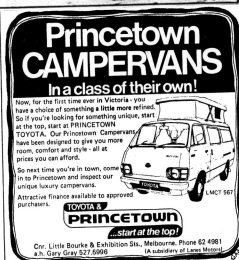

Reprinted from the Melbourne AGE

KNOW YOUR PRODUCT

After *Perfect Day,* I felt sure the Saints next album would be IT. The killer-diller. If it was anything like *Perfect Day,* it had to be.

However, on first hearing *Eternally Yours,* I thought *Perfect Day* must still be the Saints finest achievement; that the impetus and momentum it had built was lost. But I was wrong.

Perfect Day is great, of course, I'm not trying to take anything from it. But it's history. The Saints have got a new approach, new aims. It's like this: if *Perfect Day* was the Saints *I Gotta Right,* then *Eternally Yours* is their *Kill City.* (Or like *Garageband* and *Clash City Rockers?*) It's that kind of transition. The emphasis is as much on music as it is effect.

If nothing else though, *Eternally Yours* proves the Saints to be one of the most adventurous and imaginative (and courageous) groups around. But maybe they move too fast.

The Saints have tried to do a lot here, sometimes it works, sometimes not.

Their ideas are not so much totally new as they are developments on older, established foundations, which they're taking to the limit. (Indeed, many of the songs were written some time ago, though now they're virtually unrecognizable). The result of the Saints experimentation is a much and varied set — straight ahead rockers (some great riffs), ballads, and oddities like *Orstralia* and *International Robots.* It is, at times, quite stunning. Ed's guitar work is brilliant and hilarious — like himself it's dry and deadpan — he can take what might be stock-in-trade phrases and make them work as something new and perfectly fitting. Alisdair's bass playing is right up there, interesting in itself, and Ivor's well behind everything.

Chris's vocals bear down on the whole thing — at best his lyrics are bright, subtle and funny, at worst they degenerate into real banalities and cliches, which I thought I'd never hear from Chris Bailey. His obsession is Us (i.e. Chris) versus Them, which is not surprising considering the treatment the Saints are getting.

They deserve better. It's up to you.

Clinton Walker
Reprinted from *PULP 5*

THE SAINTS second album, "Eternally Yours," was released, and the band continued to play Britain and Europe.

THE NEON STEAL (nee Grudge) originated in the architecture faculty of Queensland University. Inspired by The Saints, they began covering Saints as well as Sex Pistols and Stooges songs. (Pic: Jim Goodwin)

THE LEFTOVERS suffered all the setbacks befitting a band of their nature, but they were persistent enough to play on, and even recorded eventually. (Pic: Scott Bolland)

RAZAR (above) next to the Neon Steal and the X-Men, were one of the first of a second generation of Brisbane bands, and if they were marginal musically (carbon copying English punks) at least they addressed some of Queensland's political problems.

FILTH (above left) were to some the truest punk band of all, to others nihilistic and talentless. Either way, they could be witty, even though they could barely play, and their performances frequently ended in violence. (Pic: Brad Franks)

THE LAST WORDS (left) having signed to Wizard Records, recruited a rhythm section and began playing live. Pictured at the Grand Hotel, a renowned punk pit. (Pic: Darian Turner)

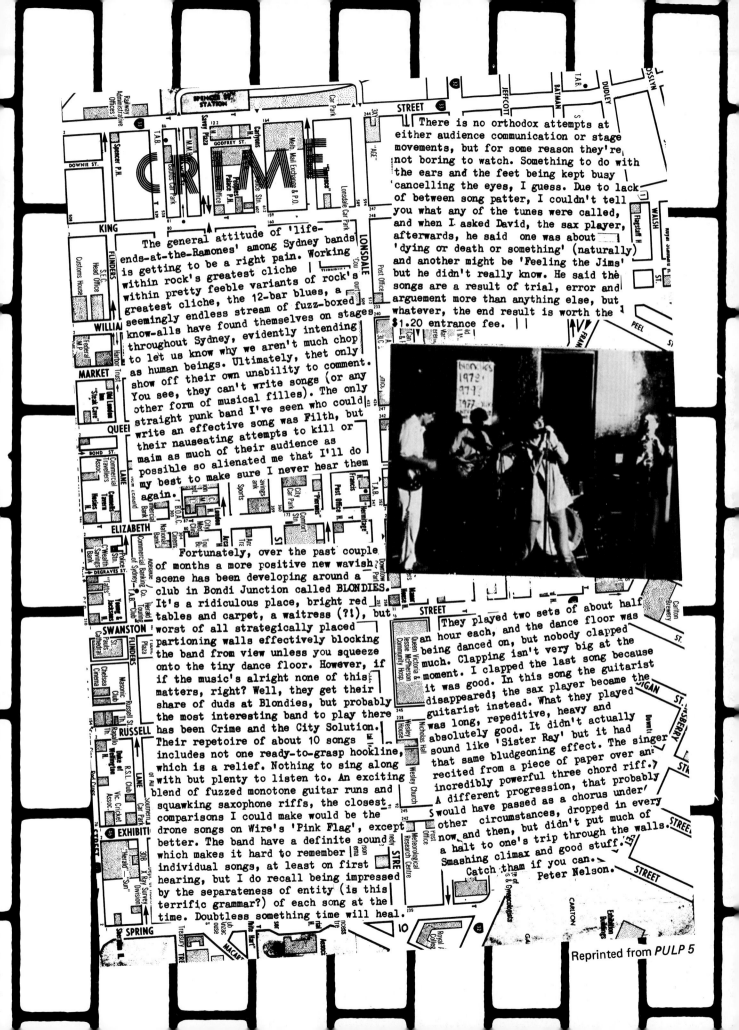

CRIME

The general attitude of 'life-ends-at-the-Ramones' among Sydney bands is getting to be a right pain. Working within rock's greatest cliche within pretty feeble variants of rock's greatest cliche, the 12-bar blues, a seemingly endless stream of fuzz-boxed know-alls have found themselves on stages throughout Sydney, evidently intending to let us know why we aren't much chop as human beings. Ultimately, thet only show off their own unability to comment. You see, they can't write songs (or any other form of musical filles). The only straight punk band I've seen who could write an effective song was Filth, but their nauseating attempts to kill or maim as much of their audience as possible so alienated me that I'll do my best to make sure I never hear them again.

There is no orthodox attempts at either audience communication or stage movements, but for some reason they're not boring to watch. Something to do with the ears and the feet being kept busy cancelling the eyes, I guess. Due to lack of between song patter, I couldn't tell you what any of the tunes were called, and when I asked David, the sax player, afterwards, he said one was about 'dying or death or something' (naturally) and another might be 'Feeling the Jims' but he didn't really know. He said the songs are a result of trial, error and arguement more than anything else, but whatever, the end result is worth the $1.20 entrance fee.

Fortunately, over the past couple of months a more positive new wavish scene has been developing around a club in Bondi Junction called BLONDIES. It's a ridiculous place, bright red tables and carpet, a waitress (?!), but worst of all strategically placed partioning walls effectively blocking the band from view unless you squeeze onto the tiny dance floor. However, if if the music's alright none of this matters, right? Well, they get their share of duds at Blondies, but probably the most interesting band to play there has been Crime and the City Solution. Their repetoire of about 10 songs includes not one ready-to-grasp hookline, which is a relief. Nothing to sing along with but plenty to listen to. An exciting blend of fuzzed monotone guitar runs and squawking saxophone riffs, the closest comparisons I could make would be the drone songs on Wire's 'Pink Flag', except better. The band have a definite sound which makes it hard to remember individual songs, at least on first hearing, but I do recall being impressed by the separateness of entity (is this terrific grammar?) of each song at the time. Doubtless something time will heal.

They played two sets of about half an hour each, and the dance floor was being danced on, but nobody clapped much. Clapping isn't very big at the moment. I clapped the last song the guitarist it was good. In this song the guitarist disappeared; the sax player became the guitarist instead. What they played was long, repeditive, heavy and absolutely good. It didn't actually sound like 'Sister Ray' but it had that same bludgeoning effect. The singer recited from a piece of paper over an incredibly powerful three chord riff. A different progression, that probably would have passed as a chorus under other circumstances, dropped in every now and then, but didn't put much of a halt to one's trip through the walls. Smashing climax and good stuff.
Catch them if you can.
Peter Nelson.

Reprinted from PULP 5

RADIOS TALK!

RADIO BIRDMAN RECENTLY LEFT AUSTRALIA
FOR ENGLAND. THIS INTERVIEW WAS DONE
BY ANDREW McMILLAN JUST PRIOR TO THAT

PULP: How did you find it getting
gigs when you first started as
Radio Birdman?
Dennis: Oh, y'know, we started off
playing at the Excelsor Hotel. We
ran anywhere from $16 to $22 a
night. Literally. People enjoyed it.
Rob: Yeah, people came to see us and
really liked it. We played at a
theatre resturant in the city and
did exactly the same sort of thing,
and they chucked us out, they just
didn't see us in the context of
their place at all.
Dennis: The guy from the theatre
resturant said he really dug us
when he saw us at the Excelsor,
booked us in and fired us after
the first night at his place.
Rob: That happened a couple of
times, qiute a few times.
PULP: Dennis, how do you find
Detroit has influenced you?
Dennis: Well, anywhere you live
kinda influences what you're
doing. It just seems natural to be
influenced by that city.
Mark Sisto (?): It's a very
militeristic city. They make tanks
there, they made the B-17 bomber.
High powered town. Very extreme in
a way. The thing about the music..
I think it was just...the strength
of the town. It was real emotional.
Dennis: The energy and the spirit
of this band is not only to be found
in what is strictly defined as
rock'n'roll records. Like we don't
only listen to rock'n'roll records,
we listen to a lot of other things
to find inspiration too, but there
seems to be a common thread that
we've all picked up, like Garland
Jeffries - not rock'n'roll. Early
James Brown.....surf music,
especially Jan&Dean. The energy's
in that too. People tend to put
you in a niche which is limited by
their own experience, which isn't
usually that great. Y'know, you go
to a party and people automatically
put on the Stooges or something
like that, and if you put on, say,
James Brown Live at the Apollo,
everybody looks at you and goes

what?! They're only clutching at
straws really.
Rob: Everytime someone does an
article on us, they always mention
the 5 and the Stooges, but there's
so much other stuff, like surf music,
I think that's got a lot to do
with us.
PULP: What other composers do you
cover then, besides yourself?
All: Stooges, MC5, Jan & Dean,
Pink Faries, Ventures, Remains, 13th
Floor Elevators.
Rob: Everything we do I think was
written by an American...we play
what we feel like.
PULP: But you do mostly originals,
what sorta mood do your songs
take? Goodtime, political?
Dennis: They're not political at
all, there's nothing political in
those tunes. Goodtime, I dunno,
we had a good time doing them.
PULP: Explain 'Do the Pop'.
(?): Well, I think that song is
sort of about....it's an extreme
way of dancing. That guy was just
really extreme the way he danced.
Just go right to the limit. It's
more of a song about an extreme
way of dancing rather than hero-
worship. Like, I don't worship
the guy or anything.
PULP: What relly impresses me
about the band is not just the
music, but the overall
presentation, the way you move.
Dennis: The way he (Rob) moves?
PULP: Yeah. Like at Hurstville once,
when you were lieing on the floor,
screaming and moaning, all the
security guards couldn't work out
whether you were in pain or what,
they were worried about you..
Rob: Well that's great.
Dennis: One time we played there,
the bouncers were taking swings at
me, they grabbed me by both arms
and they're trying to drag me out,
out the front into the street,
where they could beat me up.
Rob: This is while the band is
playing.
PULP: What made you jump offstage
in the first place?
Dennis: I just felt like dancing.
Because there's a part in the song
where the bass and drums just jam
away. I put my guitar down, I

RADIO BIRDMAN

wanted to do a little dancing, that's all.
PULP: You've had trouble because of the way you play.
Rob: We probably don't play louder than most bands. We don't have a lot of gear, but our music, if you regard it as being intense, managers think it is, they sometimes complain.
Dennis: We fill the spaces more.
Rob: They complain because they don't like it.
PULP: Are you still being put down by promoters?
Rob: Well, the manager of Chequers doesn't think we're the right type, doesn't like the crowd we attract.
PULP: What makes you use symbols etc People have likened them to Nazism.
Dennis: That's our symbol - nothing to do with the Nazis. It's got no relationship to any pre-existing political unit. It's a new... order. I invented that symbol.
PULP: Do you work on the image?
Rob: We don't work on the image of the band. It's not really a projected thing. There's no phony attitudes. There's nothing contrived.
Dennis: It's not worked out. It's something that's already there.
PULP: What about the Stuka dive bomber motif you've used. Is that just because it's music like that?
Dennis: Yeah, we just like that.
Rob: There's an image there.
Warwick: It's not political, but the image is there.
PULP: To me it typified Radio Birdman.
Dennis: Yeah, because Warwick did did that, he created that image and he understands our band totally, so the images he creates are naturally gonna fit in, because he's got the power to translate that into art.. One thing, we're not Nazis, don't ever say we're Nazis. We don't wanna be any type of socialists, nationalist or otherwise.
PULP: What do you wanna be?
Dennis: Just what we are now.
Rob: Getting power without getting involved in politics.
Dennis: The only reason you sometimes might see us wearing Nazi paraphenalia....it's not that we identify with the party. We appreciate the aesthetics of it. The whole thing of unity. That's the only thing we appreciate about it really. The spirit of people working together toward a common

goal. Their goal wasn't the right goal.
Rob: Theydressed it up well.
Dennis: They dressed it up in symbols and things. That's the part we like.
PULP: There's gonna be a New Race?
Chris: It's nothing to do with the races now on earth, with Nazi aryianism or something. It's something that hasn't happened yet.
Dennis: It's about the appearence of a totally new type of person... compared to the kind of people there are here now.
Rob: It doesn't have to be taken seriously. It's the sound of it, y'know. A song like that can be so open, that's what's so good about it.
Dennis: The part in there about a circle of time, everyones in a circle of time. We're talking about the possibilities of a new type of man.
Chris: Break off and take a line into unknown territories.
Dennis: Unfortunately people will hang it up with Nazism because of the blitzkreig aspect.
Rob: That's there bad luck.
PULP: You have this whole attitude of no compromise, you won't bow to anyone.What's the idealogy, how far does it go?
Chris: It keeps you clean, from getting killed. Y'know, if you submit to these other things you lose your identity, you become what other people want you to be. It's just a....survival.
Dennis: It's like, this is a unit, there's us and there's everybody else. To keep our unity, to keep our group spirit, we have our symbols and stuff. It's like soldiers.
PULP: You're trying to promote this?
Dennis: Don't care what everybody else does. It's up to them. It's just the way we wanna be. We're not trying to encourage anybody to do anything. It's just that we've got an understanding. It's our music, by keeping us tight as a unit, as together as we can. Our aim is only to do it ourselves, and to present it. It's an end in itself. There's no other motive. To make you buy a certain thing, or live a certain lifestyle. If they pick up on it, and wanna find out where we got our ideas, the records we got a lot of inspiration from, well that's great.

SIGN TO SUICIDE OR SUICIDE TO SIGN?

As offered, a Suicide contract is for 5 years at 5% of gross, 30% royalty on performance, and 50% on publishing. Suicide's minimum obligation is 2 tracks (i.e. 1 single) per year.

And that's what all the fuss is about.

Recently in the Adelaide paper *Roadrunner,* Suicide was accused of "ripping off" its contracted artists.

THE BOYS NEXT DOOR

Quick to come was a reply in *Juke,* chastising the writer and insinuating he was little more than an upstart who knew nothing of the recording industry.

Alright, I'm not going to leave myself open to that kind of criticism, and maybe I know nothing of the recording industry myself, but I can see things I'm positive only a blind man couldn't.

Right from the outset, Suicide's intentions appeared pretty obvious. Monopoly. It's simple: the more bets they placed, the greater chance of picking a winner. And the losers? Well, with a contract that demands only 1 single a year, it's not a heavy obligation, is it? And it's the only obligation — no promotion, no live gigs, no nothing — so Suicide can effectively control anyone. And by now, this is more than mere conjecture — the Negatives are already

dissatisfied, because they know they're far from the top of Suicide's list of priorities. Just wait and watch . . .

But all this is getting away from the point in question here, which is Suicide's debut release, the *Lethal Weapons* compilation album.

No matter what they thought of the whole Suicide schmere, nearly everyone I know grabbed a copy of *Lethal Weapons* the minute it hit the shelves. Because despite Suicide (or because of it?) some good groups have become involved, and they shouldn't be judged according to the business ethics of their management or record company. Trouble is, it's impossible to separate the two, such is the hold Suicide has on its roster of artists.

Suicide is determined to present things their way — artists are simply a

means to the end of fulfilling the Suicide vision. Which mightn't be so bad (it's despicable), if only Suicide had the slightest inkling of what's really going on, what's really needed. Of course it goes without saying they haven't, and I find *Lethal Weapons* only an embarrassment because (yet again) it reinforces Australia's position as a world backrunner. While it (and don't ask what it is, you know what I'm talking about) is in its death throes overseas, here it's still having birth pains. Suicide have simply duplicated everything they saw happening in England — 12 months ago. The whole concept is not only out-dated and unoriginal, but also quite unnecessary in its excess. Besides which, it reeks of a K-Tel crassness — the (unintentionally) kitsch packaging (which only maintains the inaccurate image), the nauseating and often in-correct credits, indeed the entire campaign.

So what chances has the actual music got? Out of white vinyl grooves, it battles valiantly. Sometimes.

A popular misconception might be

THE SURVIVORS

THE NEGATIVES   (Pic: Tanya McIntyre)

that anyone and everyone involved with Suicide feels hard done by. Not so. Most of the groups signed with few res-ervations, and most of them are still quite happy. Which may be because they're getting a chance they otherwise wouldn't have. Indeed, some have sug-gested this as a justification for Suicide — I certainly don't accept that (it's only Suicide's lack of any kind of perception that determined their choice of artists anyhow), but it is true that while some are going to move onto bigger and better things, others are going to dis-appear. The losers. Get it?

XRayZ are truly horrific, the less said about them the better. And the Survivors and Wasted Daze would appear to be little more than token representatives from outside Melbourne. Wasted Daze are/can be an exciting R&B group live, but here, on record, the energy is lost. Their two tracks are boring workouts on badly chosen material. And the Survivors — though an adept bunch of pop musicians — do tend to plod in this, an album context. I wonder if these groups have much

more to offer.

Also with a not-too-rosy future are
the Negatives — through no fault other
than time itself — their brand of Stooges
inspired punk is no longer in great
demand. Evidently, Suicide felt simi-
larly, and therefore decided to add to
the Negatives track, *Planet on the Prowl.*
The band consented to producer Eric
Gradman adding violin, but nothing else.
They weren't allowed to hear the final
mix, and when they did they were surprised to hear the violin was mixed so
high (too high), and that sound effects
and Eric Gradman's voice were added —
without their knowledge! So what you
hear is not fairly the Negatives.

No doubt though, more will be heard
from JAB, the Teenage Radio Stars and
the Boys Next Door. JAB are a group
who have 'higher' pretensions than *Let's
Go* might suggest, at least they can be
described as, err, unique, though it's not
really captured here (which many would
consider a blessing). Their contribution
is largely throwaway and lacklustre.

The Teenage Radio Stars actually
open the album, and theirs will be the
first single lifted from it. And if you
thought the name Teenage Radio Stars
was somewhat derivative, then what
about *I Wanna Be Ya Baby?* You may
well be forgiven for thinking it was
another mistake, but the Radio Stars do
actually take credit for writing it. The
story goes that Suicide heard the Vibra-
tors' *Baby Baby,* decided it was good
material for the Radio Stars, and sug-
gested they rewrite and record it. The
result is characterized only by the excellent production, probably the best on
the album. The Teenage Radio Stars are
firm favorites with Suicide — they're undoubtedly saleable — so we can expect
to see more of them, be that good or
bad.

Finally, there's the Boys Next Door,
who in my humble opinion (and I'm
never humble about my opinion), are
the best working group in Australia, and
along with the Saints one of the best
groups to have emerged in the last year
or so. But once again, thanks to
Suicide's shortsightedness, their potential is not only nowhere near being

JAB at Blondies (Pic: John Wickens)

realised, it hasn't even been given a chance. The Boys themselves describe their three tracks — *These Boots are Made for Walking, Masturbation Generation* and *Boy Hero* — as embarrassing. *Boots* and *Masturbation Generation* are easily the worst songs in the Boys' repertoire, they remain only on Suicide's insistence. Ordinarily, they would have been long dropped, since they've updated and improved themselves to their present standard. *Boy Hero* is a newer song — only it is remotely indicative of what the Boys are capable of, and even then any judgement is unfair because of the production. In the studio the straight takes were quite good, but Greg Macainsh set upon them and reduced them to the flat, limp pieces of wetness they are now. So don't take them as representative of the Boys Next Door. Still, their wit, intelligence and imagination can hardly be suppressed, and given the freedom they could produce something very good. In fact, I dare say the Boys Next Door are the only Suicide act capable of making anything of both commercial and artistic worth.

Suicide are going to need a lot more than just the Boys Next Door firing. They've spent over $20,000 (some say a

lot more), and there's no way *Lethal Weapons* will recoup that. As they say— they're going to have to break at least two of the artists nationally within the next year to keep on living.

But if they continue on their merry way — they've been asking for this pun all along — they'll be committing suicide, and unfortunately taking with them their acts.

Naturally, *Lethal Weapons* is not a terribly good album, but surely its lowest points are those where Suicide asserts its right to divine intervention — like the Boys Next Door doing *Boots* and the Teenage Radio Stars doing *I Wanna Be Ya Baby.* The sort of attitude that says, ''I don't believe it's the right of a rock paper . . . speaking to the bands.''

Obviously, they see some kind of potential here, so they should realise it can't be determined by bearded, fat old businessmen. But they never learn.

It's the age-old story, isn't it.

Clinton Walker
Reprinted from *PULP 5*

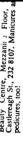

It's about time X started getting the kind of crowd they deserve. It should have
★★ been obvious from their early gigs at the Paris that given the right venue they
could give the people what they wanted — a genuine and unprentious new wave band.
Their only appearance at the Graand Hotel proved that a genuine rock and roll feeling
counts for more than all the safety pins and slogans. They're the only band I've
seen get three encores at the Grand. They gave life to a scene that ~~seemed to be exhausting~~
had lost its impetus. Not that they're anything more than a rock and roll band, but
they don't pretend to be. You realise that when you see them down on the floor at
the Unicorn with no image gap between them and their audience.
        The band is a four piece — Ian Late on bass, Ian Later on guitar (after Bondi
Masonic Hall you know why) Stevie Generator vocalist, and it looks like Steve X is
back on drums and Eddie Upset(not quite Angry) has left. They play mostly their own
songs but do great versions of "Runaway" (about as good as the Saints), EAsybeats'
She's So fine and the Stones' Paint it Black. Their own songs like Degenerate Boy,
Slash Your Wrists (slashyourwrists), YouDon't like Me, One Last Chance and Hate City
are short, mostly made up of the chorus and put across by Stevie. He doesn't move much
but stands with his hands on his hipsand leans over the mike, shouting down into it. As
THe set wares on at the end of the songs he has to sit down he gets so exhausted.
        The bass and the guitarist work off each other but in a different way to most
otherbands. the bass is a lot more prominent and Ian Late is obviously the best bassplayer in Sydney. I remember the first time they played at the Paris when the
guitar amp exploded five seconds into One Last Chance and the bass carried the song
and no- one realised what happened. The guitarist's got his own style too that uses a
lot of feedback. He's everything that Kevin Boridge could never be- a bona fide
rock and roll guitarist. And the only reason he takes his shirt off is because
he sweats so much. He's also very thin.
        X don't advertise all that widely but where they're playing usally spreads by
word of mouth. theyRe probably the best rock and roll band in Sydney but I wonder
if they want to break out of the pub circuit.

31

THE THOUGHT CRIMINALS took
up residency at the Native Rose Hotel
in Sydney, and with this and an EP,
soon won some attention for their
speedy, almost slapstick punk.
(Pic: John Wickens)

THE ACCOUNTANTS (above)
archetypal Adelaidian punks.
(Pic: Eric Algra)

YOUNG MODERN (left) next to the
Warm Jets, emerged as Adelaide's first
post-JAB "new wave" band. And with
their strictly 60's influenced power-pop,
they were soon to become Adelaide's
favourite sons.
(Pic: Eric Algra)

TWO WAYS TO GO

Two new Melbourne bands are quickly gaining a reputation for startling originality in lyrics, music and presentation. To call them new wave wouldn't be fair; perhaps modern would be a more fair description of what they are on about.

Two Way Garden are a 3-piece: Philip Riley on guitar and vocals, David Bowler on drums and Stephen Rea on bass and vocals. The emphasis of their songs is a clean rhythm sound with full guitar chords laid on top. The main vocals (a job shared between Stephen and Philip) are backed by close harmonies whilst the drums and bass pound along supplying the beat.

Their original songs, which comprise the bulk of a performance, are far from derivative. Certainly the influences can be heard, but it takes more than clever plagiarism to write the sort of material they come up with. What's more, the songs are concerned with modern life, experiences and feelings.

The Young Charlatans are Rowland Howard and Ian "Ollie" Olsen on guitars and vocals, Janine Hall on bass and Jeff Wegener on drums.

Their performances are quite unforgettable. Ollie stands stage right almost rigidly at attention, eyes looking straight at the audience, a new facial expression for each word. The slashing, jerky rhythms coming from Ollie's and Rowland's guitars are hypnotic. The guitar solos are both exciting and experimental.

Janine is not a "cute chick" in the band. Her presence onstage is certainly justified by her solid bass patterns and backing vocals.

THE X-MEN (top, pictured at Brisbane's AHEPA Hall, with guest vocalist Mark, of the Disposable Fits) played "stuff from the new wave as well as from the 60's." (Pic: Jim Goodwin)

TWO WAY GARDEN (bottom right) had been together nearly three years before they made their first public appearance! When they began regular gigging, their intricate, more melodic rock was quick to earn a small-but-dedicated following. (Pic: Philip Morland)

THE YOUNG CHARLATANS
(Pic: Tanya McIntyre)

↑→↑ (left) (Pic: Tanya McIntyre)

More than any other rock drummer, Jeff holds a greater respect for the true geniuses of percussion — Krupa and Belsun (those boys from the forties). And it shows! Jeff plays offbeats and slashes, with enough economy to not only give the Young Charlatans their backbone, but to become an exciting performance in itself.

Ollie and Rowland began writing songs together last year. They fired off each other so successfully that they decided to leave their bands and form one together.

The Saints put them onto a crazy Brisbane drummer called Jeff (the professor in *Know Your Product.*) Jeff packed his kit and left for Melbourne. They clicked together and moved to Sydney where they could isolate themselves and rehearse. Janine sat in on one rehearsal and joined that day.

The completed Young Charlatans returned to Melbourne in January and began playing an assortment of venues from small clubs to the large pub dances and universities.

Rod Runner
Reprinted from *ROADRUNNER*

RADIO BIRDMAN got to Britain, put down an album's worth of material at Rockfield Studios in Wales, and then toured Britain and Europe with the Flamin' Groovies before dissent set in and the band split, mostly returning to Australia.

THE SAINTS (right) almost broke up before "Prehistoric Sounds," their last album, was recorded, but stayed together (long enough) to finish it.

THE LAST WORDS (below right) recorded an album for Wizard which was never released. A single was, but the band left for England anyway.

47

PRACTICING PSYCHO-SURGEONS

After getting Dave, Mark and Stan from the Psychosurgeons drunk in a mansion in North Adelaide and spending 45 minutes waving a microphone under their noses, the truth came out.

"We think interviews are bad because you tend to start to perform for the interviewer. You say things that get totally misunderstood. Everybody out there is just making up their own minds about what we're saying. They don't let us have complete control. They're just rats — I can hear them now. One of them will think one thing and another

THE PSYCHOSURGEONS (above)
(Pic: John Wickens)

FILTH's Bob Short (left) whose self-destructive tendencies were a contributing factor to the band's eventual dissolution. (Pic: Matt Dickson)

THE PROFESSORS (above right) took their name from the Saints' "Know Your Product," the line "Where's the professor? We need him now." Their 60's influenced punky-pop was a short-lived attraction in Sydney.
(Pic: Brad Franks)

THE KAMIKAZE KIDS (right) mated rock'n'roll classicism with the impetus of punk and Julie Mostyn's powerful voice. They were a big draw at the Civic Hotel in Sydney.
(Pic: Patrick Bingham-Hall)

X (below right)
(Pic: Patrick Bingham-Hall)

will think another but basically they're all the same cause they're just robots tuned into mechanisms of the environment or something. How's that for a philosophy and that's why we hate giving interviews. That's why we like hard and fast music, because that way we feel we can ram what we really want down their throats while they're in a vulnerable position. That is strewn out in horizontal action beneath our feet as we play. We think the only position to be in is lying on your back writhing around like a maggot on the bread of life. That's when we see where we're all at. We use our music to attack the audience — we like them to be overwhelmed by what we're doing and then to think. To think about themselves and their position in society. We can't tell you what about — it's too complex, which is why we write songs. We wouldn't write them if we could tell you. We'd write books instead. We don't want to stand up and tell people as then we'd sound like a bunch of lecturers. We want people to have a good time — dancing or whatever. We like them to concentrate with their bodies and their minds. We communicate by writhing around on stage. We play rock and roll because we enjoy it."

Heather Venn
Reprinted from *ROADRUNNER*

CRIME & THE CITY SOLUTION playing a party in Melbourne just prior to taking up permanent residence there, and undergoing significant line-up changes. Sadly, the band would break up before committing anything to vinyl, or tape. (Pic: Tanya McIntyre)

THE MANIKINS (above) formed out of the ashes of the Cheap Nasties, and quickly established themselves as an excellent post-punk pop rock band with the single, "I Never Thought I'd Find Someone Who Could Be So Kind."

THE GO BETWEENS (left) gathered immediate acclaim with their debut single, the folky post-punk pop of "Lee Remick," which was surely the first example of the Brisbane Sound.

50

THE BOYS NEXT DOOR'S BATTLE

I think that certain Australian papers are neglecting these groups, which are really important groups — in Melbourne anyway simply because of the Suicide label and certain hostilities towards the people who direct the label. We're not getting publicity because of the label. There's so much concentration on Suicide and not on the bands. We're never treated as individuals. People even think that JAB and the Boys Next Door play the same music.'' — Nick Cave, vocalist for the Boys Next Door.

The Boys Next Door fill the Suicide sandwich in more ways than one. Not only do they receive middle billing between the Teenage Radio Stars and X RayZ, but they are the only act to exhibit any really unique flavour.

The initial impact with the Boys Next Door is visual. Drummer Phill Calvert and guitarist Mick Harvey appear distinctly angelic. Bassist Tracy Pew is the contrast for the animation Nick Cave displays. Nick Cave is the focus for the band — dynamic and frantic.

"I really enjoy performing," said Nick. "We're basically concerned with music but I get a real kick out of performing. I don't just dance around, most of our songs are kind of tragic little songs and I try to put that across sometimes by breaking into tears and things like that. I've really got a fascination with the real corny kind of performers like Barry Manilow with the way he kind of skips across the stage and does all these sort of really flamboyant gestures."

The Boys Next Door have a strangely full sound for a 3-piece band: bass guitar and drums. They're not punk. "I don't even like the term new wave, because from that title people expect your music to be new and I don't think that new wave music is necessarily new, not in the formal and technical sense of music anyway. That's being explored

THE BOYS NEXT DOOR (top right) (Pic: Tanya McIntyre)
JAB (below right) not long before their final split. (Pic: Tanya McIntyre)

THE SAINTS (top) "Prehistoric Sounds" was released — a monumental album, one of the finest bar none of 1978, and one that's been criminally neglected. The band then split, mostly returning to Australia.

NEWS (nee Babeez, left) were Melbourne's answer to the Ramones with a political conscience, and as such were one of the few bands in Melbourne to resist Suicide. They played mostly benefits and campus gigs rather than pubs. (Pic: Graham Aisthorpe)

in a totally different area," explained Nick. "We're not a buzzsaw band and have never really been a buzzsaw band," added Phill. "Not a band that just goes on and plays chord, chord, chord, brrch and the sound is just a blur. I mean, we play fast but we haven't ever really fallen into that category."

Each song has its own subtle melodic variations and deft rhythm changes, founded upon Phill's crisp fast drumming, an unusually open guitar sound and a deep chanting bass. The Boys Next Door feel they've almost exhausted the 3-piece line-up and will be adding a piano synthesiser-player soon. "We have a unique way of handling a musically

THE DAGOES (top) introduced their "greasy pop" to Adelaide. (Pic: Micheal Hope)
TACTICS (bottom) formed in Canberra, where their then-embryonic sound met with apathetic reaction, though next to Myxo they were the leading if only "new wave" band in town. (Pic: Peter Nelson)

3-piece set-up, covering holes and things like that. There is no shortage of gaps or drops in our music," said Phill.

The musical aim for the Boys Next Door is musical exploration to "go boldly forth where no man has gone before," according to Phill. Apparently in the eight months since the band has seriously been approaching music the songs are "getting a lot more complicated, the words are getting more abstract and interesting. It's sort of a tragic-comic sort of thing. We look at everything in a lighthearted way," said Nick. "The songs are kind of sad and tragic but they're treated with a sort of sarcasm. When I make these gestures or cry that's done with a certain amount of comedy. We don't expect other people to cry when they see us."

The Boys Next Door have three tracks on the *Lethal Weapons* album: *Boy Hero, Masturbation Generation* and their single, *These Boots are made for Walking.* "With *Boots,* it's catchy and we originally did it because it's a bit of a joke because it's an old song and we've rearranged it so it sounds really forceful and the audience react really well to it when we play live," said Phill.

Is there the freedom within the Suicide contract for the Boys Next Door to do, record and play as they wish? Nick feels there could be problems with musical direction. "Whether they'll still support our music no matter what direction we go in. Basically I think it's a commercial label and my ideas of music aren't commercial. There could be problems there if we went out of that and started to add other instruments and become more complicated and experimental which I can see happening."

The Boys Next Door are just brimming with style, vivacity and cleverness. They just could be the most exciting thing since the Beatles filmed *A Hard Days Night.*

Jillian Burt
Reprinted from *ROADRUNNER*

IRVING & THE U-BOMBS (left) brought to Adelaide the curious mix of reggae/rock and a 60's American punk influence. (Pic: Eric Algra)

THE MODELS (above) grew out of the respective splits in the Teenage Radio Stars and JAB. (Pic: Tanya McIntyre)

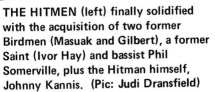

THE HITMEN (left) finally solidified with the acquisition of two former Birdmen (Masuak and Gilbert), a former Saint (Ivor Hay) and bassist Phil Somerville, plus the Hitman himself, Johnny Kannis. (Pic: Judi Dransfield)

YOUNG MODERN'S BIG BEAT

Young Modern were (and still are) nice boys. Nice, young, solid middle-class Australian boys who wanted to play rock and roll. Theirs was every school-boy's dream — to be in a rock and roll band, playing great music and having loads of adoring (mostly female) fans clambering around the stage, all interested in them. They wanted to be on *Countdown,* on the radio, regular *TV Week* centrefold pin-ups, guests on the *Mike Walsh Show,* headliners at the next 2SM outdoor extravaganza, recognized in the street, immortalized on a million bedroom walls, screamed at, and on the front page of every newspaper in the country when one of them was spotted with a female celebrity.

As you may already know, this didn't quite happen. Young Modern's first single *She's Got the Money,* backed with *Automatic,* did receive sporadic airplay on better radio stations and I did have their poster on my bedroom wall, but that's about as far as it went. Oh yeah, and John Dowler's next door neighbour did ask him one day if he played in a band — I guess that's recognition.

Young Modern played their first show on November 26, 1977. They supported Radio Birdman at Adelaide's Unley Town Hall. Chuckie Suicide reviewed them for Adelaide's fanzine *Street Fever* and had these immortal words to say: "The support band, the Young Moderns, played to an audience· of a single drunk swaying on the floor in time to the music (?). I didn't like them either." Things got better.

Steadily Young Modern became an Adelaide institution. As Dennis Atkins, from the *Sunday Mail,* once wrote: "It just wasn't a Friday night in Adelaide if Young Modern weren't playing at the Tivoli."

YOUNG MODERN (top)

THE ACCOUNTANTS (left) released a cassette recording of their performance, plus the U-Bombs and the Dagoes, at Marryatville. (One of the first Australian cassettes.)
(Pic: Eric Algra)

Young Modern's was music of the early sixties played in the late seventies. Like the Flaming Groovies, theirs is music that sounds like an amalgam of 1965 Beatles, Rolling Stones, Kinks, Byrds and Who if these bands had lived through the last 20 years in Australia and had only recently begun to play rock and roll.

They dress with that clean, untarnished style that characterized the Beatles before flower power. Just like Mum laundered all their clothes before they played. John Dowler looks like a healthier version of Brian Jones, his blonde mop-top haircut with its straight fringe dangling dangerously close to his eyes, never out of place. Cider bottle at his feet. He looks kind of awkward on stage, sort of half-dancing, half-walking but singing well, if a little monotonously, while the band play twanging, exhilarating melodies behind him. They're not the greatest musicians to ever grace a stage but wait'll you feel the rhythm and the sound, like when the first chords start your feet tapping and a few bars later you're dragged willingly towards the dance floor.

Things got so good that they went to Sydney. But alas, Sydney wasn't Young Modern's town.

"Play faster," they used to say. "Come on you wimps, play faster." All the time. The P.A. wasn't cranked high enough. And geez mate, you call those guitar solos? You must be kidding. As for the singer — poofter if you ask me.

No, Sydney wasn't Young Modern's town. Of course, there were a few devoted pop fans and music lovers, but they weren't enough to sustain the fragile personalities within the band. In desperation they turned to alcohol — a drug they never could handle.

Every so often they went to Melbourne, a town much more sympathetic to their endeavours. The end came at Rags on Saturday, July 21,

THE MANIKINS (top) toured the eastern states and created less than a sensation, though they still reigned supreme in Perth, and released the "Live Locally" cassette. (Pic: Mark Green)

THE NUMBERS (nee Near Steal, below) probably the biggest band in Brisbane, were playing more of their own material which revealed a strong 60's/English bent. Their debut "Sunset Strip" EP made a good impression.

1979. Not a happy evening at all. It was their two hundred and second show.

Since then, Young Modern have gone their individual ways — mostly back to Adelaide. Their posthumous album *Play Faster* serves as testimony to one of the finest rock and roll bands Australia has produced.

The ten tracks on *Play Faster* are mostly demo tapes recorded in Adelaide. They're rough but they capture Young Modern in fine form performing just some of their classic songs. And as a bonus, both sides of their single are included on the album.

Listening to these songs again, I'm convinced that one day Young Modern will be recognized as one of the true greats of Australian rock and roll. Like much great music, it takes time for people to realise its true worth.

Young Modern were pioneers; and for this they deserve our unending respect and appreciation. They struggled where others dared not tread.

Stuart Coupe
From Young Modern's *Play Faster*

YOUNG MODERN's John Dowler (left) (Pic: Eric Algra)

THE PASSENGERS (below) first gig at the Civic Hotel in Sydney. The Passengers united an all-star band with the considerable vocal power of Angie Pepper, Radio Birdman alumnus and almost sex-symbol. (Pic: Robyn Stacey)

YOU CAN'T PUT YOUR ARMS 'ROUND A MEMORY

Funny how time slips away. How easy it is to fall into the trap of blaming the stagnancy of one-time favourite bands on your own progressing years. How hard it is to accept that it's them up there who are fleeing sideways at a dramatic rate, not you. They play the same licks for years and you worry that you are losing touch. Ha! And while Radio Birdman was a more all-consum-

ing influence on my younger days than Gary Glitter and puberty combined, that was then and this is now and with those days lost in history, the prospect of an "almost" reunion of Sydney rock's founders reads as unthrillingly on paper as it turns out to be in practice.

There's little doubting that Radio Birdman would have been where the Angels are now if they hadn't been so patently wary of overground fame. They were the first and, if my worn shoes do not deceive me, the best band in Sydney at a time when live music was *Smoke on the Water* and satin trousers. They were the original force behind at least the first abortive generation of local punk, namely the Hellcats and the Psychosurgeons. These two bands, along with Birdman, formed an elite Sydney rock mafia which, though re-

duced in influence because of the healthy diversity of venues and bands born since then, to this day holds morbid sway over that still devoted audience thriving on memories of Taylor Square and Metallic K.O. t-shirts. My interest in this waned long ago, but could I resist the Visitors' last visit before Deniz Tek racked off to America for good, especially when the bill also includes the Hitmen and a mystery band called (wait for it) Comrades of War? Well yes, I could, but I went anyway.

Egad, it's like Anzac Day in here — the crowd of motley old diggers proudly adorned with antique red and black

THE HITMEN (Pic: Graham Aisthorpe)

59

badges of courage on their expectant chests, and the tragic legend of Radio Birdman lurking up above, a war-like spirit waiting to be exorcised. Make no mistake, the formidable crowd is here to see a once-in-a-lifetime reunion gig, not the Death of the Visitors as the typically gross eagle of doom posters around town have officially dubbed this glorified wake. Anything less will be a waste of effort. Hand-written signs outside assure us that the Comrades of War and Radio Birdman are not the same band, dampening that tinge of suspense to idle away the hours, but then again maybe that's some whacky militaristic manoeuvre to throw us off guard. Exciting is not the word.

First up are the Hitmen, still sounding the same. Johnny Kannis's big break and finest hours were in the first few Johnny and the Hitmen gigs, virtually just him fronting Birdman. When Birdman went to England, the Hitmen went Farfisa organ rock for about two weeks and were great, but when Birdman split up and started filtering back to the home country, first Chris Masuak then Warwick Gilbert joined on guitars and suddenly the Hitmen were a serious proposition. Nowadays, it's very serious. Everyone in black and very low on humour. They barge through a set of morose consistency, high on faceless average Flaming Groovies pop but low on highlights. Some good riffs but not many. Their single *Didn't Tell the Man* is an adequate example of their set. Times it by 15 or so, add a little live dynamism from Masuak whose soloing particularly has improved, and you've got a Hitmen show. Gain ten marks for wanting to leave Birdman days in the past, lose five for not being able to do it.

Between sets, as the P.A. dribbled forth recordings by old codgers like Iggy Pop and Blue Oyster Cult, one contemplates the effect Iggy Pop's expressed loathing of Radio Birdman on record had on this hysterically Stooges-conscious community.

THE VISITORS (top left)
(Pic: Linda Nolte)

THE LIPSTICK KILLERS (left) took up where the PsychoSurgeons left off— grinding out an Americanized brand of heavy-metal glitter punk.
(Pic: John Wickens)

TERMINAL TWIST (top) were a large part of the Warm Jets with a new name and progressive approach to post-punk pop. Their debut EP was well received, though the band eventually split after an unsuccessful stab at the Sydney circuit.

THE BOYS NEXT DOOR (below). Their debut album, "Door Door," was finally released by Mushroom just before Mushroom released the band themselves. Unfortunately, the band was almost playing itself into a rut on the limited Australian circuit. (Pic: Linda Nolte)

Back in the real world, I clap eyes on Deniz Tek onstage for the first time since Birdman's farewell extravaganza at the Paddington Town Hall in December 1977, and listen to the Visitors for the first and last time ever. Not surprisingly, they're corny as hell and boring as purgatory, running the gamut from pompous dramatics to vacuous yeah, baby, alright nonsense. It's so hilarious to watch all these tough sneering leather freaks sing the lyrics of *Let's Have Some Fun,* even dragging special guest Peter Tillman of the Lipstick Killers up on stage to join the already overblown line-up of serious bods going yeah, yeah as if they mean it! Cannot relate to this at all. Music of this type lives and dies on its ability to be desperate, and the Visitors aren't (weren't). After four songs I retired to the back to drink and talk.

The big moment arrived. The lights are cancelled, collective breaths are drawn in anticipation of a rock time-warp, back to best forgotten days of hope and sore ankles when sucker kids revolved lives (well, weekends anyway) around the Oxford Tavern without any choking sense of history, simply using up boundless energy, worshipping guitarists of all people, and having, ahem, a good time. I shamelessly admit to being the second ever person to join the Radio Birdman Fan Club, so I gotta right to find amusement in this moment and all its dubious pretensions. Forget it, folks, it's gone and has been for a long time, I think idly, thrilled beyond move-ment as one by one the old faces line up on stage, all except for a man who earns my undying gratitude for not turning up — Mr. Rob Younger. Who knows, maybe he wasn't even asked, but he was seen hanging around earlier in the even-

THE OTHER SIDE (top left) marked the return of Rob Younger (middle). The band played predominantly covers and if for no other reason than that never approached their potential. (Pic: Robyn Stacey)

VOIGT/465 (bottom left) with, in a rare photograph, Ne/H/il of SPK. (Pic: Linda Nolte)

ing so one can only presume that he didn't complete the matched set for ethical reasons. Whatever, there is an empty space centre-mike inadequately filled by Sisto and Kannis, two men blatantly stylised in the same old Detroit jutting jaw and Pop-dancing mould that Younger perfected and all these extras palely mimic.

So it's Birdman without the man. The set contained all the predictable Birdman favourites, plus their many covers.

No prizes for guessing the encore. All these people screeching *Yeah Hup* and shaking fists, just like when I was a lad, looked really very peculiar. I had that sinking feeling down in the stomach as the chanting reached Nurembergian levels of daft devotion and mania. The kids are taking their sweet time starting this new race. What was once upon a time an incredibly naive but just fathomable belief sounds more and more like another three chord rock song every day. The alienation complete, I happily left halfway through a pitiful second encore of *L.A. Woman.*

You can't put your arms around a memory.

Peter Nelson
Reprinted from *ROADRUNNER*

WHIRLYWIRLD "grew out of Ollie
Olsen's dissatisfaction with playing
rock'n'roll with conventional instrumentation." Whirlywirld adopted an
almost entirely electronic sound, gigging
infrequently and recording occasionally,
notably an EP for Missing Link.
(Pic: Clinton Walker)

HUBBLE, BUBBLE, TOIL AND TROUBLE

Almost ever since the band's inception, the Scientists have generated an aura of supreme self-confidence and have purveyed an image which makes you feel they have and deserve everyone's respect, affirming the myth of the Scientists as musical demigods. Indeed, the band advertise themselves as the *Legendary* Scientists.

I must confess that for a variety of reasons I've never seen the band play live before, although I've derived much pleasure from their recorded offerings.

It's Friday night and I arrive early at the Governor Broome Hotel to hear the band's guitarists Ben Juniper and Kim Salmon playing a warm-up. Great, I thought, very promising. But come the first set and it seems the legend is balsa-based, not rock. Juniper begins shakily, looking uncomfortable, and seems to completely lack confidence. His hesitant manner is made more apparent by Salmon's overconfidence, which amounts to little short of hubris as he throws himself, body and guitar, into each song.

Most of the songs in the first bracket are turgid and uninspiring, apart from *Pleasure Boy,* the Monkees' *Stepping Stone, Frantic Romantic* and Randy Newman's *Have You Seen My Baby?* Did I say that most were turgid? Well, half were, and this was enough to

THE MODELS (left) began gigging constantly and rapidly established themselves as one of Melbourne's favourite bands, with their catchy, quirky plastic pop. (Pic: Mark Green)

disappoint me.

Another mundane original, *Pissed On Another Planet,* begins the second bracket and I am becoming disillusioned as fast as the legend is evaporating. However, from this point things really pick up. A great cover of *Walk in the Room* is followed by the magnificent *That Girl. Kinda Girl* is sluggy and *Girl* (lotsa "girls") is an okay medium tempo job. The New York Dolls' *Pills* is more than adequately done, and *Make It* is not bad. *She Said She Loves Me* closes the bracket and would have been the highlight of the night if not for the flat lead singing.

I figure things are about even. The band have made amends for the first bracket, but I wonder whether this will be one for posterity or a mere "yeah, not bad" affair.

It is soon apparent that the former is to be the case. The third bracket opens with the Undertones' *Teenage Kicks,* which is much gutsier than the original; *Shake* is great live; *Sorry Sorry* is quite enjoyable; so too is *Dropout; Bet You're Lyin'* is heavy pop; *Don't Lie to Me* is adopted via the Flamin' Groovies, but the Scientists' version is more powerful.

By now I'm feeling pretty forgiving. For the last set, the band recommence with the Velvets' *There She Goes Again,* followed by *Pretty Girls,* which combines melody, gutsy musicianship and neat harmonies. *Making a Scene* is another good one, and *With a Girl Like You* sees the Troggs done proud. *Destroy All Planets* is too harsh and too fast. However, it keeps the momentum up as the band climax with *Slow Death.*

Although on stage the spotlight is very much on Kim Salmon, you can't help being overwhelmed by the perfect and furious drumming of James Baker. He has confidence and presence and while he's a great drummer he would have made a great frontman.

Of all the people inextricably associated with Perth punk, James heads the list. He is the perfect representative. Bearing this in mind, I visited him the Sunday after for the following interview.

How do you see The Victims in relation to the development of punk in Perth?

Baker: "I don't know. It was really strange. I don't see them as doing much. I just see them as being a band."

I don't know about that. They seem to be the band that broke it.

Baker: "Oh yeah, they started it, but

JAMES FREUD (above) and friends at the Bondi Lifesaver on James' year off. (Pic: Catherine Hardy)

THE BROKEN TOYS' David Virgin (below). The Broken Toys were a seminal, short-lived Grand Hotel band whose neo-pop would develop beyond the band's own life span. (Pic: Darian Turner)

I think they were over-rated. They got more credibility than the Scientists, which I think are a better band, but you wouldn't tell that to anyone in the street because to them, the Victims are sacred. But if they saw the Victims today, they'd probably hate them, except that they were the Victims. People have become so critical these days of sound quality and volume and all that. The Victims were a loud obnoxious noise. Off harmonies, off everything. Today they wouldn't even get a support gig."

What role do you see the Scientists playing in the future of punk?

Baker: "Not a great deal again. I can't see the Scientists being anything but a band. I can't see us inspiring people to do anything."

I find these answers hard to take because the image you purvey is of super-confidence . . .

Baker: "We definitely have that image. We do believe we're the best band in town and that the rest don't matter. It shows in our music, even though we're not the most popular group in town at this stage."

What have been some of the influences on you over the years?

Baker: "Definitely punk rock. I'm not going to use the term 'new wave'. I hate all this new wave and punk rock. It's PUNK ROCK. The Sex Pistols were the best. The Damned and the Ramones. That's what we get our influences from: the energy of those groups. With the melodies of the Flamin' Groovies. "

Who does most of the songwriting?
Baker: "Me and Kim and Ian."
Do you write the music as well?
Baker: "No, I usually write the lyrics or get an idea for a song from something I see or read . . . watching television . . ."

THE APARTMENTS (above) set was dominated by covers of 60's hits, but they were interpreted distinctively and the band's own material was plainly excellent. Their "Return of the Hypnotist" EP was another fine example of the Brisbane Sound.
(Pic: Graham Aisthorpe)

THE GO BETWEENS (left) second single, "People Say," was as good if not better than the first and a fond farewell from the band as they departed to Britain. (Pic: Graham Aisthorpe)

THE POLES (below) were inspired to take up music by the Saints, and took it from there themselves, to become another slant on the Brisbane Sound. They were probably best described as "a wonderful slice of modern pop halfway between the Shadows and the Saints." (Pic: Joe Borkowski)

LA FEMME (top left) were essentially a heavy-metal band in glitter-punk clothing whose credibility was mainly due to their rapport with their audience and their association with Missing Link Records. (Pic: Mark Green)

THE HUMANS (above) were like Brisbane's answer to La Femme, a heavy-metalesque pop band in glitter-punk clothing. They quickly became very popular in Brisbane, and even toured the southern states.

RON RUDE (top right) was a sound engineer cum musician. With constantly changing line-ups of his Unforgettables, he ensconced himself in his own Melbourne studio at Belgrave, and produced a debut album, "The Borders of Disgrace."

Who decides which non-originals to do?

Baker: "Usually me and Kim. We try not to do too many. We've got about ten non-originals and we rotate them."

Have you found it hard to gain acceptance and earn respect as musicians?

Baker: "Totally. We get no respect from anyone."

Not even from other new wave musicians?

Baker: "Yeah, but I don't know about them. They're a bit against the Scientists these days. They think we're finished."

What are your favourite local bands?

Baker: "I like the Manikins. The Rockets. Enemy Sounds. I was really impressed with them. They were like the Damned in the sense that they drove everyone out of the place with such high energy. I enjoyed the Triffids."

How would you describe the music that the Scientists play?

Baker: "Really high energy rock'n' roll, I suppose. That's a pretty dull

statement, isn't it?"

Yes, in comparison to actually seeing the band. Sixties-ish?

Baker: "Some of the tunes are a bit sixties-ish. The lyrics are. Boy6girl, most of them. Girls and planets. Planets take a lot of beating."

Have you ever thought about playing the role of front man?

Baker: "How can a drummer be a front man?"

Dave Clark could . . .

Baker: "I am getting a mike from now on."

Do you think you'll still be a musician in five years' time?

Baker: "Can't see myself doing anything else."

Was it true that you smashed the recording meters at Sweetcorn Studios with the volume of your playing or is that another part of the Scientists myth?

His mischievous blue-eyed grin lets you know it's true.

Kim Williams
Reprinted from *ROADRUNNER*

(Pic: Clinton Walker)

FUCK DANCE, LET'S ART

↑→↑ are not your average rock and roll band. In fact, they're not a rock and roll band at all.

↑→↑ — pronounced with three clicks of the tongue — are not easy to describe; I suppose the best way would be to call them a collective of artists and musicians who, at various times, and in various guises, perform music, stage plays, screen films, exhibit artwork, and occasionally roll it all up into what the sixties called a ''multi-media happening.''

↑→↑ are a Total Enterprise. And in that sense they're not dissimilar to the Residents. They manage themselves, direct any recordings themselves, and handle all their own promotion (which extends to printing, as well as designing their posters, newsletters, and record sleeves). If they had the finance at their disposal, their enterprise would be on the same scale and therefore, I don't doubt, equally as successful as the Residents. But that's mere conjecture.

Over the past year however, ↑→↑ — predominantly, they're a 4-piece band — have been operating more and more within Melbourne's rock and roll circuit, and as a result, have attained some of the recognition they deserve.

On record particularly, the music of ↑→↑ is immediately appealing — usually catchy, well arranged, and snappily played. But their whole demeanour suggests there's more to it than that.

↑→↑ have been simultaneously linked with the burgeoning electronic music movement (because of their use of synthesisers) and the new music movement; although connections do exist, they're tenuous.

The various incarnations of ↑→↑ perform as often as anyone will let them, and always inspire a mixed reaction. I've heard comments like ''They're too young,'' and from a bearded gentleman scratching his chin, ''But they're so serious.''

''They come to see us play, we come to see them,'' said ↑→↑'s Philip Brophy. ''But they've always had this condescend ing attitude to us — that we're just kids, you know.''

↑→↑ refuse to align themselves with the experimental music movement or any other school for that matter. As they once said: ''We are not loyal to any particular music style, artform, or, most importantly, ourselves.''

''It's not a musical thing,'' Brophy began. ''The more and more it goes on, the less musical it gets. It's not, you know, 'Hey, that bass line sounds good, keep playing it . . . hey, what if we play these chords . . . hey, that sounds great!' It's not that."

"It comes down to seduction," he continued. "We're against the people who fool you with this shit; who are even fooling themselves. Like music is basically a mysterious thing. I mean mysterious in that the object of the musician — the game the musician is playing — is to give you this object, and what would basically be the main intention of it is to hide and disguise, very cleverly, how it got there. What musician gets up and says, 'Ha, you know how I did that? I did this, I did that. Look, there's nothing to it.'

"They spend 10,000 years working out these chord progressions, and they're the most mechanical thing

TWO WAY GARDEN sadly split after the lack of success of their debut "Overnight" EP, which was in fact the first Au Go Go record. (Pic: Philip Morland)

THE THOUGHT CRIMINALS (above) gradually built a higher profile with much more gigging and recording for their own Doublethink label, which itself was a growing concern.
(Pic: Linda Nolte)

IDIOT SAVANT from Sydney (left)

X (below left) (Pic: Simon Van Der Holst)

you've heard in your life. There's just so many formulas. Our music doesn't hide that. It just doesn't. We hide fucking nothing. We're showing you what a C-major harmony is. We're showing you this and that. This is what it's all about. This is how fucking easy it is, y'know. The criteria of criticism boils down to, just these simple things. You know, like your favourite guitarist plays da, da, da — of course he can play that, he's been playing that for 20 years. What would you expect him to do? That's what he wants to do, that's his job, so why be amazed?"

My real argument with these contentions of Brophy's is that the "simple things" he refers to are usually employed as a means to an end; that end is personal expression. And to achieve

70

that end requires the exploitation of a skill. But Brophy remains cynical.

"What is skill? Skill is an amount of acquired knowledge of tactics and techniques. Musicians know that certain melodies are sad, certain melodies are happy. It's just a certain combination of notes. That's structure.

"Basically, I just don't believe in expression. I'm laying that on the line. It's got to do with the transference of ideas into physical reality, and then for that physical reality to be communicative, I just don't believe there's total control."

Point taken. After all, as Lou Reed said in *Some Kinda Love:* "Between thought and expression, lies a life-time."

Brophy does have a valid thesis, however, although unlike him I don't believe his to be the only option open to a present-day musician — there's room yet to extend the boundaries of skill.

"We're acting at using the skills," Brophy concluded. "We're just gleaning the conventions and realising how they're used. We're analytical. That's all we fucking are. We look at things structurally, not texturally, not superficially, not emotionally, not meaningfully, but structurally. That's the guts of it."

Clinton Walker

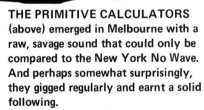

THE PRIMITIVE CALCULATORS (above) emerged in Melbourne with a raw, savage sound that could only be compared to the New York No Wave. And perhaps somewhat surprisingly, they gigged regularly and earnt a solid following.
(Pic: Clinton Walker)

THE SLUGFUCKERS (below) who nobody would dare to try to categorize and who couldn't be anyway, appear at the Sculpture Centre in Sydney, which says something in itself.

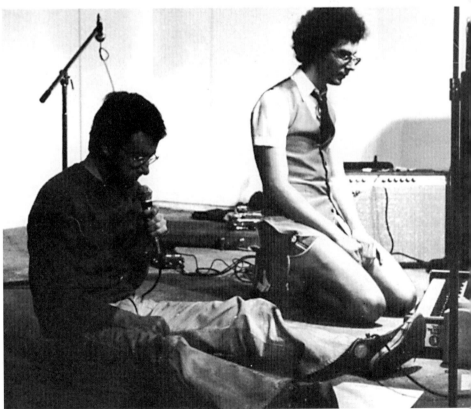

IS NEW IS . . . .

And here comes another one. Butting in amidst all this lucky country musical optimism, I righteously offer yet another indigenous digestible as the yardstick future generations will create towards.

A completely self-financed LP from a recently deceased, largely unknown group recorded on an 8-track that no one famous has ever used has left those vacant big-wigs up where they belong — staring into space — because it takes chances, because they have no one but themselves to answer to (or blame). The shaky Enigma circuit (more splits than hits, more rumours than gigs), from Whirlywirld to the Thought Criminals, at least keeps us alert. And I have faith that this Voigt/465 album

VOIGT/465 (above) (Pic: Peter Nelson)

THE N-LETS (left) came from Woollongong with their totally improvised, "free form" rock, and the 2-Tapes cassette company, which spread the gospel. (Pic: Ken West)

will be some vague vanguard for the NEW new Australian undercurrent. Hope springs eternal.

Ten tracks recorded over a weekend just two days before their final show at Rags in June, every song is a little milestone in song structuring and actual soundwise originality. Every effort has been made to experiment with standard rock noises. A small shift from the common emphasis in most cases, though any deviation after years of no-risk rock is bound to appear drastic.

F1, the least hummable, most controversial, least representative track, is 7 minutes of improvisation. Little, loud electric shrieks and vocal squeals over a steady synthesizer beat way back. It was and is both daring and effective.

Red Lock on Sea Steal, the other track you have to be in a fairly unique state to dance to, is practically rhythm and nothing else. Bass, drums and guitar pounding the least likely beat you've ever heard, that famous steel pipe being hammered for the last time in an equally eratic off-beat, before it all caves in on a couple of minutes of guitar and drum frenzy.

But don't be afraid, danceable crotchets and recognizable emotion abound in the remaining eight straightish rock songs. If it's the attractive attack of the lop-sided rhythms that initially grabs ears, then the unrelenting passion of the vocals (and therefore lyrics) will tie you down and drag you in. Passion, being no ordinary word, is also no common ingredient in popular music, requiring rather more desperation or need to communicate than most performers can be bothered with. These songs were actively inspired by specific incidents, not out of a contriving search for a good story, almost always dealing with conflicting emotions or ideas. Determined, thoughtful and a little bit angry but never depressing. And I've heard that is what it's really all about.

The music itself is fairly strident, conventional avant garde. A good solid beat, but with funny noises and slightly odd timing. Some people still apparently find this kind of thing a bit weird and off-putting but that's their problem.

So Voigt split in a decidedly unromantic, remorseless action, leaving Wednesday night barren while they seemed, after initial nasty bits, to be quite happy to all move on. Without being too grand, I think this record is important. I am definitely very biased, but I might also be very right.

Peter Nelson
Reprinted from *ROADRUNNER*

TACTICS moved from Canberra to Sydney, and immediately benefitted for it, their psychedelic/reggae-influenced post-punk pop growing more impressive.

THE PASSENGERS RIDE ENDS

There was something really magical about the Passengers at their best, something undeniably powerful and understated. It had a lot to do with Angie Pepper's voice. When she sang the Shangri-Las' *Remember (Walkin' in the Sand)* it was a moment you'd never forget.

The first time I saw them was on a really warm autumn night. There was a fan blowing from side stage and they did that song. Now I consider *Remember* to be one of the greatest songs ever written. It's a song about time and its awesome power, the elusive moment between womanhood and childhood, the impossibility of holding that second and the sadness of the loss. It's a song about virgin purity and about flesh, trust and betrayal. The horror of loneliness made so much more powerful by restraint. The meaning hints at emo-

**THE PASSENGERS' Angie Pepper.
(Pic: Cathy Croll)**

tional holocaust, the music pulls back. It's about love and preserving innocence in the face of brutal reality.

When the Passengers did it that night and they came to the chorus, the red light hit Angie, as if to freeze the moment in time, and that fan blew her hair ever so slightly and she sang that chorus with such a pure voice — like she was singing for every girl in the world who ever broke her heart. It was a moment that was removed from the

present as though sealed in a glass or painted on a canvas, universal, so minute and detailed a story and yet saying everything there was to be said.

Had they just done that one song that night, it would have been more than memorable, but the Passengers had a great many other surprises in store then and over the ensuing months. Originals like *Sad Day, Take me Back to the Dance, I'm in Love with Your Boyfriend* and others, and terrific covers like *Riot on Sunset Strip* and a version of the Ronettes' *Do I Love You* which bettered Phil Spector's.

Angie had a special quality that went with her great voice, a quality that so few singers achieve: conviction. When she sang a cover version, she made it her own. There were times, particularly during their farewell gig, when it seemed she was on the verge of breaking down. And that's what real rock and roll is about: laying yourself on the line.

For all the singer's talent though, the Passengers were a band. Steve Harris on keyboards, Jeff Sullivan on guitar, Jim Dickson on bass, Alan Brown their original drummer, and Gerry Jones, who played their last few gigs. The Passengers as a band were all capable of those same qualities that were most apparent in the vocals: a muted force and a commitment to exploring all the emotional aspects of a song.

It's unfortunate that Angie Pepper's leaving the country brings the band to such an abrupt halt. As she said on that last, emotional night: "We're not ready to break up yet."

Toby Creswell
Reprinted from *ROADRUNNER*

Chris Bailey (top right) returned to Australia and put together a band he called THE SAINTS, containing only one other ex-Saint, Ivor Hay, and a changeable number of others. The band did a few sellout gigs, playing mostly old Saints' hits. (Pic: Judi Dransfield)

THE RIPTIDES (nee Numbers) "pop art" — mod threads, 60's-influenced and with a contemporary awareness — had made them the most popular band in Brisbane, bar none.

NEWS (right) were almost a (political) institution in Melbourne by 1979, but by that time the band was on its last legs, and signed off finally with the "That Girl/I'm So Confused" single.

LAST 'HEE HAW' FROM THE BOYS NEXT DOOR

The Boys Next Door's career has been a turbulent one. In just two short years they've recorded for three different labels: Suicide, Mushroom, and now Missing Link; turned down potentially lucrative offers; earnt not even the contempt but the ridicule of fellow musicians; been ignored by radio, shunned by *Countdown,* barred from Bombay Rock; beaten up, arrested several times, and turned in some of the most miserable excuses for performances I've ever witnessed.

But at the same time, they've produced a handful of excellent records, and on occasion, delivered performances verging on brilliant.

It's this side of the Boys Next Door that leads me to consider them, simply, one of the finest bands in this country.

From their very beginnings, the Boys Next Door chose a path leading towards freer abstraction, and every phase of their development has been a step further along that path.

Their vinyl progression is a fair indication of this — from the punk-inspired beginnings of their contribution to Suicide's *Lethal Weapons;* to their debut album *Door, Door* on Mushroom, which found them finally entering a more sophisticated sort of ground, not unlike that which Magazine and Television were working within; to *Scatterbrain,* a one-off single given away at the Crystal Ballroom, which was a looser, more spontaneous extension of the style established on *Door, Door;* to their latest offering, *Hee Haw,* a five-track 12 inch EP on Missing Link. *Hee Haw* is the Boys Next Door's most coherent statement yet.

"The group is starting to realise its ideals," guitarist Rowland Howard said. "It's not an entirely new thing that's gone *click,* and we've started doing this, that and the other."

"It seems the more we write, the less influence of other people we're under," says vocalist Nick Cave.

"We're getting more confident, and that's allowing us to become more adventurous," adds bassist Tracy Pew.

Rowland: "There's more understand-

THE BOYS NEXT DOOR, soon to become the Birthday Party. (Pic: Peter Milne)

ing, within the group, of what we're trying to do, rather than just the person who's writing the song."

Of course, the way a song is written can determine what it will eventually sound like.

Tracy: "The songs are becoming more and more band compositions."

Rowland: "Like, nowadays, Nick tends to come along to rehearsals and say, 'I've got a new song,' and sit down at the piano and pound out this three-note little thing. My songs are always more worked out than Nick's, but still much less than they used to be."

Tracy: "Nick's offerings are getting less and less substantial. He doesn't bother composing them, or arranging them."

Nick: "It is quite true that I don't bother too much about actually arranging songs, because the group as a whole generally do it better. It's much easier, I think, to feel out an arrangement, as opposed to doing it beforehand."

So songwriting is a growth process?

Tracy: "Yeah, yeah. They come in stages. Like when Nick showed us *Hair Shirt*, which is on the EP, all he had was a sort of bastardized version of *What shall we do with a drunken sailor*."

Nick: "I had the tune, and an idea of how the tune should be played, and the words, and the vocal melody."

Tracy: "I think it's a good way to write songs. Rowland's earlier songs used to be very much the opposite. He'd start with a bass line, and build on it, layer by layer. And we had these very stolid songs like *I Mistake Myself*."

Rowland: "There's nothing really wrong with that type of thing. It just comes out with a different feeling, and that's not really the kind of feeling we want at the moment. The music I've always liked best has been the music that's conjured up an atmosphere, and had a really strong feeling about it. I've always wanted to do that; maybe we're accomplishing it now . . ."

They are. *Hee Haw* is a vindication of the band's approach. Each of the five songs — Rowland Howard's *Red Clock* and *Death by Drowning,* and Nick Cave's *Faint Heart, A Catholic Skin,* and *Hair Shirt* — capture a palpable tension. In some ways, the band has managed to escape many of the absurd constraints of the rock-song structure — these are songs of base simplicity, mobile structures (usually characterised by a recurring repetitive motif), and improvised embellishments.

Nick: "We generally work with one theme that basically runs through the whole song."

Tracy: "Sometimes it sounds really chaotic, like in *Death By Drowning,* which has a clarinet tooting away all the time, but fundamentally they're simpler

THE BOYS NEXT DOOR's Nick Cave (above) at Richmond Recorders. The band spent a lot of time in the studio putting down "Hee Haw" and a year's worth of singles before leaving for Britain. (Pic: Clinton Walker)

THE LAUGHING CLOWNS (below) were formed by ex-Saint Ed Kuepper (second from left) upon his return from Britain. After much rehearsal, the band made their debut late in the year, to a perplexed response.
(Pic: Judi Dransfield)

songs. Our songs seem to be getting simpler and simpler."

Rowland: "They're getting sparser, in a way, too. There are more spaces."

Tracy: "It's just getting into more freedom."

Rowland: "I find it really hard playing a really organised piece anyway. It's not very much fun, and it's hard, after a while, to inject any sort of energy into it. It's a lot harder for us to convey our ideas now, because they're more abstract."

Nick: "A lot more of our own . . .

obsessions, I suppose, are coming out."

Rowland: "I think the really good thing about our music is that it always has a slightly self-mocking element to it. Whatever we do, we're never totally serious about it. I mean, music's just sound anyway."

Hee Haw has met with a mixed reaction. It is, after all, music unlike any ever recorded in this country (and could only be compared to one other Australian band — Whirlywirld.)

The Boys Next Door are still playing basically the same circuit they were two

years ago, but by now their labours have become little more than a means to an end.

Tracy: "We reached a plateau in Australia a really long time ago, and we've just been rolling along ever since. The thing is that now we're doing gigs mainly with a view to getting money so we can go overseas."

Obviously, England seems like a greener pasture.

Rowland: "Well, we could sell ourselves better in any country where there's a larger population, because there'd be more people per acre that liked us. These tracks (on the EP) we're going to use as demos for record companies in England."

Clinton Walker
Reprinted from RAM by permission.
Copyright.

THE SCIENTISTS (top left)

THE MODELS (below) broke up, then reformed for a New Years' Eve gig at the Crystal Ballroom, and then stayed together.

UNDERGROUND OVERSEAS

All of us are only too well aware of the inroads Oz-rock is making into the international marketplace. Austalian music is nowadays a force to be reckoned with. Or at least that's what we keep telling ourselves . . .

It's actually hard to determine just how well "our boys" are going "over there." And let's not be blinded by that absurd c'mon-Aussie-c'mon sense of patriotism, huh?

It is, however, impressive to note that in England the Birthday Party have recorded a session for John Peel's BBC Radio 1 programme. Peel is one of the most popular and influential disc jockeys in all of England.

And the Birthday Party aren't the only ones — in England right now there's quite a contingent of Australian bands working within the "underground"; these bands represent an aspect of the "Australian Invasion" that's as little known as it is the source of some excellent music.

As well as the sessions for John Peel, the Birthday Party have begun gigging, and will see their debut English single, *Mister Clarinet,* released in the very near future.

The Saints have just returned to England after a "sell-out" Australian tour, and they have high hopes. But their story is well known . . . more obscure are the Last Words, the Go Betweens and Whirlywird.

The Last Words are a straight-forward punk band who actually recorded an album for Wizard whilst they were still in Sydney. Although a single, *Animal World,* was lifted from it, the album was never released, and the band left the country. They've been in England for over a year now, gigging regularly, and have had two singles released.

The Go Betweens are a brilliant if idiosyncratic band who are like a meeting of *Blonde On Blonde* period Dylan and the Velvet Underground. In Brisbane they recorded two excellent singles for the Able Label, and it was these that prompted Beserkley Records (home of Jonathan Richman) to offer the band a contract. They turned it down at the time, but have since journeyed to England, in search of new

TACTICS' David Studdert (Pic: Stephen Hocking)

ideas and other such offers.

Whirlywirld were a band "not unlike a truckie yelling and screaming as he drives slowly through a china shop." I say "were" because Whirlywirld, as such, are no longer. Six months ago, the nucleus of the band — leader Ian "Ollie" Olsen and drummer John Murphy — packed up and left for

WHIRLYWIRLD (above) (Pic: Alan Bamford)

THE PRIMITIVE CALCULATORS (left) alienated more people than they attracted, but they persevered, making original sounds and a "statement," and wielding considerable influence in the process, until they left Australia for Europe. (Pic: Janis Lesinskis)

England. Now, with two new guitarists and a new name — Hugo Klang — the band are about to embark on a new phase.

Hugo Klang are typical of the kind of band who see they have little future in this country — it's the hostile, unsympathetic reactions that drive them away.

The original Whirlywirld grew out of Ollie Olsen's dissatisfaction with playing rock'n'roll with conventional instrumentation. Olsen had served time with a couple of Melbourne's seminal punk combos, as had John Murphy — the pair joined forces to form a band that would move into the realm of electronic sound.

Whirlywirld's debut EP (recorded late in '78) was a pale representation of the band's real capabilities. Their music —an almost totally electronic environment— was evocative and intensely powerful.

By the middle of 1979, Olsen and Murphy had assembled a new Whirlywirld, with bassist Greg Sun and guitarist Arnie Hanna, and a new approach. Of the wholly electronic sound only one synthesizer remained, and Olsen had introduced his horn playing to the fray. This made Whirlywirld a band of much freer structure than its earlier editions.

Missing Link has just released a 12" EP of this model Whirlywirld.

"I was trying to finally exorcize the rock'n'roll that was inbred in me — I was not successful," Olsen said over the phone from London. (Some influences — Bowie, Beefheart and James Brown — are evident, and although the band would admit to a respect for Beefheart and Brown, they'd vehemently deny any for Bowie.) "I don't like it," Olsen continued, "it's clinical, a Dr. Kildare-like operation that was a total failure — besides creating a nice disco sound which I always wanted to do.

"The direction we're heading in now bears no more than a passing resemblance to Whirlywirld," Olsen said. "This group is totally different, and has a new name — Hugo Klang — which is only logical. I just hope maybe I can relay information to people. Back and forth. That'll be enough."

Clinton Walker
Reprinted from RAM by permission. Copyright.

Out of and around the Primitive Calculators and Whirlywirld grew a network of "little bands," purveyors of the "North Fitzroy Beat."

Above: THRUSH & THE CUNTS (Pic: Ann-Marie Rourke)

Centre right: THE ALAN BAMFORD MUSICAL EXPERIENCE (Pic: Kim Beissel)

Right: THE J.P. SARTRE BAND (Pic: Paul Dogood)

Below & right: the MANIKINS were seldom heard of on the eastern seaboard, but in Perth the band maintained their standing as they themselves remained unchanged, seeming to have missed their opportunity.
(Pic: Kim Williams)

Above: the FLECKS (nee White Riot) were Tasmania's one and only punk band (still).

Left: the YOUNG DOCTEURS became Canberra's leading light after their "Rock Against Boredom" gigs throughout 1978. Their supremacy was challenged only by the Naturals, No Concept and Quintrex Bop.
(Pic: Chris Bird)

DOUBLE-THINKING

Let's face it, for any band starting off in Sydney, or anywhere for that matter, it's just a complete and utter fight. All you've got is your usual avenues, and either way you get nowhere really."

Mark Handley is slumped over his desk at the Doublethink office. "I mean, major agencies have got 30 bands on their books," he says, "and there's just no reason why they'd put a lot of hard work and effort into supporting a baby band."

Mark Handley, along with Roger Grierson, is at the helm of Doublethink, an alternative booking agency that's recently been established in Sydney.

On Doublethink's roster is just a handful of relatively small-time bands, like the Thought Criminals, Popular Mechanics, Tactics, the Singles, Sekret Sekret, Seems Twice and J.M.M. Doublethink is also an independent record company; it's so far released two

Thought Criminals' EPs, a Popular Mechanics' EP, a Barons' EP, singles by Rejex, and the Suicide Squad, and an album by Thought Criminals.

That the Thought Criminals would seem to dominate Doublethink proceedings is no big surprise, for it was they — predominantly bassist Grierson — who originally conceived the project.

The Doublethink moniker (derived, like the term "thought criminals," from George Orwell's *1984*) first appeared a couple of years ago, on the label of the Thought Criminals debut EP.

The Thought Criminals were forced to go it alone, and go it alone they did — they slogged away, released a record themselves and, having built up a con-

siderable following, eventually managed to penetrate the inner city pub circuit.

In July last year came Doublethink's next record — the Thought Criminals second EP, *Food for Thoughtcrimes*. Not long after that the band embarked on what was termed their "Spreading Themselves Thin Tour" — playing the city pubs solidly for four weeks.

"In that month nearly every night was with a different support band," Grierson said. The Thought Criminals were handing over support spots to bands who most *needed* them, like Popular Mechanics, the Products, Tactics, The Ugly Mirrors (who became Sekret Sekret), Moving Parts, Seems Twice and Idiot Savant.

Top: THE THOUGHT CRIMINALS at Garibaldi's. (Pic: Catherine Hardy)

Right: the SINGLES were one of the bands to come out of the Broken Toys, making mod music for punk people. Pictured: an early gig at French's. (Pic: Darian Turner)

Left: J.M.M. were a "power trio" in a short, sharp but not quite so simple sense. (Pic: Linda Nolte)

Below left: POPULAR MECHANICS showcased genuine good musicianship and a pop sensibility for all the punks to see and hear. (Pic: Marjorie McIntosh)

"The support bands started getting popular as well," Handley continued, "and work started coming in for them. So when the Thoughties went off the road, bands like Popular Mechanics and Tactics kept working."

"I was in a position to get work for the bands when they couldn't do it themselves, so I didn't want to stop," Grierson said. Thus Doublethink was born.

"Everything just sort of arrived," Handley said, "none of it was really planned; never at any stage did we sit down and say, 'well, let's start an agency.' It just happened. And from there, it was obvious, what with the Thoughties recording, and Popular Mechanics recording . . .''

"The small amount of money we made out of that month we virtually lent to Rejex and Suicide Squad to do their singles," Grierson explained. "That's how the record part came about."

The Doublethink catalogue is an annoying one — doused with integrity and good intentions, it falls short in terms of actual content. The singles by Rejex and the Suicide Squad are equally appalling heavy-metal/punk thrashes. Ditto the Barons EP. Popular Mechanics' *From Here to Obscurity* EP is perhaps prophetically titled — it's nothing more than totally *ordinary* rock'n'roll.

The Thought Criminals, however, are a band that's *trying,* as their album *Speed . . . Madness . . . Flying Saucers* testifies. It charts their development over two years, having been recorded intermittently in that time.

"We just enjoy working at a relaxed pace," Grierson said.

"The album doesn't work, and it was never intended to work, as a thematic whole. It's just a representation of the stuff we've done," continued Grierson.

And it's sold a healthy 800 copies. "The records on their own aren't a viable proposition," Grierson said. "There's no way we put out records for the money."

"At this stage," Handley continued, "we put out records hoping that in selling those records, and getting some airplay, and publicity, that we'll attract more people to the gigs."

Well, it had to come to this — the "money-go-round" — sooner or later. So what is the difference between Doublethink and the majors?

"Well, we maintain that we *care* about our bands," Handley said.

Admirable sentiments indeed; and what's more, they seem to be *working*— the Thought Criminals have put the Clash's ideals into practice (which I don't see the Clash doing). Doublethink has got bands off the bottom rungs of the ladder, to somewhere just below the middle. The question is: can they push them any further? Or will the majors, who are already vying for some of Doublethink's bands, take over? In other words, is Doublethink just a half-way house?

"It's only a half-way house because we're only half-way there, if you know what I mean," Handley smiled. "At the moment Doublethink is what it is — everybody knows that. But that's because we've only been around for 6 months. In the last 6 months what we've accomplished is that we can now communicate with agents and promoters and the rest of them. They know us, and they know we've got a few bands that will work, so now they take notice."

Clinton Walker

Right: SEKRET SEKRET, like the Singles, came out of the Broken Toys, making psychedelic music for punk people. (Pic: Kathleen O'Brien)

Bottom right: LITTLE MURDERS occupied a similar position in Melbourne as the Singles did in Sydney, a post-punk band of mod influences. (Pic: Lyn Gordon)

Below: LA FEMME grew in status on Melbourne's suburban circuit, and early in the year had their debut album released.

Above: INTERNATIONAL EXILES
came from the same source as Little
Murders, but unlike them pursued a
more "modern" vision of pop.

Left: the MODELS, hype style.

SERIOUS WORDS ABOUT LAUGHING CLOWNS

When the Saints were formed in 1973 the biggest — the only — hurdle they faced was simple, mindless opposition from audiences that just weren't ready for them.

Now, some four years later, the former Saints' main-man, Ed Kuepper, finds himself in much the same situation once again.

Chris Bailey took the easy way out—he 're-formed' the Saints, and is laughing all the way to the bank with the rewards that that (acceptable) name reaps nowadays.

"As far as I'm concerned," Kuepper remarked, "the Saints broke up two years ago."

Kuepper himself is fronting an outfit called Laughing Clowns, who meet with antipathy at every turn.

"To be honest, I don't know why people react the way they do," he said. There's still this sort of disdain for good playing. Like, I reacted against the super-technician type of musician a number of years ago when the Saints started, and therefore that roughness and sloppiness was part of that statement. Now, I find pleasure in hearing things well played. Not that that necessarily needs an excellent musician, as such. Good musicianship doesn't necessarily equate with . . . well, boring music. Basically, I just think it's important to try and improve."

Ed Kuepper was in a quandary after the dissolution of the Saints in England late in 1978. He returned to Australia. It wasn't long, however, before he'd decided to re-enter the fray.

This decision was encouraged by two old friends — Wegener (who'd drummed with an early incarnation of the Saints), and saxophonist Bob Farrell — who were keen to collaborate with Kuepper.

A bassist, Ben Wallace-Crabbe, was quickly recruited, and Laughing Clowns

Above: LAUGHING CLOWNS, 4-piece. (Pic: Graham Aisthorpe)

Below: X were mostly seen at the Heritage Hotel, where they held down a Thursday night residency, but they did, at long last, release a single and an album. (Pic: Francine McDougall)

came into being. After nearly six months of rehearsals, the band began gigging in August.

"We had a lot of problems . . . reaction differed. The audience seemed to sort itself out into two distinct groups — those that hated us, and those that liked us.

"I think the main problem — well, it's not really a problem, but it seems to be — is that the music is quite 'singular,' for want of a better word, and, like, you can't really compare it to anything that's catching on overseas, and yet at the same time we're not doing anything Australian bands are doing," Kuepper said.

"It can't easily be classified, into really obvious categories," Wegener added. Because Laughing Clowns are unique — a band that really does defy categorization.

"The music's only parallel lies in latter-day Saints," Kuepper said, "and in a way that's a bad state of affairs."

While Laughing Clowns' music is a logical progression from the Saints' *Prehistoric Sounds,* at the same time it's a departure, a foray into new territory.

This is the result of the band's growing awareness of the avenues open to them. The five members of the band — they've since added a pianist, Dan Wallace-Crabbe, Ben's cousin — have a *diversity* of influences.

"Say, as far as the saxophone goes, Bob doesn't play like any other rock sax player I can think if," Kuepper said, "and whereas he's jazz-influenced, he doesn't sound like any particular jazz sax player. And I think that's fairly true of everyone in the band — there is a reasonable amount of individuality. Whle nobody is technically brilliant, it still manages to work well."

At various times, Laughing Clowns' songs can be fast, or they can be slow; they can be simple, or they can be complex; they can be melodic, or they can be disonant; but what's most important is that they create a mood and a tension, and that the band have room to move, exploring these nuances.

No one instrument dominates the proceedings; rather, they're all in the front line, jostling for the lead. This includes the drums — Laughing Clowns are a very rhythmic, very percussive band.

"I think a lot of people who play music play *roles,*" Wegener proffered. "They don't really think about the whole point of what it is to play an instrument. As corny as it may sound, it's got something to do with making some sort of statement, and being creative, or expressing something. And all of us are egotistical enough to want to make a statement."

Eventually, after months of sporadic gigging, the band realised they were fighting a losing battle, and that the only way to be properly heard was on vinyl.

"Basically, we just *needed* to record. I'd started to get a bit impatient, because it was getting onto two years since I'd recorded last," Kuepper said.

Laughing Clowns entered Richmond Recorders, and after just thirty hours emerged with six songs that would make up a 12 inch EP.

The result is a record unlike any other ever made in this country.

Contrary to aural appearances Laughing Clowns' songs *are* structured — very structured, in fact — though on the EP they retain the apparent open-endedness they possess live. The cavernous production allows the band even more space within which to extend themselves, with a vitality and intensity that's rare.

TACTICS further refined their unique musical vision which was mated with David Studdert's personal vision, and played more often to more people. (Pic: Stephen Hocking)

"It's got an immediate appeal," Wegener began, "but it's got a lot of subtleties in it too; perhaps they're lost on stage.

"I think every instrument — every player — makes some sort of statement about their . . . 'individuality,' I guess."

In many ways though, Laughing Clowns are but a vehicle for Ed Kuepper's vision. His vocals have always posed a problem, but on the EP they're perfectly audible, which makes his lyrics all the more demanding.

Kuepper's incisive philosophy can't be ignored, and it makes most rock'n'roll lyricists look as trite as they really are. In *Lucky Days* he sings: "The things I'm looking for, don't walk right in through an open door."

It's this kind of attitude, plus an unshakable belief in what they're doing, that makes the success of Laughing Clowns almost inevitable.

Clinton Walker
Reprinted from RAM by permission.
Copyright.

Top: LAUGHING CLOWNS, 5-piece
(Pic: Kathleen O'Brien)
Right: Chris Bailey's SAINTS settled on a steady line-up, and with a well-received EP behind them, embarked on a national tour, then returned to Europe again. (Pic: Francine McDougall)

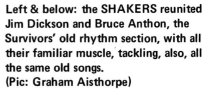

Left & below: the SHAKERS reunited Jim Dickson and Bruce Anthon, the Survivors' old rhythm section, with all their familiar muscle, tackling, also, all the same old songs.
(Pic: Graham Aisthorpe)

Centre left: the TOY WATCHES were typical of Brisbane bands in that they appeared suddenly, shone briefly and then disappeared.
(Pic: Graham Aisthorpe)

Left: the HUMANS, with the departure of the Riptides, increased their status in Brisbane, but they would break up before the end of the year.

RISING RIPTIDES

The first thing that strikes you about a Riptides performance is the number of people dancing. The Riptides' music seems specifically designed to inspire movement. Never mind that you've just been subjected to another crushingly boring day. Here is joy, movement, the atmosphere of happiness, bar none.

The Riptides are now Sydney-based, with the ink still drying on a six-album recording deal with happening record label Regular, plenty of work in Sydney and the occasional trip to Melbourne. When they returned to Brisbane to open 4ZZZ's new venue the Heritage Hotel they attracted 800 people and were hailed as conquering heroes.

But, as is usually the case with all "overnight success" stories, there's a lot more to it than that.

The Riptides started out as the

Grudge in early 1977. The members of the Grudge were all studying Architecture at Queensland University. The initial inspiration behind forming a band was provided by hearing the Saints' *I'm Stranded.*

Through various line-up and name changes the band finally became the Numbers, comprising Scott Matheson, singer Mark Callaghan, drummer Dennis Cantwell and bass player Rob Vickers, a line-up that has stuck together, apart from the replacement of Vickers with new guitarist Andrew Leitch, ever since (Callaghan now plays bass). As the Numbers, the band recorded one independent single, *Sunset Strip,* which was reissued under the name the Riptides when the band changed names, due to "confusion" with the Sydney band and with fellow musicians the Go Betweens formed the Able Label.

"Stranded was still fresh in everybody's mind — fresh enough for people to think you could record a single, send it away and get a record contract. I

remember when we listened back to *Sunset Strip* in the studio . . . we said, 'Oh, it's great, it's going to be No. 1!' About a month later we thought, 'Oh dear (laughs) that's dreadful!' " says Scott Matheson.

"We were recording about the same time as the Go Betweens. They were planning to do a record, as we were, so rather than having two small labels we thought we'd do it on the same one. And that was how the Able Label came about. Then the Go Betweens did another record and the Apartments did one," says Matheson.

The Go Betweens escaped Brisbane and made it to the UK, where they have a single out on Postcard Records, but few Brisbane bands are so successful. Why the high accident rate?

"It's strange, it's the whole atmosphere

THE HITMEN simply refused to die, like old soldiers, even going so far as to make a stab at the disco market with the "I Want You" single.
(Pic: Catherine Hardy)

Above: the SHY IMPOSTORS were a band in the Passengers' mould, a tough ensemble fronted by a tough but tender female vocalist, Pennie Ward.
(Pic: Patrick Bingham-Hall)

Left: the LIPSTICK KILLERS lived on.
(Pic: Robyn Stacey)

up there . . . it's hard to describe. Like when you live there you take the police harrassment of dances for granted. We used to hire a hall in the suburbs with two or three other bands, cause that was the only way you could get to play. But we gave up doing that because the police would always arrive by nine o'clock and half the audience would spend the rest of the night in jail. Down here Queensland is just a cartoon on page three of the newspaper. It's a joke. But it's deadly serious up there."

Paul, the Riptides' manager, chips in: "Bands get destroyed just because the atmosphere is so oppressive. Work is impossible to get because of police harrassment."

"It's sad," says Matheson. "So many bands fall by the wayside. And there have been some great Brisbane bands. I think one thing though — if you do manage to get out of it you have to be pretty tough. It made us even more determined I suppose."

Against such a 1984 background it might strike listeners as strange that the Riptides' music is so poppy and danceable. The two singles that the band have released to date, the aforementioned *Sunset Strip* and *Tomorrow's Tears,* which landed the band a spot on Countdown earlier this year, were both rather lightweight in

the old lyric department. Matheson agrees, but points out that when you've only got one day in the studio you tend to opt for your catchiest, poppiest tune, "in the hope that it might land you some work in Sydney or something."

"When we first started out we were doing overtly political songs. At that time we were all marching in the anti-uranium marches and getting beaten up in King George Square. We had songs like *Advance Australia Fair* which was about the police raid on the hippie commune at Cedar Bay. Odd that all the songs that have got on the singles have been so lyrically . . . shallow. We've got a lot of songs with more substance than those . . . A lot of songs about Brisbane. There's one called *Lonely Old Sunday* which is about how deserted Brisbane is on a Sunday or *Growing Up in Brisbane* which is about all the pressures you face up there. *The Eternal Flame,* one of Mark's songs, is an anti-RSL song."

What about the suggestion, made in the press just after *Tomorrow's Tears* came out, that the Riptides were perhaps Australia's newest "mod" band?

Matheson laughs. "I've always fancied mod. We've always fancied button-down collars and suits and ties. We were actually wearing clothes like that before we ever formed a band. We'd always be wearing suits in the

middle of summer while people at Queensland Uni would be getting around in stubbies and T-shirts."

His wild pair of wicklepickers are proof enough that the mod overtones have not gone out the window.

The Riptides are still fairly new to Sydney and they'll be working on building a live following before venturing onto the vinyl market again. They are justifiably excited about how everything has fallen into place so quickly after they've had to struggle for so long. They're still paying off debts accumulated in Brisbane but it shouldn't be too long before they are going to be earning a wage. And for Matheson at least, Sydney is the next best thing to heaven after the Deep North.

The simple things most of us take for granted. Perhaps we don't know how lucky we are.

Donald Robertson
Reprinted from *ROADRUNNER*

THE FLAMING HANDS, like the Shy Impostors, were of the Passengers' ilk, only with more soulful influences, plus the distinctive voice and presence of Julie Mostyn. (Pic: Dare Jennings)

MODEL POP

This over-clouded afternoon is one of those when Sean Kelly is definitely not looking the part of the pop star; face pallid and bearing the signs of what looks like near-terminal road weariness, he's describing how he's realised just how far his band Models have to go before they become household names.

"When we were playing in Adelaide the last time, there were usually only forty or fifty people in the audience."

"It really brought us back to earth," interjects bassist Mark Ferrie. "We don't mean anything much outside Melbourne yet."

In Melbourne, Models certainly do mean something; a band that answers the primitive tribal longing for style, colour and inventiveness and not mere headbanging release.

It's a position they've arrived at in the most circuitous possible manner. Models have never had a hit single and have no intentions of releasing a forty-five. They've merely kept playing solidly for two-and-a-half years. And with the release of a debut album that ignores all commercial ground rules they seem about to expand their appeal nationally.

"If we've proved anything with the album," says Kelly, "it's that persistence pays off. I've been with the Models two-and-a-half years now, and in that time I've seen so many bands who were going to be the next big thing but

THE MODELS

they just didn't sustain."

In that time Models have negotiated plenty of shifting currents both within the band and in the fickle and competitive Melbourne rock scene.

Their roots lie in the Teenage Radio Stars. When Kelly split from the Radio Stars, it was with the remains of JAB that he joined forces.

The prime musical forces behind JAB were drummer Johnny Crash and synthesizer enthusiast Ash Wednesday. Crash and Wednesday had sufficient innovative ideas to ensure that their partnership with Kelly in Models would either alienate diehard punks or else succeed in no mean fashion.

Above: the SUICIDE SQUAD spear-headed a revival of one-chord wonder punk in Sydney, followed by the Rejex and the Bedhogs, making the Rock Garden their home. (Pic: Peter Nelson)

Top: the PARTICLES were probably the longest-lived band in all of Sydney, having been together in one form or another since early 1977, though it wasn't until 1980 that they were "discovered," by Melbourne audiences! (Pic: Darian Turner)

Right: SEEMS TWICE played more songs, faster, in a shorter period of time than any other band in Sydney. Sort of like an Australian Wire. In an appropriately short career, the band made an EP for Doublethink containing 12 songs.

95

As things turned out, it wasn't long before the band began making a considerable impact. Kelly flourished as a singer/guitarist in his new environment, rapidly developing that scrawny vocal style that relies as much on wordless screams and sighs as it does on clear enunciation of his skeletal lyrics and which has since become a major Models trademark, while Ash's layered keyboard playing added the other necessary distinction to the band's jagged attack.

The final piece of the Models jigsaw came with the arrival of bassist Ferrie.

It wasn't roses all the way. Accusations of contrivance and of the band being more interested in visual style than music weren't long in arriving, and Kelly admits the obvious conflict of aims in the early version of Models.

Ash left the band in early '79 but his influence lingered on. Replacement Andrew Duffield from Whirlywirld had only minimal experience of playing live, and took some time to make his presence felt.

"The sound of the band is definitely the product of what all four of us contribute, so naturally Ash had a major influence," says Kelly. Duffield's more delicate approach to the keyboards which have always been the dominant Models sound took some time to come through, and further internal strains were imposed by the release of a giveaway single, *Early Morning Brain,* a scrappily produced artifact that some band members felt was more damaging than representative of the Models' sound.

The band broke up, but weren't long in reforming. The impetus to continue was an offer from Vanda and Young to record some demos (one result of which was *Progressive Office Pools*.) And this time around the band were determined to do things properly. 1980 has seen the Models become virtually unstoppable on their home turf. The culmination of their progress has been their debut album, recorded painstakingly, and at the band's expense, at Melbourne's Richmond Recorders.

AlphaBetaCharlieDeltaEchoFoxtrot-Golf is definitely not the kind of no-risk debut expected of Australian bands. The band have used available technology not to fashion safe product, but to synthesize sounds, influences and rhythm into a set that's both cohesive and nebulous. "One of the things we tried to do with it is to show where everyone's coming from," says Ferrie, and in that aim at least it succeeds. Ferrie's own acidic bit of ockerbilly *Pulled the Pin* is a jaunty highlight of the record; elsewhere you'll find plenty of evanescent Kelly pop rhythms and edgy guitar as well as exploratory percussion and synthesiser quirkiness from Johnny Crash and Duffield.

Accusations of Models self-indulgence won't be laid to rest by the album especially as the band have chosen to avoid including their more obvious onstage pop favourites. "We did all those songs like *Keep It a Secret* and *Whisper Through the Wall,*" says Ferrie, "but we just found that the newer stuff had more sparkle, including the tracks we

improvised in the studio. And even though we use all the technical bullshit imaginable, I think it still has a warm feel."

"The fact that it doesn't have a potential hit on it doesn't worry us; we don't feel like being typecast at this stage," Kelly says.

If *AlphaBeta* demonstrates anything it's Models ability to work successfully by committee. "One of the reasons I think we've stayed together apart from the fact that we want to be rich and famous," says Kelly, "is that we do work so well together."

It's an attitude that leads to an extreme volatility onstage: without a real focus to the music that can be provided by a dominating member, Models gigs tend to fluctuate between the sublime and the mediocre with extreme frequency, but it's a price they're prepared to pay. "Sometimes when we're playing I can feel that the band is going to drop right off the edge, but even when we're really awful I reassure myself that there's someone out there

THE JETSONNES beat the Models and the International Exiles at their own game, and then some. Their clever post-punk pop was lighter, bouncier (rather than funkier) and very infectious. Sadly, the band would split before realizing most of their potential, a brief Melbourne delight. (Pic: Robert Miles)

Top: ZERO were clever but not clever-clever. Their set was mostly covers, though the band was making an obvious attempt to express themselves musically and even moved into extra-musical presentation. (Pic: Graham Aisthorpe)

Above: the SWELL GUYS were Brisbane's clever-clever answer to their English near-namesake, the Swell Maps. After making a single, the Swells split for Sydney, where they still surface erratically. (Pic: Tony Milner)

Left: the TRIFFIDS were Perth's leading progressive post-punk outfit. (Pic: courtesy the Triffids)

enjoying it. ''

And Kelly goes on: ''One thing that amazes me is the number of formula bands in this country who think that audiences are complete, unperceptive idiots. And I don't think we're like that. It's 1980 after all and audiences are prepared to accept something different from formula good time rock'n'roll, or guitar solos . . .''

Adrian Ryan
Reprinted from *ROADRUNNER*

Top: the EARS aped the old Boys Next Door better than anyone else, and for that reason became extremely popular in Melbourne at the Crystal Ballroom. (Pic: Philip Stott)

Left: JAMES FREUD (& THE RADIO STARS) biggest year was 1980. A debut album ''Breaking Silence'' was finally released, and a single from it, ''Modern Girl,'' was a big hit. Freud travelled to England to cut an album under Gary Numan's aegis, but the project fizzled out and so did the Radio Stars, who by then were known as Berlin.

"THE NEW ADELAIDE BANDS"

A tasteful, pleasant, safe little city is Adelaide, an Athens of the South, a centre for the arts. Everyone knows absolutely everyone here, and surprises don't come easy.

In such a climate adventurous rock bands generally piss into the wind. There's nothing much the rest of Australia would know about from the past couple of years, Young Modern and Terminal Twist aside.

Suddenly things have picked up. Off hand, I could list a dozen bands who stand the test of several viewings. All play mostly (or all) original sets, record whenever possible, and receive good air-

play on 5MMM-FM (which is probably the key to the whole resurgence).

There have been nights when 300 to 400 person venues are packed with excited people along to see local bands. Mid-week, too.

At the forefront is the handful of groups who will be known for the purpose of this article as "the new Adelaide bands."

Since everybody likes a beginning, let's pretend this revival took root early this year, when word got around about Nuvo Bloc, a band featuring sacked Terminal Twist vocalist Peter Tesla. A demo recording of Peter's *Fun Times,* a song "whose distinctive sax and vocals paint delightful swirling color on

a canvas the eye never tires of beholding," gained the band instant notoriety.

The song charted on Triple Em for about three months. It demonstrated that Peter was more willing than ever to experiment with his voice, and that Nik Filips was an adventurous saxophonist.

Vonnie Rollan, vocals, percussion and synthesiser, Ted Thornberry, vocals and guitar, Michael Liferaft, vocals, drums and synthesiser, and Nigel "Auto" Function, vocals and bass, completed a group generally older, more experienced and wiser than most young bands.

Few groups anywhere could boast six individuals of their talent. Peter and Vonnie, who sing more songs and stand

Top: NUVO BLOC (Pic: Steve Keogh)

Right: the LOUNGE were almost as much a "collective" as a band, boasting a large, changeable line-up, and a changeable approach to their "living room sound." They took Adelaide by surprise, and maintained interest by selective gigging. (Pic: Steve Keogh)

their keyboards back-to-back, tend to be focal points, but Michael, Nigel and Ted all sing lead too, while Nik dresses and plays colorfully enough to ensure his share of the limelight.

The sound? Well, with five singers, six songwriters from musical backgrounds ranging from jazz to punk, and a mass of instrumental resources and ideas on how to use them, things like

bound to defy classification. Shades of Bowie, Roxy Music and particularly Eno creep in, but so do rhythms of Africa, free-form jazz and the sounds of a circus. Collectively, Nuvo Bloc sees itself as "experimenting in electronic and rhythmical instrumentation, bending the rules of existing rock formats."

Since drawing 480 to its first gig, Nuvo Bloc has maintained a big following here. Next important step comes with the release of a first single, *Atomic Fiction*, written by Vonnie and highlighting her finely-stretched modern voice supported by purposefully unclustered musical backing. At first listening it suggests over-reliance on subtleties, but after that gains stature until thumbs point most definitely upwards.

Stephen Hunter
Reprinted from *ROADRUNNER*

Left: DESPARATE MEASURES were a "new Adelaide band" perhaps a little less original than the others, obviously influenced by contemporary British rock and ska. (Pic: Eric Chalmbers)

Below: SYSTEMS GO were a "brief but delightful Adelaide experience," and like the Lounge, like a collective in the changeable roles within the band. (Pic: Steve Keogh)

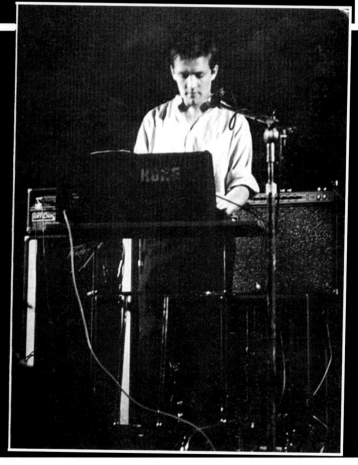

EQUAL LOCAL emerged as the brightest star in Melbourne since the Birthday Party left town. Their sparkling post-punk of jazz-rock was a breath of fresh air in jaded Melbourne.

POP AND SOUL AND A PRESENT-DAY SNARL

And now, my favourite live Sydney band of the moment — the Flaming Hands. If you haven't seen them play yet then your life isn't as enjoyable as it could be!

The Flaming Hands line-up is: Julie Mostyn (vocals), Jeff Sullivan (guitar), Paul Bryant (sax and vocals), Michael Hiron (drums), Steve Harris (keyboards), and Richard Allan (bass).

Last week I sat around with Jeff, Julie, Paul and Michael listening to old soul records and finding out the band's history and views on the state of the universe.

The band had only been playing seriously since Jeff returned from a visit to America. "We actually did three shows before Jeff went overseas," Julie said.

"Paul joined while he was away. The band was formed by me, Steve and Jeff with the idea of just doing one gig for fun," she said. "But everyone liked it so we decided to continue." Jeff added.

The Flaming Hands debut was in February.

Background-wise they come from diverse areas. Michael drummed for five shows with Brisbane punk "legends" the Leftovers. Paul has been playing sax for four years but he's convinced himself that this is the first "real" band he's played with.

Jeff and Steve have played in a trillion Sydney bands. Both were in the Passengers and Steve has spent time with the Hitmen and the Visitors — playing bass. Richard began playing bass two months ago and has never played in a band before.

Julie, who possesses an extremely strong, emotive voice (although her articulation could be a little better) used to sing with the Kamikaze Kids before getting involved with Flaming Hands.

The band already has a record out — a single on the Phantom label containing two cover versions, the Soul Incorporated song *I Belong to Nobody* and the Marvelettes *The Stranger.* The single was recorded in February, three weeks after the first line-up was settled.

"When I was with the Passengers I realised how cheap it was to do a single so we thought, why not?" Jeff said. "It took us four hours one night."

One of the band's earliest breaks would have been supporting the Dead Boys on their Australian tour but the tour was cancelled at the last minute. The band was also chosen to play at a

2JJJ party to celebrate the introduction of FM. "We were incredibly lucky because it was our second gig," Jeff said. "They'd just heard our test pressing," said Michael.

So what sort of things do they do on stage? Well, visualise a band with a large degree of personality, who move a lot on stage, playing a mixture of pop and soul music. "It's really soul stuff roughed up," Michael said.

Or as Paul sees it, "We add a present day snarl to it."

There's three originals in the repertoire — *Wake Up Screaming, Love Execution* and *Sweet Revenge.* They're all written by Jeff.

The rest are cover versions. A look at the best ones and their original sources should give you an idea of what Flaming Hands are on about.

There's two Animals songs — *Don't Bring Me Down* and *That Ain't the Way It Is;* the Grass Roots' *Pain* and *Midnight-Confessions;* the Shadows of Knights *Shake;* Spencer Davis Group's *Gimmee Some Lovin'.*, the Golliwogs' *Walking On The Water;* Martha and the Vandellas' *No Where to Run;* Wilson Pickett's *Night Owl;* Aretha Franklin's

FLAMING HANDS' Julie Mostyn. (Pic: Cathy Croll)

The TEENY WEENIES (right) a variation on the Perth Sound, were reminiscent of nothing so much as early Blondie. They were probably the first Perth band to make a permanent move east.

The SCIENTISTS (below) gigged infrequently, and put down an album. (Pic: Kim Williams)

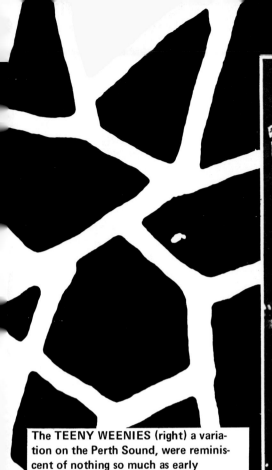   

Right: the ROCKETS were in the shadow of the Scientists and exponents of the Perth Sound, a ballsy form of rock'n'roll in the mould of the New York Rockers. (Pic: Kim Williams)

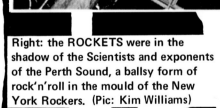 

See Saw; and the Ids' *Watch Out.*

And that's just a few. "There's also a mid 60's psychedelic song by Balloon Farm called *Question of Temperature,*" Jeff said.

What do they all have in common? Played live by the Flaming Hands, they make some of the best danceable rock'n'roll I've heard in this city for a long time.

The selection of covers is one thing that impresses me about the band. They all have that familiar feel but aren't the obvious and done to death covers that most bands play. The Flaming Hands seem pretty happy that people often aren't sure whether a particular song is an original or a cover.

At this stage they all agree on what songs they'll cover and are all keen to eventually replace a good proportion of the covers with originals. Jeff, in particular, has an amazing ability to write fantastic, catchy pop rock'n'roll songs and the inclusion of more of his material couldn't hurt.

The Flaming Hands went into the studio this week to record their second single which will be two originals — *Wake Up Screaming* and *Sweet Revenge.* It was recorded at EMI with Cameron Allen producing.

The band seem happy to continue working around the pubs until something happens. Basically, they seem content to keep playing and having fun. Their live shows exude an air of passion and goodtimes. They play every song for all it's worth but look like they're enjoying the experience of exhausting themselves performing.

"We're really just learning," Julie said. "No one's in a hurry and we're content to take it as it comes."

Stuart Coupe
Reprinted from SYDNEY SHOUT

The RIPTIDES (top left) created near-hysteria when they returned to Brisbane to open a new venue at the National Hotel, though a Regular Record debut was delayed for innumerable reasons. (Pic: Graham Aisthorpe)

The SUNNYBOYS (bottom left) breathed some freshness and vitality into Sydney's stagnating post-Birdman scene. The Sunnyboys were young and they sounded like it, and were rewarded with an immediate positive response. (Pic: Cathy Croll)

Above: the MARCHING GIRLS arrived in Melbourne from New Zealand with their 60's influenced, very English post-punk pop.

LITTLE MURDERS (top) grew and grew in stature, as Rob Griffiths' songwriting matured, if within its own narrow precepts, and the band itself gained much confidence.

JUMP VISION (right) were ska/soul influenced. The trio extended their appeal with a link-up to the newly formed Basilisk Records.
(Pic: Simon Bullard)

BACK FROM THE BACKLASH

The Saints, back in town for the "Beware of the Pygmy" tour, arrive for our interview late, and without Chris Bailey. It seems it's just a ploy to emphasise the band at his expense.

We buy drinks, break the ice and talk, among other things, about their recently completed and heartening tour of France — the Saints are big in Rouen, by the way.

Birmingham and Barrington (guitar) make up the English contingent in the band. Janine Hall from Melbourne is on bass, and Chris Bailey, from Brisbane, stolling in 45 minutes later, is, of course, the singer.

The original Saints went through numerous line-up changes. But it was always Chris Bailey and Ed Kuepper's band. When Chris Bailey returned to a hero's welcome in Australia with the Saints name, Ed Kuepper was struggling against the tide in his new band, the Laughing Clowns, there seemed to be a strong feeling against Bailey in some quarters.

"It was in fact a very difficult time," says Chris. "All that sort of nonsense is fairly upsetting — one can't avoid that. 'A lot of people talking, but not many of them know' is a quote from an old blues song that is quite appropriate."

The Saints last tour here was an unqualified success, aided firstly by reputation, and no doubt, by their magnificent EP. The band, minus guitarist Cab Calloway, returned to England where they've spent most of the last six months.

This time around, the tour seems to have a much lower profile, probably because there is more pressure on the band to really establish themselves.

"There's a strange natural progression that's happening with us," says Chris. "I like it. It's sort of building to the level where I suppose the aim is to be a local band in as many places as possible.

"Ed Kuepper's an extraordinarily talented songwriter. But I find the songs we churn out, with the influences that are on us now, personally more interesting.

"I tend to write mainly when I get away from things. There's things you soak up that you don't realise — you go through life like a happy idiot. Then something will happen and you'll stop for a second. That's when I tend to write songs most, in those whinging moments away from the bottle."

The next night, the Saints kick off their tour at the Rock Garden. The start is spirited and exciting. Chris Bailey, with his animated mock-rock antics and inebriated lunges to and away from the

THE SAINTS' Chris Bailey and Barrington. (Pic: Graham Aisthorpe)

microphone, has the crowd eating out of the palm of his hand. An entertaining showman and a perfect frontman, he is totally involved with the audience. He gives away a drink, and he gets one in return.

The remainder of the set had its ups and downs. Barrington, while a more than competent and able guitarist, was very loud and flashy, and on the night, simply lacked sensitivity and subtlety. The sound of the band as a whole could have done with a lot more variation, more light and shade, and that's why Ted Pepper's sax was so welcome.

I was certainly disappointed, and I sensed a similar feeling in the audience as well.

Chris Bailey's Saints are now a fact of life. There's no big contract, (well maybe, just a small one with Larrakin Records for a single and an album). But there's certainly no managers. They deal, says Janine, with people they get

THE MODELS' Sean Kelly (Pic: Mark Green)

THE SURFSIDE 6 (below) were essentially a part-time, fun band put together by a couple of writers, friends and relatives of the stars and others. Surf and destroyı

LAUGHING HANDS (above) began life at the CHCMC, but soon attracted a rock audience with their improvised music of shifting electronic currents.
(Pic: Sebastian Gollings)

Philip Brophy of ↑→ᵀ (left), who also ran Innocent Records, virtual house label at the CHCMC. (Pic: Mark Green)

DAVID CHESWORTH (below) solo artist, member of Essendon Airport and the Dave & Phil Duo and co-ordinator of the Clifton Hill Community Music Centre. The CHCMC was a performance space for "new music" (of the experimental kind), which was unacceptable elsewhere.

on with. And they handle the business side themselves.

Chris Bailey seems unchanged. He still sounds a little cynical, but his conversation is more that of a man with an all-round drinking education. Relaxed, cryptic and well versed in the ways of the world. One has to, after all, manage somehow.

"At times," he says, "I can be embarrassingly serious about things. But the only way my attitude's changed is that, if you're taking the risks, and paying the bills, then you sometimes have to get up at ten in the morning and think about it. And that's a pain.

"That slight amount of responsibility we feel as a group to shit like that is necessary. Being in a band is a fuckin' good idea. I like it."

Richard McGregor
Reprinted from RAM by permission. Copyright.

The **LAST WORDS** (right), obscured by English fog. The band made a few singles and an album in England, though they made little impression.

The **BIRTHDAY PARTY** (below) With an album collecting the year's singles and EPs just made available, they returned to Australia to tour and record.

TACTICAL TRIUMPHS

According to the tourist brochures, the Rocks area of Sydney, down by Circular Quay, is "the Birthplace of Australia." It's perhaps ironic, then, that when Tactics made a return to live appearances recently, it was at the Governors Pleasure, a pub in the Rocks. Because Tactics are a band aware of their heritage, a band Australia and only Australia could have produced . . .

Tactics begin their set with *Long Story*, a song from their debut album *My Houdini*, that they've never before played live. And it's quite superb. David Studdert tells *"a long story along familiar lines where a mirror's held up against a real life"*; that *"there are certain ways things can be resolved,*

TACTICS (left) (Pic: Stephen Hocking)

The THOUGHT CRIMINALS (below) played their last ever gig at Chequers in Sydney late in the year.

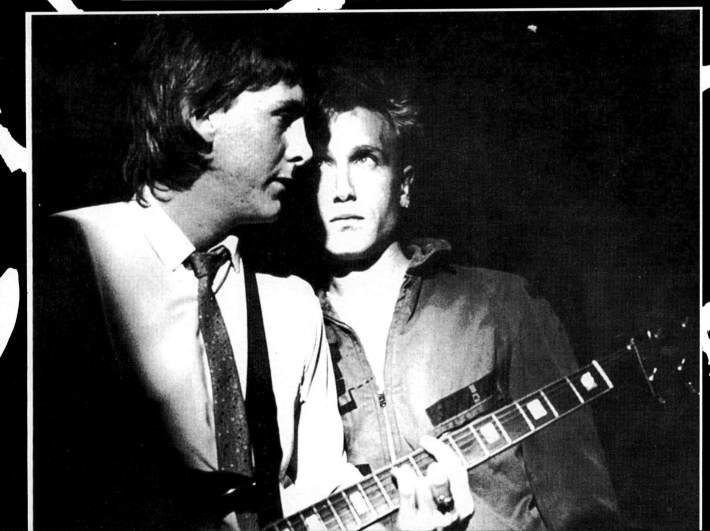

PEL MEL arrived in Sydney from Newcastle with a clutch of English bands'
songs in their set and a wide-eyed
ambition to establish themselves as an
accessible and credible post-punk
progressive outfit.
(Pic: Kathleen O'Brien)

certain ways in certain lives."

Studdert jerks like a marionette run
amok, arms and legs flailing, his voice a
shrill, staccato howl, his guitar a frantic
thrash that bears only passing resemblance to the reggae that's influenced
him.

Angus Douglas is Tactics' *lead* guitarist, his more controlled, fluid lines
offset Studdert's dementia. Pianist
Ingrid Spielman adds dollops of colour,
while the Geoff Marsh/Robert Whittle
rhythm section provides rock-
steady support — Marsh with his pro-
truding bass lines, "Rover" Whittle with
his strong, certain drumming.

Even though Tactics' influences are
distinct — the Velvet Underground,
Burning Spear, Neil Young, early Talking Heads, Love, Television, Roxy
Music — they've been thoroughly assimilated and subsequently transcended;
Tactics have created a sound of their
own, an urgent, insistent sound without
likeness in Australia or anywhere else in
the world.

The Governors Pleasure gig was to
coincide with the release of *My Houdini*,
which comes after three years of Tactics.

David Studdert formed the band in
Canberra late in 1977. "I just wanted to
do something apart from the 9-to-5,"
he said. "I mean, it's as banal as that.

"Rover was an old hippie, y'know.
And we sorta taught him to drum. And,
like, the bass player had never played
before." At that stage a quartet, only
Angus Douglas had had any previous experience, playing with a high school
band or two. "When I started writing
songs," Studdert continued, "I didn't
want to learn how to play 12-bar, 'cos
everybody else played 12-bar. I just
figured that the only way to do something different was to sit down, without
going through all this shit, just sit down
and do what you want to do."

Tactics gigged in Canberra, until their
"big break" came when they supported
the Thought Criminals, in mid '78.
Impressed by the band, the Thoughties
invited Tactics to visit Sydney. By early
'79, Tactics had assumed permanent
residence in the Harbour City, and were
gigging regularly.

It was then that I saw Tactics for the first time and I hated them! I thought they sounded like a Buzzcocks single at 78.

But their reputation grew, and I kept going back, and slowly found myself being converted. Nowadays I consider Tactics one of the finest bands in Australia.

It's David Studdert's vision that really propels the band. He writes all of Tactics' songs, and they're some of the best, most Australian songs I've heard since . . . well, I don't think Australian rock'n'roll has ever had a writer like Studdert.

Studdert's songs capture the atmosphere and images of life in this country, where our short, brutal heritage is never far away, like the aural equivalent of a Sidney Nolan painting. "There's two sorts of mainstreams of the way people write, right," Studdert began. "There's the Romantic, which is subjective, and particular, and there's the Classical, which is general and . . . objective, and I'd rather write like that. You take the Aborigines," Studdert seemed to be flying off at a tangent, "the way they view their society is completely different to the way we do ours. They glorified ordinary things, and they were

very understated lyrics, and they were very plain, simple, descriptive lyrics. And, like, I would rather write those sort of songs than . . ."

The telephone interrupts Studdert's train of thought . . . .

As a quartet Tactics released two platters: the *Long Weekend* EP and the *Outdoors/Hole in my Life* single. It was when Ingrid Spielman joined the band, early in 1980, that they began work on *My Houdini.* Nearly eight months later they'd finished.

The album was recorded mainly at Basilist Studios in Sydney, where owner/engineer Martin Bishop allowed the band much free time. "It was the sort of situation where we could spend

The SYSTEMATICS (left) had grown from a one-man band to a duo, making mutant electropop on record for M Squared and occasionally even on stage.

(MAKERS OF) THE DEAD TRAVEL FAST (below) were the first of many bands to emerge on M Squared. They had a surprise "hit" with the "Tael of a Saeghors" single, then started playing live and recording their electronic mood muzak.

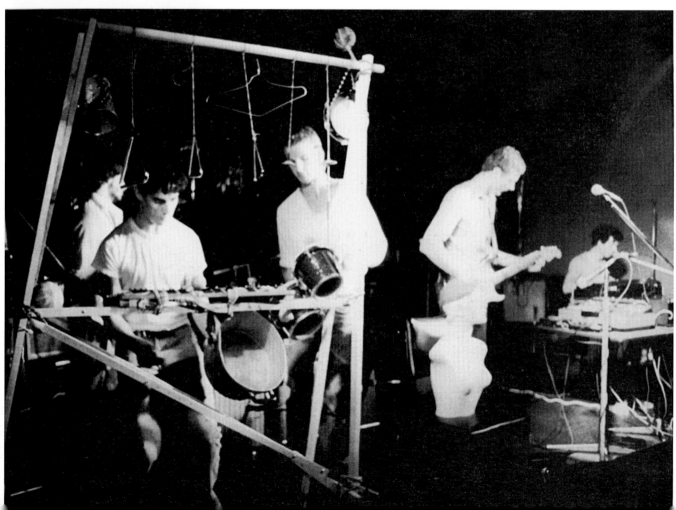

four hours getting a guitar sound," Studdert said, "and if we didn't like it we could go back and fix it up. And that was good, because I like that idea, of *crafting* everything."

Indeed, Tactics make not a particularly *emotional* music. Rather, it's a journalistic sort of music. *My Houdini* culls 10 songs from Studdert's catalogue of over 50, and happily the time in the studio was well spent. *My Houdini* is one of the most impressive Australian debut albums released in recent years. It captures Tactics in all their intricate detail, and although theirs is a unique sound, it's not inaccessible; melodies, if understated, are plentiful, and the rhythm is to be danced to.

I remark to Studdert that the overriding impression the album made upon me was one of *entrapment.*

"It comes from living in Canberra,"

he replied matter-of-factly. "A lot of those songs were written in Canberra, it's extremely claustrophobic.

"In Canberra, the difference between what Australia really is and what Canberra is, is really obvious. I mean, Canberra is a very apt capital for the country. In a hell of a lot of ways it does represent what Australia is — the idea of one culture coming out to this country and forcefully asserting itself upon the country, despite what the country's like."

So how do you validate your own existence here?

"I don't really know; that's what I'm trying to work out."

Whether or not a widespread Australian audience will, or rather *can,* accept Tactics' determination to face our failings remains to be seen.

"If they're frightened to see that, or they're upset by it, then that's their fault," Studdert said. "I don't care. I mean, I don't care about 'success.' What I care about is whether or not it's on our own terms."

Clinton Walker
Reprinted from RAM by permission. Copyright.

SCAPA FLOW (nee J.M.M., above) played gigs that impressed with their power and authority. (Pic: Linda Nolte)

WILD WEST (nee God: The Movie, nee Grab-A-Guitar, right) were the logical inheritors of Voigt/465's former mantle, an obviously progressive band in the English mould. (Pic: Annette Jones)

LAUGHING CLOWNS added a trumpeter and entered a new phase, that of the Laughing Clowns' Big Band, which culminated in a soaring performance at the Paris Theatre with the Birthday Party and the Go Betweens. After that, the band fell into disaray.
(Pic: Linda Nolte)

THE GO BETWEENS, having made a single for Postcard Records of Scotland, recruited a drummer, began gigging (pictured at the Rock Garden in Sydney) and then recording for Missing Link. (Pic: Graham Aisthorpe)

EQUAL LOCAL EXCEL

A slow miserable Saturday Night Fever existence is what most Ballroomites live in.

Both sides of the Ballroom were displayed on this night. Decrepit young men relying on their reputation to produce crowd frenzy only displayed what Led Zeppelin were clouted around the ears for a couple of years ago by Johnny Rotten. That was the torn, dulled clothing of the night. A strong, sinuous body was vamping around the

The BIRTHDAY PARTY completed another Australian tour, put down a new album and then got out of the country, fast. (Pic: Cathy Croll)

INTERNATIONAL EXILES' Laine (left) (Pic: Mark Green)

EQUAL LOCAL (below left) took audiences' breath away time after time, soon to go into the studio to record for Missing Link. (Pic: Lyn Gordon)

place, successfully though — Equal Local had arrived and they were here to stay.

Ring out the old, ring in the new.

Equal Local are the fashionable ones now. They are the trendsetters, the ones to be seen seeing.

Equal Local took the stage. They presented themselves anonymously with casual sincerity. In other words their appearance and behaviour were boring though not in the least offputting.

The beat is a different matter. Some suave rhumbas gone haywire and a few electronic mind turns combined to give a sound and dance throb that pulsed into the mind and stayed there, gesticulating madly, yet making complete, calm sense.

Twelve Ways to Go opened the set with a notewise drift that halted just before the inner reaches of ambience. It was soft and clear as well as being obvious in its aspirations. The influences are non existent, yet the band still has to find the power to make every song an entity and not let some songs slip easily into a waste basket of useless categories.

Cowboy Mouse has a classically oriented be-bop/funk infiltrated sense of fuzz tongue lolling.

Lamp That is laziness and exists merely for the drum machine cum rhythm maker. *Hard as Count* continues in the tradition of predictable pre-set flourishes. They continue the newness with a distinct lack of variation — toneless and meandering. *Punjab* halts the rot with some real cool guitar funk workovers that are subtly cooled down by a neatly deployed mechanical beat which is then, God save us, torn to shreds as Mick Hause's saxophone grows roots in the dance floor to bloom in dripping, organic horn lines. In the remaining songs the guitar goes from fresh disco funk to hippy wholesomeness, the keyboards move to and fro from obvious portentous struttings to clever iconoclastic motifs and the sax is serene while Bryce Perrin's double bass consistently shifts the show from right to left and back again. At times it's obvious and at other times it's not, yet

↑→↑ at long last, began to receive the serious critical attention they deserved, with new projects such as the Asphixiation disco installation, "Television Works", the "Spaces", video soundtracks and others.

the whole sense of shuffling rhythm the band depends upon is supplied by the bass and to a lesser extent Phillip Jackson on synth/computer. Melissa Webb's Korg/synthesiser could be forgotten but because of the texture and depth it adds to the picture it is impossible.

Equal Local are a vital, new force. With time and the perception maturity should grant them they would seem to be a band not to be ignored in both circles cool and circles not so cool.

It was obvious when walking into the Birthday Party's performance that things were not well. The vibe was subdued and the funk flat. What committed sounds there were ended up being wasted within a tired set of stale constructions. Normally *Friend Catcher* opens with a thunder clapping bass line. Not this time — maybe all the alcohol in Pew had softened his fingers. From then on the proceedings got more dire and flaccid.

Only *King Ink* and *Figure of Fun* displayed true conviction. These stalking instrumentations were honest in their intent and both climaxed in a frenzy of purpose. It was a performance which should only be remembered as an odd slur on an otherwise nerve juggling set of Australian performances.

The night ended with International Exiles — it's a wonder the nights haven't ended them yet. In all the months they've existed I can't see how I failed to perceive them as the single minded, keyboard infatuated clowns their toneless thrashings set them up as. Frequently they fool people into thinking they are fresh pop, but beware, that they are not.

A quick fall back to the emptiness of a blank Sunday morning in Melbourne with only a brief moment of Equal Local magic in mind. Unfortunately the bad always slurs the good. So tonight we were washed out.

Craig N. Pearce
Reprinted from *ROADRUNNER*

THE BIRTHDAY PARTY's Nick Cave (top left) (Pic: Cathy Croll)

RON RUDE (left) sat in the front window of Missing Link Records' store in Melbourne on a hunger strike until radio station 3XY would play his new album, "The Vorpal Blade," which they never did . . . (Pic: Reynold Carlson)

DEADLY/
SERIOUS

That's BULLSHIT!" cries an irate voice from the crowd.

"Could you redefine your terms, please," the lanky figure of Dead Travel Fast person Peter Richardson replies politely.

The Dead Travel Fast were more than half-way through their set before they were so rudely interrupted.

The Dead Travel Fast (name via Bram Stoker's *Dracula*) are simply the best new thing in Sydney. They've only

SCATTERED ORDER (right) was the studio band/production team of Michael Tee and Mitch Jones (pictured) and Patrick Gibson (of the Systematics), who also ran the highly successful M Squared Records.
(Pic: Lyn Gordon)

(MAKERS OF) THE DEAD TRAVEL FAST (below) released their debut album, "The Vessels," promptly retired from live performances, then broke up. (Pic: Annette Jones)

been playing live for a few months, since the success of their debut M Squared single, *Tael of a Saeghors,* but tonight at the Graphic Arts Club, supporting Serious Young Insects, they handle the hecklers and the half-empty hall to deliver a superb set.

The Dead Travel Fast have been described as "electronic," which is perhaps more than a trifle misleading. Certainly, they use a drum-machine and often multiple synthesisers, but with two guitars and a sax, as well as percussion, the DTF's scope is immesurably greater than the Numanesque implications of the word "electronic."

Their set began with a languid instrumental, Tim Schultz's sax appearing to glide above the guitars and synthesizers that flow and bubble like a mountain stream. This is typical Dead Travel Fast — much more than muzak, an evocative melange of melody and understated dynamics. The set was progressing smoothly — and included some "harder" songs and much singing by Shane Fahey — until the aforementioned incident. The heckler was unable to define his terms at all, however, so the band pressed on, and by the time they left the stage with *The Dumb-waiters* had the hall applauding loudly.

The headlining Serious Young Insects come from Melbourne. All the way from Melbourne, in fact, for just two gigs — the previous night at Green Records' Paddington Town Hall spectacular (with Tactics, the Allnighters, Wild West and the Systematics), and tonight . . .

I saw the band in their home-town about a year ago, and they reminded me of other trios like the Jam, Two Way Garden and Scapa Flow, as well as "pop" outfits like XTC. But what struck me most was their youth, that they had a lot of room for *growth.*

And indeed, Serious Young Insects *have* refined their approach some. Theirs is essentially a "pop" music — the influence of the Beatles is predominant now — which is infused with an uncommon freshness and vibrance. The songs are crisp, tightly structured and

The MODELS (top right) still refused to
be lumbered with a hit single, and
instead released a mini album, and then
went to England to record a second
album proper.

The EARS (right) sound was becoming
poppier. They made the "Scarecrow"
single before they broke up.
(Pic: Lyn Gordon)

DRESDEN WAR CRIMES (right) the
post-Birthday Party/Joy Division doom
merchants from Melbourne, gigged
briefly, made a cassette, then
disappeared.

hookline-laden.

Serious Young Insects are distinctive: the guitar has a clear, ringing sound that's reminiscent of the Byrds or early Public Image; the rhythm section does more than merely *support,* while the vocals are shared by all three, equally capable Insects.

Serious Young Insects are a hopeful young band; hopefully they will continue to grow. They must.

Clinton Walker

USE NO HOOKS (left) were one of the few Melbourne "little bands" to survive, and even then it was precariously. (Pic: Annette Jones)

The **SYSTEMATICS** (below) added a third member, and by gigging frequently they began to build a following, hungry for humour. (Pic: Sean Graham)

SEKRET SEKRET's (top right) neo-psychedelia met with some favour, mainly through their "New King Jack" single for Basilisk, but late in the year the band's future was uncertain. (Pic: Linda Nolte)

THE THOUGHT CRIMINALS (bottom right) had no intention whatsoever of playing live again, but they did make a second album, "You Only Think Twice." (Pic: Stephen Philip)

POST-PUNK
FUNKY FOLK

Baa, baa, ba-baa, baa/Baa, daa, daa, da-daa, baa, ba-baa, baa/Ay, yi, yi-yi, yi/ Love Lee Remick/She's a darlin'

So went the Go Betweens fab debut waxing of 1978, *Lee Remick.*

Lee Remick was a sparsely produced, poorly — if passionately — performed post-punk folk-pop song. It was ridiculously catchy and ridiculously romantic and it bounced its way into my heart. And it could well have bounded its way

THE GO BETWEENS (top, pic: Moss)

THE END's (left) influences were all-American and undeniably Birdmanesque, yet the band built upon this to make a contemporary rock that was much appreciated in Brisbane. (Pic: courtesy Brett Myers)

into every other Australian heart (given the opportunity — a perceptive major label A&R department would have signed the Go Betweens immediately, re-recorded *Lee Remick,* released it and had a hit on their hands). But this was not to be . . .

Reaction to the single elsewhere, however, was very favourable — the British press liked it, and Beserkley Records liked it enough to offer the band a contract. But nothing much amounted of all this attention, and the Go Betweens disappeared from view in the backwoods of Brisbane.

Until the arrival of a second single, *People Say,* in '79, again on the Able Label. Not as irrepressibly chirpy or immediately infectious as *Lee Remick, People Say* was, however, a maturation of the Go Betweens' style — a more sophisticated statement.

"People say I'm mad to love you." *People Say* saw the more confident Go Betweens adopt a thicker sound, as opposed to the thin, acoustic sound of *Lee Remick.* But alas, it seemed to have

THE SUNDAY PAINTERS (right) were based in Woollongong. Their primitive neo-Velvet Underground sound was an "attempt to provide both radical entertainment and alternative politics."

THE BAD POETS (above, pic: Heather Venn)

*** *** (right, pronounced by coughing twice) took audiences in Canberra off guard with their fierce and ferocious complexity.

SCRAP METAL (left) made the transition from covering Buzzcocks and Sham 69 songs to writing some of their own plus covering the Jam and Echo and the Bunnymen. Other bands in Brisbane on a similar level were the Perfect Strangers, the Hostages and JFK and the Cuban Crisis.

PERFECT STRANGERS (bottom left, pic: Mark Louttit)

less effect than *Lee Remick,* and once again the Go Betweens disappeared from view.

Until now. The band have just returned to Australia from Britain, where they recorded a new single, *I Need Two Heads/Stop Before You Say It,* which is yet another step forward, yet another simply superb single.

It's with this single that the Go Betweens hope to finally make some real impression on Australia. And even then any success they find will be belated . . .

I actually saw the Go Betweens first-ever performance, over three years ago, at Baroona Hall in Brisbane.

Robert Forster had been at university, "failing in arts," and he "just played guitar a bit." He taught his friend Grant McLennan what he knew about bass, and a little later the pair got up at Baroona Hall and played two songs Forster had written.

With a transient drummer, the Go Betweens began occasional gigging, a lot of songwriting — influenced most by the Velvet Underground and Bob Dylan — and occasional recording — the two Able singles. But it wasn't long after *People Say* that Forster and McLennan left Brisbane and went to Britain.

To Virgin, to begin with, but there they were kicked out after performing an impromptu *People Say* on acoustic guitars. Then Rough Trade, where they weren't quite "heavy" enough. Eventually it was a new Scottish independent called Postcard that *found them.*

Postcard has just released the Go Betweens' Scottish-recorded single *I Need Two Heads/Stop Before You Say It,* and already it's climbed to sixth spot on the British alternative charts.

I Need Two Heads/Stop Before You Say It evinces the Go Betweens admitting more contemporary, often black, influences.

"Yeah," Forster agreed, "the music they were listening to in Scotland we just hadn't considered. Like . . . Donna Summer, Stax and bits of disco."

"It also came out of seeing the Gang of Four," McLennan added, "and the similarity in our rhythms. That's the thing we really came back with — the interest in rhythm."

Indeed, on first hearing the new single I found it not unlike Talking Heads — the Go Betweens sound very much more *electric,* and funkier, punchier, although it's with a delicacy and understatement. "It's a very clear, clean sound," new drummer Lindy Morrison commented. "It's not that soft — it's brittle, there's an edge to it. And there's a lot more subtleties."

The Go Betweens also retain their own, very individual identity, propelled by Robert Forster's vision — *Stop Before You Say It* was written before the band went overseas, about "the inability to say what you want to say, so you don't say anything." *I Need Two Heads* is about being overwhelmed by a new environment (namely Britain). So what did the Go Betweens return to Australia with in their heads?

"Mainly confusion," Forster laughed

THE RIPTIDES suffered yet another line-up change, but managed to finally finish a single and a mini-album for Regular. By the end of the year, the band was in turmoil.

"But it sorted itself out after two or three months.

"I think it's made us more aware of just being ourselves really.

"Going overseas we could finally compare our sound to overseas bands," McLennan added, "and I think we felt it stands up. I did come back confused, but that was due to . . . *openness.* So many things had opened up to me. I mean, apart from music. And in a lot of Robert's songs I think that comes out now."

Since coming back to Australia the Go Betweens have spent most of their time, first, finding Lindy Morrison (who left the very promising Zero to join the band), then integrating her.

"Just getting a drummer, that's probably been the biggest thing," Forster said. "Like, I consciously feel that this is the first group, that this is just the beginning."

Forster is still writing the majority of the Go Betweens' material, although McLennan contributes some songs, and they're all arranged by the band as a whole. I wondered then what Forster's *intentions* were. (He'd told me once before, in a previous interview: ". . . I like the music to be emotional, and reckless, at the same time . . . it's whatever situation you're in, and you're trying to explain it to yourself . . .")

"It's an attempt not to be vague or general in any sense. I like to be . . . *clear.*" Forster enunciates that word

with fitting deliberation. "So that means the style is *understandable,* as opposed to dropping words like 'decade,' 'fall' . . . stuff like that.

"But it's hard to describe. It's definitely bright. Oh, this is stupid . . . it's not universally bright, I couldn't stand it if it was all bright." Simply, the Go Betweens express the contradictions and conflicts of life itself.

The band have just finished a national tour supporting Birthday Party, and the new single is about to be released here, but beyond that they have no real plans.

"I think what we've got to do is just establish our identity — this is the way we are, this is the way we sound — and hope that people will understand it," Forster said.

"We'd like to get to the stage where we're putting out records and making money," McLennan added. "Before, people have said that we don't take it seriously, but we do take it seriously, if we didn't we'd be playing out in the beer barns.

"We've never compromised — that's the thing I'm proud of. But as a result, we haven't got as much . . . 'exposure' as perhaps we should have."

This will change soon. (Claim the Go Betweens for your own before the British do!)
Clinton Walker
Reprinted from RAM by permission. Copyright.

SOME WORDS FROM PEL MEL

"It didn't cost us anything," says Pel Mel's Judy McGee of the recording of the band's first single, *No Word From China/Ipaneema Mon Amour.* "2JJJ had invited us to make a tape for them to play on air, and when they started playing it, a lot of people started to ask for it in the shops.

"Then 2JJJ asked us back to remix the songs for a special they were doing on the Machinations, Wild West and ourselves; it sounded great, so we decided to use it. All we had to pay for was the mastering and pressing."

Pel Mel are one of several young Sydney bands whose work in the nether regions of rock music has been exposed

PEL MEL
(Pic: Peter Nelson)

THE LIMP (top right) were a Pel Mel offshoot that marked the beginning of "little band" activity in Sydney, to supersede that in Melbourne, which was on its last legs. Other Sydney "little bands" were the Tame O'Mearas, Monotony Phaides and Via Venito. (Pic: Peter Nelson)

WILD WEST (bottom) added another former Voigt person, Rae Macron Cru, and cut back gigging, preferring to record at their own pace. By the end of the year the band had broken up. (Pic: Annette Jones)

to the public through the enthusiasm of Sydney FM station Triple Jay, and the band are grateful. Pel Mel (Judy McGee on vocals, synthesizer, sax and clarinet, sister Jane on guitar, Graeme Dunne on guitar and vocals, Lindsay O'Meara on bass and Dave Weston on drums) are, along with Laughing Clowns, probably the most popular of the crop of Sydney new music bands. Their sound is a brilliantly contrived mixture of pop dynamics, musical understatement and lyrical force; Pel Mel are, in their own unique way, a rather catchy band.

"We all think we're rather commercial," explains Dunne. "But it's hard when you're not with an agency or a major record company."

Slowly but surely the band are reaching a wider audience. Originally from Newcastle, they've moved to Sydney full-time.

With *No Word From China* receiving heavy airplay on Australia's alternative radio stations, offers of work have increased and the band seem, if anything, quite pleased if a little bewildered.

Dunne recalls their early days. "When we were starting to play, a year and a half ago, we did a lot of covers which everyone liked because no-one else played that sort of stuff. We used to do Joy Division, Wire, the Fall, the Cure — all those bands. We don't do any now, because we're getting better at playing."

It's this improvement in playing, they claim, that led to the sacking of their former bassplayer (who plays, incidentally, on the single), and since October the bass-playing duties have been attended to by Lindsay O'Meara,

formerly of Voigt/465 and Crime & the City Solution. Says O'Meara, "I liked the look of Pel Mel onstage before I joined. They're really honest."

It's not easy for a band to retain control of its destiny in the Australian music scene, particularly one such as Pel Mel. They've been fortunate to have the help of 2JJJ and resident engineer Ron Minogue and they're managing to broaden their audience without agency work or a major record deal.

Ed St. John
Reprinted from *Rolling Stone*

LITTLE MURDERS (top) with a mod cult springing up around them in Melbourne, made what was claimed to be the most expensive independent single ever — "She Lets Me Know" — but still awaits real success.

The **SETS (left)** emerged from the Sydney mod scene with their modern R&B, making a bid for across-the-board appeal.

The **ALLNITERS** (below) consciously aped the British ska movement. Their fans in Sydney were skinheads who touted Union Jacks and spoke in a Cockney accent. But the Allniters were certainly proficient, and never failed to incite a dancing frenzy.

ON THE SUNNY SIDE OF THE STREET

No matter what time of the year it is, Sydney always has one or two, or even three, great bands playing around the city. They stand out amongst the average and appalling bands like punks at a Mormon picnic.

The Sunny Boys are currently the most spirited dance band in Sydney.

The SUNNYBOYS (top, pic: Cathy Croll)

The HITMEN (right) all revved up with nowhere to go. A band by now a few years out of date, their long overdue debut album was a flop, and their prospects dismal . . .
(Pic: Patrick Bingham-Hall)

The SEVERED HEADS (left), with Wet Taxis and Negative Reaction, led a trend in Sydney towards cassettes, predicted by the N-Lets. Otherwise, these bands had little in common, though they all tried to avoid standard commercial and musical practices. (Pic: Tasso Taraboulsi)

The MACHINATIONS (bottom). Despite appearances, they put electronics in a broader context, making an accessible electropop that was on par with any anywhere. After a year of gigging in Sydney, their debut single, "Average Inadequacy" extended their standing considerably.

The METRONOMES (below) were an electronic duo, and occasionally trio, who never play live but record their thematic muzak for Cleopatra.

The PROTEENS (right) revived the art of girl-group pop, in the Dixie Cups mould, as opposed to the Passengers' prototype. Despite constant line-up changes, the band became a fixture in Sydney.

The SAINTS (below right) after another successful Australian tour and the release of their debut album "The Monkey Puzzle" returned to Europe. (Pic: Cathy Croll)

They're young, energetic, dynamic, powerful and all those other journalistic cliches used to describe great bands.

They're impossible not to dance to and have an enormous stack of catchy rock'n'roll songs that make you realise that if you've got what it takes a couple of cover versions are all you need.

OK, take a touch of Iggy, some Remains, a bit of Kinks, some Detroit power, a wonderful sense of melody, a tinge of Beatles, a bit of the Hitmen before they returned to being a heavy metal band, some Flamin Groovies, put them all together and you've got some inkling of what to expect at a Sunny Boys gig.

Oooooops, and add lots and lots of sweat cause this band is POPULAR. I repeat POPULAR. Going to see them play anywhere you're assured of being very familiar with the 20 people cramped around you. You'll have trouble moving more than a foot in any direction and so will they.

The Sunny Boys line-up is Jeremy Oxley (guitar and lead vocals), Peter Oxley (bass), Bill Bilson (drummer), and Richard Burgman (guitar).

It all began a few years ago when Jeremy and Peter used to play together in high school bands. Bill also went to the same high school and they estimate that they had four or five different bands during those years.

Three quarters of the Sunny Boys reside in Newtown, an inner-city Sydney suburb, and it was there that I met Jeremy and Peter for this interview.

Both were excited, and apprehensive, about their impending tour of Melbourne. Seems this Gudinski fellow has offered them a contract, making them the first Sydney-based Mushroom act.

Whether the Sunny Boys actually autographed the contract I'm not sure but there certainly was/is interest. And Mushroom were paying for the band to record demos at EMI's 301 Studio.

They'd put down 17 songs there with Lobby Lloyde producing. "That's just about all the original songs," Jeremy said.

Lobby Lloyde also produced the Sunny Boys first vinyl outing, an EP for Phantom with four of Jeremy's song — *Love to Rule, Alone with You, What You Need,* and *The Seeker.*

Let's face it, things have happened VERY fast for the Sunny Boys. The day of the interview they'd only just played their 50th show. And they're not rock'n'roll veterans. Jeremy, who I consider one of the finest rock'n'roll songwriters in the country, is only 18. Yep, 18.

"Our first gig was August 15th," Jeremy said. "It was at Chequers and we played with Trans Love Energy, ME 262 and the Lipstick Killers."

"Our roadies still don't have a set list," Jeremy said. "We always throw them out after every show. Every show has been different."

The Sunny Boys have 23 songs that they can call on. On an average night they play 17 or 18 of those. They're all originals written by Jeremy, although two, *Let You Go* and *Thrills* he co-wrote with Peter.

Cover-wise they regularly do the Remains classic *Why Do I Cry* and sometimes the Kinks' *All the Day and All the Night.* They've also been known to do the Fab Four's *Birthday.*

Boy/girl love songs are very common in the Sunny Boys set, but don't worry. It's only on a few occasions that they border on the mushy side of true love and romance.

The Sunny Boys only manage to get one new song down per practise. "I like to get the songs down whilst the confidence is there," Jeremy said. He writes all the music as well as the words, and Peter helps with the arrangements.

It didn't take the Sunny Boys long to obtain the nod of approval from the fickle inner-city cliques but now they're attempting to win audiences in the suburbs. "A lot of kids in the suburbs know us from the EP. We see them get up and dance when we play those songs."

The EP sold 1000 copies in 2½ weeks which ain't too bad. In fact it's better than any single or EP that a major company would sell.

I was interested in how the Sunny Boys felt about attracting many of the fans that Radio Birdman once had. I remarked to myself one night that the Sunny Boys were everything the old Birdman hordes had been waiting for.

"Well, we know certain tricks," Jeremy grinned. "We can play hard and heavy, or soft. The Birdman cult are only after energetic bands. There's very few around."

And the Sunny Boys don't copy no one. Hearing them blaze through the EP songs and other originals like *I'm Shakin', Tunnel of my Love,* and *My Only Friend* ("a slow song where people hold hands and kiss and cuddle") is to experience the true spirit of rock'n'roll.

Their attitude was perfectly summed up when I asked what they felt about tackling Melbourne audiences. "We're just going to play our guts out," Jeremy said. "Basically it's just dance music. We don't dress up or anything like that. We're an energetic pop band."

And a damn fine one too. If you want rock'n'roll spirit they've got it.

Stuart Coupe
Reprinted from *ROADRUNNER*

The NEW RACE (top left) brought together: 3 Birdmen, a Stooge, and one-fifth of the MC5; lots of old Birdman, Stooges and MC5 chestnuts; and all the old phallic connotations and fascist implications. (Pic: Lyn Gordon)

The "Legendary" DAGOES (left), a veritable institution in Adelaide, looked eastwards to spread the legend. Their American-oriented rock'n'roll met with good response, especially in Sydney. (Pic: Eric Algra)

BAD POETS SING ANOTHER SONG

Well, the Bad Poets are back on the road. They supported Laughing Clowns at the Governor Hindmarsh a couple of weeks ago, showcasing a new guitarist and playing an almost entirely new set.

For those who don't know the Bad Poets, they formed in January of 1980 and did their first gig at Adelaide University on March 30. The band then consisted of Jade D'Adrenz (D'Adrenalin was too long for forms) on vocals, Marcus Jarrett on guitar, Brogs playing bass, Tim Nicholls on drums and Troy Spasm on guitar.

Troy left in August due to "musical differences" (as usual) and the search that led to guitarist Martin Rigby began.

In those days the Bad Poets were very enthusiastic, very new and very drunk. It was the end of the punk rock

thing and they were exciting, energetic, sloppy, but more than that. They wrote good songs. Songs with usually excellent lyrics and interesting melodies. And they had Jade up front, belting it out, or crooning, or standing in the middle of the stage looking a little lost and gazing at the ceiling.

Potentially one of the best bands Adelaide has produced, they attracted people's interest but their enthusiasm was qualified by the Poets' erratic behaviour. After a debauched, screwed up final gig at Flinders University, they went off the road.

The new Bad Poets is different. They've retained only three songs from the old days: *Sing Another Song* (a World War Three marching song), *The Job* and *Faking As One* (about that desperate urge to couple, to be "in love"). Jade says it was almost as if the whole band broke up, and four of them decided to join with Martin Rigby. Five people are writing songs now whereas

The BAD POETS

135

before it was really only two.

I saw them at their first reappearance and was surprised. They were subdued and sober. But Jade's presence is as commanding as ever. The sound is tighter and more polished, and they work together instead of fighting each other. They are still very strong — just not sloppy. I was impressed and so were most people. As Brogs said, "People expected the Bad Poets to be more rocky, but that's behind us now, so we should be ok."

Jade continued, "In the old days we'd go on . . . I used to think it was a great thing to do on a Friday night. Now we like doing the songs more. It takes a while to work out what you like best and what you want to do."

The songs are what I call story songs or picture songs. They evoke images and tell stories about people, places and feelings and a lot of them are political. But not sloganising. When I asked Jade about being understated and evocative rather than outspoken, she said:

"If you emphasise things too much . . . I dunno . . . I find the Clash a bit insulting to the intelligence. Like if you say 'Peace not War' it offends the audience's intelligence. In *Ronnie Has a Vision* I saw this guy on TV and he was talking about China and he kept saying 'it's so simple', *Famous Beaches* is about the same thing . . . simplicity is dangerous."

Heather Venn
Reprinted from *ROADRUNNER*

The LOUNGE (top)

NUVO BLOC (left) devolved from a sprawling 6-piece to a quick, concise trio. (Pic: Eric Algra)

FLAMING HANDS (above) underwent
a complete reshuffle during a period
of hibernation, and then re-emerged
with a new single, new songs of their
own and an ambition to really make it.

FAST CARS (right) played a Tuesday
night residency at the Sussex Hotel in
Sydney, building a mod following. With
that, they broke out, enjoyed much
attention, then nearly broke up.

ZOO-MUSIC!

Nick Cave got a tattoo when he was in Australia. A great big skull-and-cross-bones, smack on his right bicep. Now, that may not be any big deal, but it was significant to me, because it seemed somehow symptomatic of the *change* the Birthday Party have undergone . . .

The BIRTHDAY PARTY made another excellent new single, "Release the Bats," after "Prayers On Fire" was released, and it was with this that the band began to make a real impact in England and America.
(Pic: Peter Milne)

HUGO KLANG (left) led an almost completely submerged existence in London, surfacing occasionally to play live and recording erratically. Pictured at Heaven.

The FOUR GODS (above right) became the latest purveyors of the Brisbane sound early in the year with their light, delicate pop. Pictured at the Queensland Institute of Technology. (Pic: Mark Louttit)

OUT OF NOWHERE saw Peter Walsh take a step towards realizing his full potential. The band played a jazz-influenced brand of post-punk pop, moving to Sydney to broaden their bases.

XIRO (above and right), after a short period as a trio, stabilized as a duo , and made a cassette before resuming live performances.

The Birthday Party are no longer boys next door: the Birthday Party have shed the last vestiges of false middle-class decency. Now they *confront.*

And this is only possible because, in their "liberation," the Birthday Party have become a better band.

Prayers On Fire is, perhaps, a certain coming-of-age. Their best record so far, it's also the best Australian album since the Saints' monumental (and criminally neglected) *Prehistoric Sounds* (with very little in between — only Tactics' *My Houdini* and Laughing Clowns' mini-albums come to mind immediately), and one of the best albums released so far this year anywhere in the world.

Prayers On Fire makes even previous Birthday Party triumphs like *Mr. Clarinet* seem positively pale.

The Birthday Party have loosened up. Stoicism gives way to Swing.

With *Prayers On Fire* the Birthday Party have reached a pinnacle of near-primitivism. *Zoo-Music Girl* — a virtual rewrite of the band's own, unrecorded *Let's Talk About Art* — opens the album, and could almost stand as a manifesto: *Don't drag your orchestra into this thing/Rattle those sticks, rattle those sticks/The sound is beautiful, it's perfect/The sound of her young legs in stockings . . . I want the noise of my Zoo-Music Girl . . . Oh! God! Please let me die beneath her fists.*

Zoo-Music Girl throbs with a sort of animal intensity that permeates all of *Prayers On Fire,* and will doubtless be likened to the "tribalism" of *Antmusic* and Public Image's *Flowers of Romance.* To me, it's more like the Cramps.

The songwriting on *Prayers On Fire* is distributed among various Birthday Party boys — predominantly Nick Cave and Rowland Howard — and their friends, so there's diversity, and inconsistency, though ultimately there's also a cohesion of vision that's uniquely and collectively the Birthday Party's.

The excellent drumming of Phil Calvert and Tracey Pew's heaving basslines create the space within which Cave, Howard and Mick Harvey play.

SCAPA FLOW remained almost "undiscovered," although they were without a doubt one of the most impressive bands in the land.
(Plc: Kathleen O'Brien)

Nick Cave's earlier obsession with religion has become the Birthday Party's obsession with the grotesque, the evil, the primitive . . . the primal.

Cave is indeed Nick the Stripper; he howls and yelps and on *Yard* even blows a squeaking sax.

King Ink, like *Yard,* was perhaps inspired by the Stooges, and it has that sort of menace. *Dead Song* betrays the influence of Pere Ubu, as does *Capers.* Mick Harvey's one composition *Just You and Me* is mock grim. *Cry, Figure of Fun* and *Dull Day* wouldn't be out of place on *Hee Haw.* Rowland Howard sings one song — the chilling *Ho-Ho,* which is like a meeting of a sea shanty and the Doors' *The End.*

Nick the Stripper (which has been released as a 12″ single) is a definitive statement on the performer/audience relationship, and probably the best song on the album. Play it back to back with Teardrop Explodes' *Reward!* Play it loud and try to resist . . . the sideshow alley atmosphere, Equal Local's horns, Rowland Howard's sprinklings of guitar like so much ground glass . . .

Prayers on Fire is like a rite.

For too long now Australian music has met with ridicule and, worse, apathy in England. In *Prayers on Fire* the Birthday Party have made an album that's not only magnificent but also has been rapturously received in England, and hopefully that will open the door for Laughing Clowns, the Go Betweens, Equal Local . . . I could go on.

Clinton Walker

Reprinted from RAM by permission. Copyright.

LAUGHING CLOWNS (top right), after a period of turmoil, stabilized as a trio augmented by other musicians, and moved closer towards their ideal' The band gigged regularly and recorded consistantly, yet widespread recognition still eluded them.
(Pic: Ken West)

TACTICS (bottom right) campaign to convert Australia continued with more diverse gigs and recording a second album. **(Pic: Stephen Hocking)**

SARDINE — SQUEEZING OUT SPARKS

Ian Rilen is something of a revered figure. Cold Chisel's Don Walker has called him one of the best songwriters in the country, but don't hold that against him. Walker was referring to the material Rilen pens for Rose Tattoo, a band he was a founder of, but don't hold that against him either.

His previous band, the notorious X, I never liked much — but when word got out about Rilen's new band making their debut at the Rock Garden late in 1980, I went along. And it was good, a very impressive debut. Since then, Sardine have gigged fairly consistently around town, though I kept on missing them. Until this gig at the Governor's Pleasure . . .

And once again, I wasn't disappointed. The promise of Sardine's debut was true; they're one of the best new bands I've seen in Sydney so far this year.

On stage, Ian Rilen cuts an impressive figure. Wearing an impeccably tailored light blue suit, his hair slicked back and thick make-up, Rilen *leans* into his guitar. To his left, on keyboards, his wife, Stephanie, elegant as ever in a white evening dress, and to his right, lanky young bassist Phil Hall, dressed sharp too. Behind the drums, another youngster, Greg Skehill.

Sardine's music moves in slow motion. At root, it's as simple as hell — a melodic, understated simplicity, that gains by repetition and subtle variation.

Easy comparisons: the Cure, Public Image, the Gang of Four. Underlying it all, however, was a fairly strong rock traditionalism, the natural result of Rilen's years of experience.

Sardine skillfully integrate old and mostly new. Their set has complete cohesion and, within that, diversity. They emit light and shade, they can sound thick then thin and sparse.

They jump— and they're usually led by Phil Hall's nimble fingers — from a swishy jazz feel to Detective Riffs. Rilen's guitar is like a meeting of Hank

SARDINE's Ian Rilen
(Pic: Francine McDougall)

Marvin, Keith Levene and Angus Young — yes, Angus Young! — and it's wor ing! From an almost Indian raga — Sardine often have that hypnotic effect, which is especially enhanced by Stephanie Rilen's (literally) minimal contribution on keyboards — to a strange form of heavy metal that denies comparisons with the usual crassness that is heavy metal because of its richness and resonance. Ultimately, it spells a sort of brooding power.

Because of its very nature, Sardine's music is very reliant on execution. Occasionally does a song fall flat on its face, simply because the band don't play well enough, but that's the exception rather than the rule.

Sardine's only other real weakness lies in Rilen's lyrics: I mean, lines like *I've been hearing all round town/I've been hearing you been getting round/ Whether it's right or whether it's true/ I'm stuck here, I'm stuck on you* aren't exactly revelatory, but then perhaps that's the key to Sardine — perhaps what they're doing is putting the gunslinger ethos and the blues into a kozmic — as in *space age* — kontext.

Clinton Walker

The TABLEWAITERS (above left) were highly able musicians undeniably influenced by the English school. Their preoccupation throughout the year was recording an album, though they did play live in Sydney occasionally. (Pic: Peter Brennan)

The YOUNG DOCTEURS (left) moved to Sydney from Canberra, and presented themselves in ways outside the norm, such as the picture here.

THE PLANTS (bottom right) were either 'pretentious new noise or simply a Perth band influenced by the English sound, who were individual mainly in their presentation and image.

WILDLIFE DOCUMENTARIES (top left) marked the return of Ivor Hay to the stage. The band brought together eclectic influences and made a very promising impression with their first few gigs. (Pic: Judi Dransfield)

KILL THE KING (centre left) almost did justice to the term "jazz-punk." Theirs was a crude, savage sound offset by wailing horns, which only really confused Sydney audiences. (Pic: Clinton Walker)

UPSIDE DOWN HOUSE (left), a sprawling ensemble playing free form country and western swing were ready to debut in Sydney by the end of 1981. (Pic: Lisa Walker)

HUNTERS & COLLECTORS COME OUT AT NIGHT

Ever since the Birthday Party left Australia, Melbourne has frantically tried to find a new focus. For the latter half of 1980 and the early part of this year, Equal Local were it, with their sparkling post-punk brand of jazz-rock. But even though Equal Local have improved with age, they've already been superseded. Right now, Hunters & Collectors are the Hip New Thing in Melbourne.

Hunters & Collectors have a perfect pedigree, what with four-sixths of them formerly of the marvellous Jetsonnes, and the remainder having been Birthday Party roadies. They began gigging in Melbourne only a few months ago and immediately met with a tumultuous and rapturous response from critics and (capacity) crowds alike. Then, thanks to that young maverick among promoters, Ken West, Sydney was able to witness the Hunters & Collectors phenomenon first hand.

The last of Hunters & Collectors' three recent Sydney gigs was at Redfern Town Hall, where they were supported by Pel Mel, the Systematics and the Limp. Following the Limp (appropriately named) and the Systematics (making synthesizers cute), Pel Mel arrive on stage fresh from taping *Countdown* that afternoon for their first Sydney appearance in two months. They have a clutch of new songs and get off to a good start. Pel Mel still rely heavily on their — English — influences for inspiration, only now the emphasis has shifted from Joy Division to A Certain Ratio. But as the set progresses its initial promise is dissipated; be it due to the material or their playing or whatever, Pel Mel allow themselves to slip back into their formula approach to pop (for Pel Mel are pop, not progressive, contrary to popular opinion).

Hunters & Collectors bound on stage radiating vitality and colour. Before long they prove they're nowhere near as good as they're cracked up to be, but neither are they as bad as their (admittedly few) detractors would have you believe. What they have done is synthesise art and funk, as Talking

Heads did before them. Within Hunters & Collectors you can hear echoes of the Models and Chic, George Clinton and Sly Stone; still, their own character is omnipresent, with songs and words like "Loinclothing" and "Junket Head." What they don't do, however, is expand on their own base. Simply put, Hunters & Collectors seem to know only one riff, and they play it all night long. They're repetitious, as even their most ardent admirers must concede.

One song at a time, though, there's no doubt Hunters & Collectors are damn good — as good, even better, than so many other white punks on funk. Bassist John Archer, occasionally augmented by vocalist Mark Seymour playing the same instrument, supplies a rubbery bedrock, which, with Doug Falconer's sure drumming and percussionist Greg Perano's clanking gas cylinder, woodblocks and what have you, is hard and well-nigh impenetrable. Guitarist Ray Tosi repeats that riff to an almost hypnotic point, Geoff Crosby adds electronic embellishments and Mark Seymour alternately howls and croons. And if you're at all put off by the band's near-New Romantic image, don't be; once you feel the amount of humour with which Hunters & Collectors approach everything, you won't be. I mean, they smile so much.

It was for this reason — Hunters & Collectors' spirit — that as their set drew to a close I was drawn in, almost despite myself. By this time any accusations of contrivance had flown out the window. Hunters & Collectors were, as they say, cooking. It didn't matter that every song sounded the same, because that one song *is* good. They played two encores and left the stage, and Sydney, jubilant.

Hunters & Collectors are a disco band, no doubt, no art (please), and if they hope to realize all their potential — which is significant — they must be aware of this and act accordingly. A prediction: Hunters & Collectors are going to be big. You just wait and see if I'm not right.

Clinton Walker
Reprinted from *ROLLING STONE.*

NERVOUS SYSTEM (right), despite the image, assumed a more visible profile around Sydney towards the end of the year. Their sound was raw, arty neo-punk.

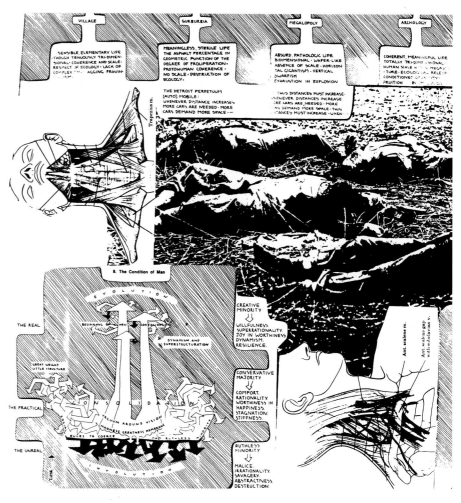

NEW SINGLE: SECOND GLANCE — OUR BOYS
APPEARING AT

ALBUM!

YOUNG MODERN
PLAY FASTER
A LOCAL ALBUM

LIPSTICK KILLERS

CIVIC WED. 24TH OCT.

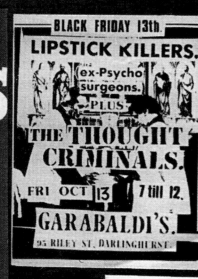

BLACK FRIDAY 13th.
LIPSTICK KILLERS.
ex-Psycho surgeons.
PLUS
THE THOUGHT CRIMINALS.
FRI OCT 13 7 till 12.
GARABALDI'S.
95 RILEY ST, DARLINGHURST.

The Boys Next
DOOR·DOOR

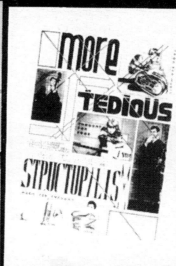

more
TEDIOUS

STPUCTUPLIST

STAGE
FRI
THOU
CRIMI
POP
MECH
TA

UGHT
MINALS

NESS
FLYING SAUCERS

primitive
calculators
+ whirlywirld
crystal ballroom. tues 15. may.

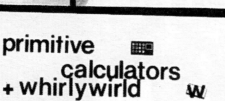

BASILISK RECORDS
NEW RELEASE
JUMP VISION
CAN'T GET USED TO YOU
"THE JUMP"
DEBUT SINGLE

LITTLE MUR
SHE LETS ME KNOW....

pŏp´-ūlar mechăn´-ics
APPEARING AT:-

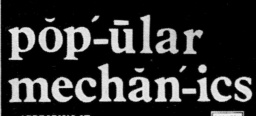

YOU ONLY THINK

VISITORS

TACTICS

THOUGHT CRIMINALS. TACTICS FRIDAYS FOREST INN

VOIGT/465
IN MELBOURNE IN MAY
WED 9TH - ANGLERS HALL (7·30PM HIGH ST PRAHRAN WITH →↑→)
FRI 11TH - PRESTON INSTITUTE (LUNCHTIME WITH →↑→)
SAT 12TH - CRYSTAL BALLROOM (EARLY)
" - UNIVERSAL WORKSHOP (LATE)
BE THERE OR BE SOMEWHERE ELSE!

THE RIDES
the go-betweens
The Humans
Friday 21st. September
Griffith University Refectko.
$3.00 & $2.50 Unemployed Students
Licensed and ZZZ subs.
Presented by Griffith Students Union.

GARB...
FRI. 5TH FLAMING HANDS
SAT. 6TH LAUGHING CLOWNS

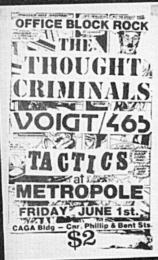

OFFICE BLOCK ROCK
THE THOUGHT CRIMINALS
VOIGT/465
TACTICS
at METROPOLE
FRIDAY JUNE 1st.
CAGA Bldg — Cnr. Phillip & Bent Sts.
$2

THE GOBETWEENS
PEOPLE LOVE 'PEOPLE SAY'
Their New Single

Les Rythmiques
the Apartments
when:
where:

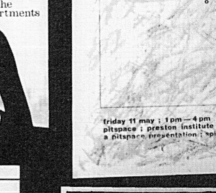

"TERMINATION........"
& VOIGT 465
friday 11 may ; 1pm — 4pm
pitspace ; preston institute
a pitspace presentation ;

Boys Next Door.

TWO WAY GARDEN

young modern

NEWS
★

RIPTIDES
single   Sunset Strip

the leftovers
with RAZAR
HAMILTON HALL
RACECOURSE RD
MAY 27 1978
BAYS 2 LATE
$4

LIPSTICK KILLERS
Fri. Oct 13 Garibaldi's 95 Riley St Darlinghurst
Sat. Oct 14 Brooklyn Hotel 225 George St
Thu. Oct 19 Sydney Uni. Cellar
Fri. Oct 20 Garibaldi's
Sat. Oct 21 Brooklyn Hotel
Thu. Oct 26 Sydney Uni Cellar

MALE MINIMALISM

MANIKIN
MODELS FOR MANKIND

THE LAST DAYS OF THE SEAVIEW

NICK CAVE sporting the Big Daddy Ed Roth T-shirt that led to the Birthday Party commissioning the legendary LA kustom kar-toonist to paint the cover for their incendiary *Junkyard* album. When Big Daddy, a practicing Christian, finally heard the album, he was incensed at its 'godlessness'. (Pic: Missing Link)

TERSE TAPES' LUCKY DIP OF QUASI-NORMALITY

Attitudes to cassettes are changing." says Andy Maine, co-producer of *Fast Forward* cassette magazine. "For so long they've been the little brother or sister of records, whereas now they're coming into their own. Things are being done with cassettes that can't be done with records."

Australia has always been slow to recognize its own achievements. But with the ever-increasing popularity of "walky" cassette players, and, in England, Bow Wow Wow's "C30 C60 C90 Go!" campaign, Island's "1+1" series and cassette-only releases such as the *NME*/Rough Trade C81, *From Brussels with Love* and the British Electric Foundation's *Music for Stowaways*, there would certainly seem to be some sort of cassette revolution, and within this development, Australia is something of an innovator.

Nearly four years ago, Dave Warner made his first impression on the Eastern

Above: While Adelaide was becoming the domain of local indie Greasy Pop, the Sputniks lit out of town and in Melbourne became THE MOODISTS when they picked up former Negatives' bassist Chris Walsh. Pictured at the Yugal Soccer Club, Sydney 1983. (Pic: Joe Borkowski)

Centre left: "Talking to Cleopatra" was a turntable hit that promised much for ESSENDON AIRPORT, but the band had to split before that promise was realised in the solo career of David Chesworth and in the formation, by the remainder of the band, of I'm Talking, the hippest new thing in Melbourne clubland in 1984.

Left: In the face of the chart action enjoyed by Euroglider/Real Life-style synthpap, or even the Machinations, the Systematics turned into YA-YA CHORAL and proved the alternative didn't have to be all grave industrial atonality. (Pic: Annette Jones)

states with live cassettes. Other bands from Perth followed: the Mannikins released their *Live Locally* set, and the Triffids have put out a slew of tapes. Now, Australia can boast *Fast Forward* (perhaps a first, being a regular cassette magazine), and a plethora of cassette labels. Terse Tapes of Sydney is probably the most prominent of these, and certainly the most active. Run by one man, Tom Ellard, Terse has just released a triple-cassette ("five album equivalent") called *One Stop Shopping*, which is a compilation of lots of Australia's practitioners of Music For Cassettes, "a festival of quasi-normality," as Ellard puts it.

Ellard specifically asked me to review *One Stop Shopping* with the following provisos: to avoid mentioning "trends in England [unavoidable, sorry, we are all susceptible to them], metaphysics and what Philip Brophy thinks. Just tell them what they get for their sixpence."

Well then, for seven dollars, you get sixty bands — count 'em, sixty! — too numerous to mention individually, from sources such as the Clifton Hill Community Music Centre (the home of new music in Melbourne), Slow Drama Music (that of the Primitive Calculators' attendant "little bands"), Painkiller Tapes, M Squared (Scattered Order, Systematics), Tapeworms (Slugfuckers, Bleeding Arseholes), Two Tapes (the N-Lets), Adhesive Records (Laughing Hands), Terminal Records (the Sunday Painters, from Wollongong) and the post-Voigt/465 push (led by Wild West and Pel Mel) as well as Terse itself (Severed Heads, Mindless Delta Children, Agent Orange, Wet Taxis, Mesh); some of these bands play on the rock circuit, most don't; some have records out, others don't; and in Ellard's words "no band was rejected because of style or recording quality."

As a result *One Stop Shopping* is inevitably a mixed bag. What it really reminds me of in a way is Zappa's *Weasels Ripped My Flesh* (and that's meant to be a compliment). Naturally, it's impossible to label the music in any single way, but it is fair to say it's most commonly characterized by "low-tech" sound and instrumentation, equal parts electronic and acoustic, an amateurism bordering on naivety and occasionally pretension, spontaneity, vigour and (often black) humour. It's a sort of primitivism, and sound collage is popular. As to whether or not it's experimental, I daren't say, but it's nothing like anything you hear on radio. This is music in the league of — and here come some Easy Reference Points — Cabaret Voltaire, the San Francisco of Ralph Records and Chrome, Industrial Records, Factory Records, David (Flying Lizard) Cunningham's various projects, and the Fall. And it stands up. *One Stop Shopping* is one moment hackneyed and dull, the next inventive and exciting; but that's forgivable considering the breadth it presents.

Ultimately, perhaps the best thing to say is to echo the sentiment expressed on the cover of the accompanying booklet: "1. Convince some friends to record on a cassette."

C.W., reprinted from *ROLLING STONE*.

Below: SEVERED HEADS, Tom Ellard (centre). Pic: Juilee Pryor, with video by Ian Andrews.

Above: Few Australian musicians are as peripatetic as SAINT Christopher Bailey. After a solo stint in Paris, Bailey got together a new lineup and album, *Casablanca*, in London in 1982, before heading 'home' to tour.
(Pic: Iain Sheddon)

Left: The LAUGHING CLOWNS line-up that toured Europe in 1982 was disbanded shortly afterwards, leaving behind the sludgy "Everything That Flies" 12" single as the legacy of an ill-fated summer (Pic: Red Flame).

REMEMBRANCE AND HOPE

It's fitting that when the Go-Betweens added a new member to their three-piece line-up it turned out to be Rob Vickers, an old Brisbane boy (and a former Riptide too) who'd been holed up in the Big Apple for the last five years.

The Brisbane-born Go-Betweens, presently resident in London, are a band smitten by all things New York — the Velvets, Dylan circa '65 to '66, then the School of '76 — Patti Smith, Television, Talking Heads — and on. Even the cover of *Before Hollywood* harks back to *Highway 61.* But the Go-Betweens aspire not to make music *like* their heroes, rather as *great* as.

And with *Before Hollywood* they almost have. This is an album that positively glows. It was recorded in Brighton, England, for Rough Trade, during a bleak winter in 1982, and producer John Brand has captured a Go-Betweens looking homewards at the same time as they were looking towards the future with wide eyes. It's an album of remembrance and hope. If *Send Me A Lullaby*, the debut Missing Link album, was very much "Songs of Innocence," *Before Hollywood* begins the loss of innocence process.

Where *Send Me A Lullaby* was fragile and occasionally faltering, while still possessing an uplifting resonance, *Before Hollywood* is more a complete album. Endearing as their vulnerability was, the Go-Betweens now play with confidence and solidity, though still with an edge. The songwriting is now equally shared by guitarist Robert Forster and then-bassist Grant McLennan; they offer ten deceptively simple pop songs that pack an emotional impact just barely below a skin of finely wrought and realised melody and rhythmic attack. McLennan's are the really catchy ones, of classic structure, his voice almost doe-eyed. Forster's are more quirky, more obtuse, while his voice has developed from a strangled style to a penetrating pitch.

Australian record companies were wary of taking on the Go-Betweens because they were "too old" and/or without a palpable image, which is incomprehensible to me, because apart from the fact that *Before Hollywood* is full of potential hits, it appeals to our

best romantic instincts and as such crosses all over. I could pick nits and say I don't really like the Al Kooperesque organ, or that in my opinion a couple of the songs are comparatively weak, but what's that when you're dealing with an album as affecting as this one? Romantics who are often confused and hurt by the world, the Go-Betweens know where they're from and dream of a perhaps unobtainable perfect love, while they do their best to cope with the way things are.

There's no need to scrutinize this album song by song — save to say that the single from it, "Cattle and Cane," is

a classic and quintessential Australian record and has to be a hit. Each person who hears *Before Hollywood* will be uniquely touched by it.

C.W., reprinted from *ROLLING STONE.*

THE GO-BETWEENS were a three-piece (above; pic: Tom Sheehan) when they arrived in the UK in 1982, but soon after they recorded *Before Hollywood*, Grant McLennan was able to hand over bass-playing duties to new member Robert Vickers (below; pic: Clinton Walker).

Left: If ROB YOUNGER's return to the stage with the New Christs was in any way reluctant, he was increasingly in-demand on the other side of the desk, producing new acts like Died Pretty, the Hard-Ons and the Eastern Dark. And the Christs, despite only sporadic activity, and despite fresh competition from the likes of Brisbane's Screaming Tribesmen, are still the most creative exponents of Australia's so-called Detroit Sound. (Pic: Francine McDougall)

Centre: Leading lights of the Sydney 'little band' scene, PEL MEL joined new label Gap, the Australian Factory/Joy Division licensee, and produced a modest debut album that saw the band pursuing a lighter, funkier approach. (Pic: Phil Turnbull)

Below: After "New King Jack," SEKRET SEKRET had the world in their hands, but the eccentricity and volatility that made the band great also contributed to its decline. (Pic: Peter Nelson)

DANCE TO THE DEAD-BEAT ON
FRIDAY 13!
SPY v SPY, le HOODOO GURUS
Hoi Polloi, Introverts, Scientists
PADDO TOWN HALL.
7pm - 1am
[BAR AVAILABLE. NO B.Y.O.]

CONNECTING WITH ROCK'S SPINAL CHORD

(Pic: Dean Bateup)

The Moodists may have more detractors than believers, but any band that polarizes reaction like they do must have something going for them. I'll declare where I stand, straight off: I reckon the Moodists are the best new group Australia's seen since, well, Hunters and Collectors.

The Moodists' strength lies in the fact that they've invented a language of their own that's tantalizingly so near yet so far from anything we already know. In the last two or three years, a handful of Australian groups have broken through with original voices — the Birthday Party, the Go-Betweens, Laughing Clowns, Hunters and Collectors — but nothing much has happened since then until the appearance of the Moodists, who connect brilliantly with rock's spinal chord. They remind us that rock must reassociate itself with its roots, rechannel them into a new form that's far less *removed*, rather than hiding behind production and image. We need music that may be rough and simple, certainly honest, economical and direct. The Fall are like that; so are the Gun Club — and so are the Moodists.

Coming to Melbourne via Adelaide in 1981, from the backwoods of home-town Mount Gambier, the Moodists deny any country roots, but there is nevertheless a simple, rural honesty about them. Their first single, "Where The Trees Walk Downhill" (on Melbourne independent Au Go Go), evinced their punky-poppy predilec-tions. After that, with the addition of bassist Chris Walsh to the remaining line-up of singer Dave Graney, Steve Miller (guitar) and Clare Moore (drums), and a second single. "Gone Dead," the group moved closer towards its ideal.

"Originally," says Graney, "we had a bass player who really inhibited what we wanted to do; he was interested in being like Serious Young Insects or something. Around that time there were a lot of really serious, Joy Division-type bands around, and we were playing a fairly physical sort of music. It wasn't very popular, but it was what we wanted to do, even though we didn't have a very clear idea. Chris joining the band changed it

into what we really wanted."

The Moodists' latest record, the *Engine Shudder* mini-album (again on Au Go Go), is little short of a classic. So impressed was visiting Englishman Dave Kitson that he signed the group to his Red Flame label. Red Flame released a Moodists' compilation, which garnered excellent U. K. reviews and leapt into the English independent charts at number 19. The group have just left for London, and it's my opinion they'll be Australia's next success there.

"We're looking forward to going to England," said Graney, not long before they left, "where somebody is prepared to invest money in us and put us into a studio. We want to make a really decent album, and tour. I think we can make a much better record than *Engine Shudder*."

No doubt they will, yet *Engine Shudder* remains a unique and glorious vehicle for the Moodists' music, a vehicle stripped down to an alloy chassis housing a supercharged V-8, with independent suspension, and sheetmetal body panels.

'Minimalism' is a word I hesitate to use, but it's a measure of the Moodists' class that they can get away with the Bo Diddley beat. Chris Walsh is an out-standing bass player and Clare Moore drums like rolling thunder. Songs have been reduced to repetitive lines. Ensemble playing can be bludgeoning, yet because of the space between the musicans, and their intimate rapport, there is no lack of light and shade, or creative punctuation. Steve Miller is one of those rare players who knows when not to play. And now, with the

addition of new guitarist Mick Sick, he has more scope. ("Mick's given us a whole new lease on life," says Graney. "The sound of his guitar has made it possible for Steve to play less. It's opened up the sound.") Just as in his offstage demeanour, Graney weaves in and out of the mix in slow motion, soaring, swooping, stumbling. And the melody — for there is melody — you can sing along with! Graney's lyrics and the music commune perfectly, with the songs generally containing no more than a few lines. Yet, as in "Kept Spectre," remarkable perceptions emerge through repetition and juxtaposition. The imagery and implications a Moodists' song evokes is deep, scary, absurd and funny.

"We don't jam," Graney says. "I just write a lyric and we usually just muck around with a couple of chords that anyone brings along. I don't think we've ever set out to do anything really consciously. Most of the songs are about pretty real emotions and stuff."

The Moodists are bemused by the world, bemused but never down-trodden. With their eyes wide open, they willingly fling themselves at the mercy of life's contradictory lot. There is a calm, however, underlying their vigorous muse that denotes a benign understanding of the way things are, a strange mixture of innocence and a sort of eternal wisdom.

And they can drink anybody under the table.

C.W., reprinted from *ROLLING STONE*.

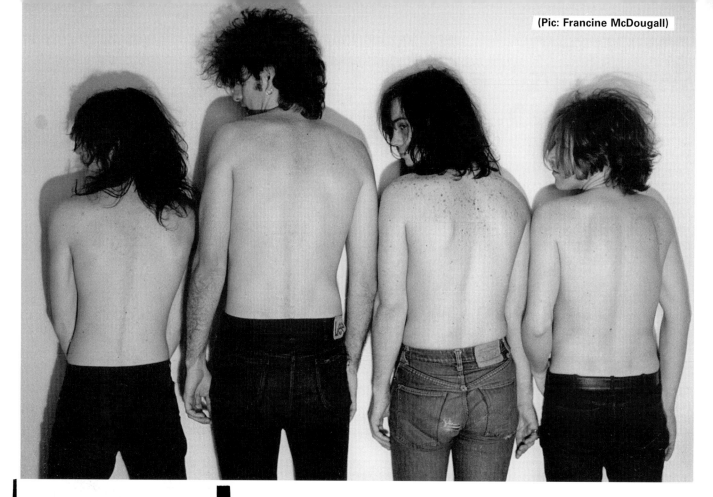

INSPIRED BY THE SPIRIT OF ROCK & ROLL

The news that the Scientists are about to leave Australia — as permanently as is possible — will doubtless barely cause a ripple in Oz-rock's Halls of Acceptance. Which, of course, is part of their reason for leaving. It's the same old story — as also experienced by the Birthday Party, the Go-Betweens, the Moodists — a group makes an original noise, records independently, finds a limited audience, but eventually becomes frustrated because there's nowhere else to go — within Australia, at least. So they head for greener pastures.

The Scientists' brand of post-punk neo-rock & roll is a snarling, wild beast, a tooth-and-claw attack that Australians at large don't seem to appreciate at all. When the group played a support gig with the Angels at a suburban Sydney RSL club late last year, they were greeted by a barrage of abuse and beer cans so thick they were forced to leave the stage. But there's no doubt the Scientists are an

important Australian group who deserve better treatment than that (anybody would!) and will just as likely find it in England.

'We've done about as much as we can do here," Scientist-in-chief Kim Salmon told me. 'I think because we play to a minority — a large minority — we're a band that's musically on the move, our sights are set ahead of us. You often find that people will come in at a certain time and identify with what you're doing, and then maybe not appreciate the changes you'll make. That's a gross over-simplification; what I'm saying is that it gets frustrating, you need to play to a wider and more varied group of people."

Indeed, the Scientists are a group that's undergone a lot of changes in their six-year life-span. Originally formed in Perth in 1978, they moved from a brash, New York Dolls-influenced base to a (power-)poppier conclusion, cutting a couple of singles and an album before they broke up in 1980. Drummer James Baker would eventually join the Hoodoo Gurus in Sydney, while singer/guitarist Kim Salmon set to assembling a new Scientists. With Tony Thewlis on guitar, Boris Sujdovic (formerly of the Rockets) on bass and Brett Rixon on drums, the group left Perth for Sydney late in 1981,

a different group to the Scientists of yore.

They looked different, to begin with, different to *everything*, a quartet of shaggy-topped, lean torsos wrapped in supremely tacky, psychedelic outfits. The Scientists had wilfully grown ugly.

I asked Kim Salmon if he thought it was a different group.

"Not in ideals," he replied. "The approach and the sound were different, but the ideals were the same."

"Ideals" is a word that crops up a lot in conversation with Salmon, as does "spirit"; even though he's shy and a reluctant orator, it's obvious he's a man totally dedicated to realizing his vision of rock & roll, a vision shared implicitly with the rest of the Scientists.

It was 1982's "Swampland" single (on the Melbourne independent label Au Go Go) that really established the Scientists (it's still sitting near the top of the indie charts). Comparisons with the Stooges, Suicide, the Cramps, even the Birthday Party, were to be expected but the Scientists occupied a niche of their own, and they were digging deeper.

"There's a Scientists sound itself. Some people have just got it. There was an awful lot of them in the Fifties, and," he laughs, "there's been less and less ever since. You listen to something that's got that style about it, that class, and you identify with it. And it inspires you; you think, I'd like to do that. But you don't do it by copying, you do it by trying to capture that spirit."

And that spirit abounds in the Scientists. The *Blood Red River* mini-album, released early last year, was a consummate achievement, the Scientists' coming-of-age. Bass and drums thundered, guitars wailed, Salmon howled. A great part of the Scientists' strength lies in the chemistry, for want of a better word, that exists within the group; their rapport makes possible musical flights — the Scientists actually do improvise on stage — that transcend the structured. The Scientists are a driven group.

Song titles like "When Fate Deals Its Mortal Blow," "Burnout" and "Rev Head" tell part of the story. "Anybody who writes songs sets out to convey some sort of feelings," Salmon admits, "but if you asked me what a song was about I couldn't tell you. Besides, the songs are supposed to do that; that's what they're for."

Since the release of *Blood Red River*, the Scientists have maintained an accessible profile, but it's because so few challenges remain, or present themselves anymore in Australia, that the group must leave. They played an under-publicized farewell tour late last year, so there won't be another opportunity to see them. But a new single, "We Had Love" — possibly the most relentless racket the Scientists have yet made — has just been released, and a new EP is completed, for release shortly. The recent tendency with the Scientists is to shorter, more concise songs; how would Salmon describe the EP?

"Well, really, it's just closer to what we've always wanted to do: it's a process of perfection. It's got a sense of humour about it, and it's really wild and over-the-top, and it's irreverent — the way we've always liked to do it really."

Finally, on the eve of the Scientists' departure, what sort of hopes does Salmon have?

"I'd like to be big," he smiled. "Successful! Isn't that what everybody wants? And to make money our of it as well. I mean, devotion, and love of what you do, can get you so far, but the rewards have to start coming in soon."

They should. It's just a shame the Scientists have to go to England to look for them.

C.W., reprinted from *ROLLING STONE*.

Right: Even before the Beasts of Bourbon in Sydney, Melbourne's SACRED COWBOYS were a post-punk swamp rock supergroup. Led by former Negatives front-man Gary Grey, they almost crashed the charts with "Nothing Grows in Texas".

Below: When THE MODELS moved from Melbourne to Sydney to work under the wing of INXS manager Chris Murphy, Murphy asked them, "Do you want to be a toy band like Talking Heads, or a real band?" James Freud rejoined and electronics whiz Andrew Duffield left, though not before his "I Hear Motion" gave the band its chart breakthrough.

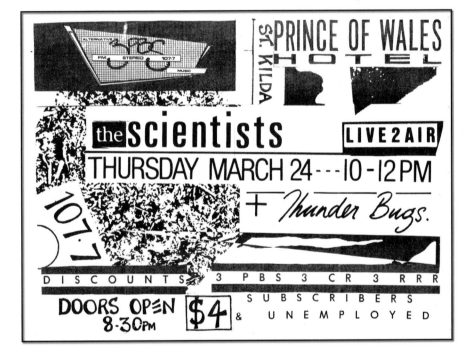

Above: Driving an imaginary '57 Chevy, Boy King DAVE LAST poses for the cover of *Asleep at the Wheel*, Au-Go-Go Records' 1984 Melbourne compilation that defined an era with the post-Birthday Party/hillbilly grunge sound of the Olympic Sideburns, Feral Dinosaurs, Corpse Grinders and others.

salon bon ton/new music/the club/thursdays

SALON bon ton

only $4.00!
beer & wine
FREE till 9.30!!

une spree president

thurs nov 25
soldiers of fortune
(ray tosti ex-hunters)
and all the way from
sydney australia in their
debut melb performance
le hoodoo gurus
plus
no dance—a film by ➤↑→

thurs dec 2
ash wednesdays modern jazz
plus guests tba

thurs dec 9
essendon airport
plus guests tba

thurs dec 16
ya ya choral (syd)
plus guests tba

des talent modernes

pour des genes nouveaux

The CLUB

132 smith st collingwood ph 417 4425

THE SAINTS

LIVE!!LIVE!!ALIVE!!ALIVE!!A LIVE PERFORMANCE!!

Chris BAILEY, <u>alone</u> with guitar.

Where: LEICHHARDT HOTEL, 126 BALMAIN RD. LEICHHARDT.

When: Thursday 10th February.

Time: 8.30--10.30

How Much: $3.00

NEW CHART FOR INDEPENDENTS

Let's face it, the charts are the biggest marketing tool the record industry has. They dictate," says Martin Jennings, of Sydney independent Hot Records, the man behind the new Australian Independent Charts.

"There was a hulking great void," says this 35-year-old Englishman and former WEA executive, known affectionately as Motor Mouth by his colleagues. "I suppose it was due really to the importance of the indie chart in England, the fact that it's grown and developed to a point where you can look at the Top Three and know that if they're not big acts today they will be tomorrow — bands like New Order and Aztec Camera."

So if it's good enough for England it's good enough for Australia, and if it's good enough for the majors it's good enough for the independents. Obviously, the credibility and accuracy of any chart is always open to question. In England, chart rigging is a standard practice and chart positions lower than 5, 10 or 20 (depending on whom you talk to) simply cannot be trusted. Whatever the methods of constructing a chart might be, it's just plain naive to put a great deal of faith in it. The situation is not very different in Australia, where over the years a number of record companies have been convicted of varieties of chart manipulation in cases which never seem to attract a great deal of publicity. The fact that record companies refuse to divulge sales figures —unless they're claiming gold or platinum awards — means that totally accurate charts must remain a pipe-dream.

A Melbourne record store employee reports that they sometimes become aware of chart-rigging activities. "We carry major-label stuff, Top Forty as well as independents, and you can *feel* when a record has nothing behind it except a lot of push from the record company. There is just no interest in the public in buying it."

But while chart rigging in Australia may be difficult to isolate, there is another kind of injustice going on that's quite clear. Which is that independent records never figure in the charts, no matter how many are sold, simply because they sell mostly in non-chart-return stores. Given the deflated nature of the major marketplace, an indepen-

158

dent record will often sell in sufficient quantity to qualify for a chart position. "The Celibate Rifles' seven-inch, 'But Jacques the Fish?' would be in the Kent Report, if there was any justice," exclaims Jennings. But when nearly all of its sales are in specialist stores it misses out; thus the Independent Chart.

"It reflects a pattern of music buying which is not reflected anywhere else," says Jennings.

Until now, there was no real record of sales by independents. There were precedents, however: 3RRR-FM in Melbourne compiles a weekly chart, which due to the nature of the station, includes independents on an equal footing with majors; in fact, this chart has held some sway, but it was inevitably inaccurate because it was based on air-play. Other non-commercial radio stations have published their own charts to less effect. Scratches, a small specialist store in Newtown, Sydney, has been putting out its own chart, which in a way was the immediate predecessor to this new one.

The chart coming out of Hot Records' back room is compiled from actual sales figures for independently distributed records. These figures are obtained over the phone from participating specialist stores around the country. Doubts about accuracy remain, as they must, but as for the potential for corruption, Jennings hotly denies the possibility.

So what does it mean to get onto these charts? How many records do you have to sell? On this question Jennings is evasive: "I mean, we know we sell 500 copies of the seven-inch reissue of 'But Jacques the Fish?' at Hot (who distribute it), so obviously it's going to go straight in at Number One and its going to stay there while it's selling out, for a couple of weeks, then it will disappear because there won't be any left. The total numbers — well, this is where I'd like more shops to come in and be counted."

The chart is still in its infancy but it is snowballing, according to Jennings.

"I see it as the establishment of a list of records that should be in people's attention," he says. "Not only is it supposed to provide a meaningful list of what there is, how it ranks and how long it's lasted, but it's meant to create some sort of leverage as well."

Already, there's been a significant response to the chart. Agents and promoters have become interested in bands that figure well. Suburban record stores have placed orders with Hot, which of course is one way Hot itself stands to benefit; but penetration of the faraway suburban market has always been a stumbling block to inner-city independents, so the chart should be of benefit to all of them, not just Hot. Penetration of the larger chains is a larger task. Radio, which determines so

much, is an even stiffer hurdle, In England, one function the independent charts serve is as a proving ground for major label A&R departments, and given the cautiousness of depressed Australian record companies, here's no reason that that wouldn't also happen here.

"I'm hoping, by developing leverage with the chart, we can say, look, you can't ignore the Scientists," Jennings concludes. "You can say to somebody in a radio station that this particular album has been in the indie charts for fifteen weeks. Now, a radio station, in my language, has got to take notice of that. So maybe they'll play the Scientists between 10 p.m. and midnight on a Monday night — that's a foot in the door.

"I mean, maybe the Scientists have got what it takes to become a Top Thirty act, maybe not."

At least now there's a better chance that we'll be able to find out.

C.W., reprinted from *ROLLING STONE*.

Hailing from Sydney's northern beach suburbs, the CELIBATE RIFLES were surf punks as likely to quote Sartre as the Stooges, Bill Bonney as Birdman, and they forged an allegiance with new independent label Hot Records to launch both in 1983. (Pic. Francine McDougall)

IRONY AND DISTANCE

The Triffids fairly well defy convention; their seeming contradictions only make them stronger. They come from Perth, capital of raunch'n'roll and birthplace of the Scientists and the Hoodoo Gurus (sort of), but they are a very different kind of group — the Triffids are song-orientated; their sound is light, delicate and melodic at the top end, anchored by a tough, sinewy rhythm section at the bottom. Their muse is modest yet insidious, ironic but optimistic. Triffids songs are vignettes, stories of life and love, detached but by no means objective, rendered sensitively yet stridently.

There is a contained passion to the Triffids. Like the Go-Betweens, they are more an extension of folk-rock than punk-rock; the Triffids, however, are unafraid to dredge up covers of Eddie Cochran and Sixties' ravers when they need to flesh out a set. Pragmatists more than romantics in every respect, the Triffids are a totally self-contained, self-sufficient organisation that belongs to no school or clique. And although they're still very young — mostly around 21 — they possess the maturity and wisdom of an older outfit because they've been together for so long.

David McComb and Alsy MacDonald joined forces initially in 1976, in a naive 'experimental' duo called Dalsy. They made tapes, did paintings, wrote poetry and a book called *Lunch*. By 1978 they had become Blok Musik, then, for a day, Logic, and then the Triffids. With a core consisting of McComb, MacDonald and McComb's brother Robert (on guitar and violin), the Triffids played around the traps in Perth for a number of years. Their prolific output of cassette releases has documented every phase of their career; while in Perth the group also made a single ("Stand Up") and an EP (*Reverie*). When the inevitable move east occurred, the Triffids were snared by the White Label in Melbourne, and although the relationship was not particularly fruitful it did produce another single and EP ("Spanish Blue"/"Twisted Brain" and *Bad Timing and Other Stories*).

The Triffids are now well established in Sydney. At the end of 1983, their first album, *Treeless Plain*, was released, and if it hasn't rocketed the Triffids to stardom it's certainly another involving chapter in the Triffids' continuing saga — and a minor masterpiece in its own right.

Above: After starting life in Sydney as a pre-industrial experimental 'cassette band', the WET TAXIS devolved back to the garage, beating all the post-Birdman Detroit bands at their own game with a sound that was raw, dynamic and totally free of posturing.

The following interview with David McComb and Alsy MacDonald was held at the Triffids' residence in Surry Hills, Sydney, in autumn 1983, as the group were recording *Treeless Plain*.

What does it mean to be a group from Perth?
DAVID: It's a bit like being in an incubator, being bottled somewhere. And there's some factors, like — what is it? — 20 per cent English population, immigrants, and there's a very large, aggressive skinhead scene, like pre-punk skinheads, boot boys. At the time of punk in Perth it was all typical middle-class punks like the Victims, y'know, from Catholic schools. And they were the first bands that I saw live. The first band I saw in a pub was the Victims, and anything after that was an anti-climax. They were great, incredibly aggressive.

The outside influences were more from going to record stores after school. The cliché about formative periods, when all those first records from New York bands were coming out, not that I look back on those days sort of wistfully or anything, but I found out what sort of music I thought was important.
The influence of that classic early New York stuff — Patti Smith, Television, Talking Heads — was pretty obvious.
It's really funny, because the Scientists, all those guys who were now also the Hoodoo Gurus, they were all part of this heavy New York Dolls-influenced thing. Those guys were like our big brothers, those were the bands we used to see and really like. But because they're five years older than us they have the idea of rock'n'roll closer to their hearts, which I sorta like, but then I started liking . . . more sort of funny groups.
You started playing when you were 15.
We started off, the really early stuff was hilarious. We had a group called Dalsy, which was just the two of us. I played one-string guitar and Alsy played drums, and we made tapes. I guess the main influence was punk/Velvet Underground stuff, but it was just totally humorous.
You've got a number of songs — like 'Too Hot to Move' and 'Spanish Blue' — that are obviously about Perth.
All those songs were just really logical. It's a real insult to think that to reflect anything about Australia you have to be like Dave Warner or Austen Tayshus or something like that. I thought just to cut it back to the most basic things about Australia . . . the weather in Perth is so debilitating in the summer, it's so hot.
Yeah, apart from just the title 'Spanish

Blue' they often seem to have a sort of Spanish feel, in the way, say, Love occasionally did.
It was pushed down your throat in geography classes, the place is Mediterranean.
Is it?
Yeah, absolutely. And I mean, it sounds really flippant to say our music has a Mediterranean feel, but it is true, we're quite aware of it, and there's about four songs like that, one called 'Hell Of A Summer', which is less sweet. I guess it's up to people what they want to see in it, but it does go deeper into things than just the climate.
The songs are permeated by a sense of suffocation/desperation/ennui.
Yeah, exactly. 'Hell Of A Summer' is an extension of that. And it was written in Melbourne. We felt more suffocated in Melbourne than we ever had in Perth. In Perth I never felt, I never felt like busting out of it, I really quite liked living there. [But] it's just not practical.
So the Triffids had to leave Perth just to keep going?
We couldn't stay in Perth and remain the Triffids. There's just too few people and they have too old an expectation of you. It's like the people have such a vested interest in the band, an emotional vested interest, that they are part of you. I'm sure that happens to lots of so-called cult bands.
Did that stifle you?
Slightly, but you'd have to be fairly . . . not pathetic, but just a bit weak to let yourself be swayed that much by your audience, and let yourself be constricted, because if you've got enough gumption of your own, and you know why you're in a band in the first place, then you know what sort of music you like and what sort of music you want to make.
How did leaving Perth affect you?
It was an eye-opener for us to come east. We caught the bus over here last year, and I got here the day Hunters and Collectors, the Birthday Party and Pel Mel played at Sydney University. And seeing bands like that, and the Laughing Clowns, made me respond to Australian music for the first time.

The thing is though, bands here tend to follow precedents. We haven't chosen to go against that, like, there's been lots of good independent bands in Australia, but we don't feel we have to follow them.
Why not? Do you think those precedents aren't so good?
It's not that they're not so good, just that they're not us. Like, you can see the logic of bands like the Birthday Party going overseas, and it makes sense. We could

Pic: Francine McDougall

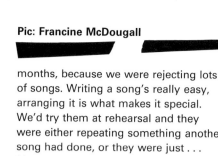

Pic: Francine McDougall

months, because we were rejecting lots of songs. Writing a song's really easy, arranging it is what makes it special. We'd try them at rehearsal and they were either repeating something another song had done, or they were just . . .

You said that at one stage earlier on you found a lot of your songs "annoyingly delicate", and now they're a lot tougher. How did that change occur?

The songs just came out like that. They're much more satisfying to play now. I sort of see them as complicated, they take longer to write, the lyrics are more intentional than they used to be, but it is more simple music really. As they say, it's what you leave out rather than what you put in.

There is a lot of light and space in your music.

Wide spaces, yeah. Someone once told us that they never really understood us until they played one of our tapes in the country. Because I never thought of our music as being inner-city music at all, but we couldn't be dishonest and say we're really down-home either.

Still, sometimes you do have a slightly country feel.

What I like is when Bob Dylan went country and everyone said he'd sold out, and I reckon those records are just great. Then I started listening to Hank Williams.

But how does that apply in an Australian context?

When you've been across Australia six times by road . . . You just look at it very unromantically when you're crossing the Nullarbor.

How does all that travelling affect you?

ALSY: You can go from Sydney to Melbourne in the space of a week, and it could be the difference between being happy and depressed. And if that's happening at such a rate, especially like last year, when we were moving around a lot, it very directly affects you.

Although you two have remained pretty constant, the Triffids have undergone a lot of line-up changes. Has that altered your approach at all?

DAVID: The overriding thing we've always had with the band is that technique should always be subservient to feeling, you should never let technique be an end in itself. But then you should never disregard technique, as a tool. We play as well as we possibly can play for the atmosphere and feeling we're trying to create. It's quite a pleasant surprise to find you can play better, it's good. We

do that, but we'd never really rush into anything. We don't feel a part of that, and we don't feel a part of anything like the Riptides either, anything supposedly more mainstream.

Are you in a position you're happy with now in Sydney?

Financially, we've come to a strange but efficient sort of thing. Like, most of us aren't on the dole, so we do have to survive by playing live, selling tapes. We've got this system down where we depend on almost no one. We keep overheads to a minimum, keep everything streamlined, otherwise we wouldn't survive.

Is this approach reflected in your music?

The other thing independent bands get into is that they feel there's certain things they can't do, like attempt a big production. By big production I mean like bringing in a string section on the recording of 'Red Pony'. A lot of independent bands would feel that's beyond their means. It only takes a lot of pugnaciousness, and if you have an idea . . . We knew that song was special, so we wanted it to be really special, have something different about it, and once you have an idea like that it's a trick to be persuaded against it because you're a 'small' band.

That's why we stopped using producers; we've got a much clearer, more purposeful sound by ourselves than we

ever did with a producer.

ALSY: I think there's a long way we can go, within the framework of the band, just being very streamlined and just surviving, and not being so outwardly ambitious, and channelling everything into the idea of going overseas straight away or something like that. We can be here and do all the things we feel are important. It would be presumptuous to expect to be somewhere else in six months.

DAVID: The other trap you can get into is wanting to be at a certain stage by a certain time. Not that we don't want success or anything, but we think more in terms of, y'know, getting records out, and we've said this before, once we've made a record we think is a perfect Triffids record, that would be a good time to end the band. Because we consider all our records are not quite getting there. That's what we're always aiming for, making a record that's a bit better than the last one.

You're obviously a very prolific songwriter. How many have you actually got?

At last count, a hundred and something. A lot of them are really early ones, and I used to write an average of one song every two weeks, and lately it's only been one every two months or so.

How do you gauge a good song?

That's why it's only one every two

can use violin, and stuff like that.

There's a great idea, that's stayed with us, to do with music that's so lacking in bombast, so lacking in self-importance, music that can be just very ready-made, anywhere, anytime, by people who just pick up a guitar, just getting up and playing, which to me is as revolutionary as punk was. You just learn that you don't have to have this whole set of obligations and things before you can play.

You've just made your first album. What were your intentions with it?

ALSY: That should be put into context, like, the album comes at the end of a string of EPs and singles, so in some ways just getting the album out provides a much broader insight, there's more variety.

DAVID: We have a thing with variety in our music, which gets us into a bit of bad water — some people see it as a lack of direction. Like, we have really dirgey songs, and we have melody, and people can't see which sort of band you want to be, this or that, so we've always battled against that. We say, "Why can't we be both? We like both.'

I've always liked melody, obviously, the whole band's based on melody. Totally. In the music, and the rhythm, the lyric, the voices. But melody without tension is a waste of time, it just goes nowhere. Something that affects you is not the most pristine, sweet, white-boy melody, it has to connect with tension.

Given the variety in your music, what holds it all together?

That would come down to something more lyrical, I suppose. I'm not sure. I think that's the common denominator, if there's a quality in the lyrics. Which I find even harder to talk about. It's even harder with lyrics. You try to make them as plain as possible, almost unsubtle, so people . . . then it's entirely up to the person. There's no point in trying to explain what they're about, because that seems like another insult to people. It's like it's just really important with our band that the audience does the work.

We used to do a lot of things with really sweet music and a more dark, sinister lyric. We used to have songs that I thought were the most depressing songs ever. Like 'Close To The Sun', which was a really in-the-pits song, and people used to say, 'What a great surf song! That really reminds me of the beach!' And I thought, 'God, we've really failed there', because I was trying for an irony. Even 'Spanish Blue' is supposed to have a fairly dark underbelly, that will

stop the music becoming too innocuous. Obviously, we've failed sometimes in the past. We haven't failed in creating a sense of languidness or ennui.

You often seem quite detached in your songs.

A good way to do things is to take something that matters to you, or some part of your personality, and then force it to be more extreme, distort it beyond what it was, almost fictionalise it.

Well, I do think there's a strong narrative tendency . . .

Not so much a story, you try and make it stronger than it originally was, because if you just say, 'Oh, I woke up and felt bad', it's just too weak, so you make it extreme so it's like another character. David Byrne is one person who does that really well. It almost sorta seems more real, with a narrator.

Does the narrator take a stance?

It may be emotional, but never sentimental . . . We feel, obviously, by nature, we must be idealistic, or insane, because you don't go on getting $80 a week, that's not much . . . Generally, I suppose there's a pessimism, but there's humour in it as well. We've never been as extreme as some groups I like, but we've always had irony, all the way. Everything we've always done has always had a strong strand of irony, each song you can look at one way or another, you can laugh at the narrator, or you can get immersed in it.

Does the album capture the group in a way you're pleased with?

ALSY: The album's not meant to be an accurate representation of what we're like live . . . we've done some sort of adventurous things with the production.

DAVID: We really hope it comes across as a strong collection of sort of stories. Each one is a little point of view of someone. It's like a whole lot of little confessionals. Not from us, just from people we could be.

What does the future hold, given your youth?

ALSY: We just turned 21, but we don't think of ourselves as young, because we've been doing it for so long.

DAVID: But, like, I always thought it was a terrible thing just to rely on your youth. I'm not sure that it's important for rock music to keep a strong element of the juvenile. There's one band like that, the Sunnyboys, their whole original appeal was based on innocence, and look what happened to them, people didn't want them to get older. That's a fairy story.

C.W., reprinted from *THE NEXT THING.*

(Pic: Judi Dransfield Kuepper)

SEND OFF THE CLOWNS

It's an old adage that worthwhile art only arises out of conflict. Friction, after all, is what generates the sparks that light the fire. It may not be so bad, then, in rock 'n' roll terms, that the members of a group dislike one another. The Who, for instance, was notorious for backstage punch-ups, and look at its achievements.

The Laughing Clowns may not be so open about it, but it too is driven by an undercurrent of hostility. And there can be no doubt it is one of the most important Australian groups of the early '80s.

After nearly five years, Laughing Clowns has arrived at an effective mode of operation. Always a vehicle for songwriter Ed Kuepper, Laughing Clowns is now less a fixed group and more a name Kuepper can apply to variable line-ups under his leadership.

The current edition of Laughing Clowns is the same one that toured Australia last year, comprising — as well as Kuepper (vocals/guitar) — stalwart master-drummer Jeffrey Wegener, saxophonist Louise Elliot and bassist Peter Milton Walsh. I asked Kuepper how he felt about the group.

"Never been happier. I mean, we've always been a cheery, easy-going bunch," he replied, with a supercilious smirk. Jeffrey Wegener, sitting opposite, fidgeted, not uncomfortably, but as if to emphasize his indifference. Laughing Clowns seems to survive on

a staple diet of sarcasm and innuendo. Thrive, even.

With a new single, 'Eternally Yours', and a new album, *Law of Nature*, just released, the Clowns will appear, as part of a national tour, at Melbourne University on Sunday night (with hot Sydney band the Celibate Rifles and the premiere of Ollie Olsen's new Skin and Bones Orchestra) and at the Seaview Ballroom on Monday night.

Law of Nature marks something of a return to form for Laughing Clowns, and certainly a return to a more straightforward approach. "Maybe there's been too much emphasis on the way we've changed," Wegener said. "To me, Ed's songwriting has developed, but I don't know if we've changed that much . . ."

"Still churning out the same old rubbish," Kuepper added, as if to goad his critics.

Mr Uddich-Schmuddich Goes to Town, Laughing Clowns' last album in 1982, was a confused affair. The songs were excellent, but they were marred by cluttered arrangements and frequently indulgent passages of improvisation. It was, however, the Clowns' most successful album to date, and propelled the group to England. Its initial appearances there were poor, though, and Kuepper broke up the group. But before that it cut the *Everything That Flies* EP, which, while it may have been more frugal, was unfortunately sluggish.

Kuepper then assembled a new Laughing Clowns to tour Australia last year. Its sound was pared-down and more pointed, a rockier Laughing

Clowns than any line-up since their very earliest days, which Kuepper describes as deliberate. *Law Of Nature*, recorded at the ABC Studios in Sydney after the tour, captures the group well. Yet while Kuepper's songs remain involving, it is his flat singing that drags this album down, especially since the playing is otherwise scintillating. Asked for his opinion of the album, all Kuepper could offer was: "It's good. It sounds better. They're good songs."

After finishing the album, Laughing Clowns headed for Europe, where they played in Austria, Holland, Germany and Czechoslovakia.

"We played brilliantly . . . it went really well," Wegener commented cynically.

"We've probably got a lot more potential in Europe [than England]. It's generally not as depressed," Kuepper said.

But, as Peter Allen puts it, Laughing Clowns would "still call Australia home." The band is now being promoted by Sydney independent Hot Records, while its own Prince Melon label seems to have gone into retirement.

"I think the interest that's been generated should sustain and continue," Wegener proffered. "There's enough progression there to keep people entertained."

The Clowns set will be basically the same as last year. "That's necessary because this album's got to be promoted," Wegener explained, "and people do appreciate a live set that includes some material they know. We've often had a problem in the past when an entire repertoire has been relatively new."

Kuepper: "It will just be more planned, like the last time, I guess. And that seems to work with this line-up of the band anyway, slightly tighter."

And after the tour?

Kuepper: "Well, y'know, the band's always been in a state of flux; that's really the way it's always worked. People tend to get a bit hysterical when there's a line-up change, and yet that's been the norm. Yeah, we'll see how things go at the end of the tour . . . After every tour we've always had a break. I need time to write, and the other people in the band do other things."

All the indicators are, however, that Laughing Clowns will dissolve finally after this tour, so if you don't see it now you may never get another chance. At least, not until Ed Kuepper finds a new backing band.

C.W., reprinted from *THE AGE*.

LOVE'S LONELY CHILDREN

It may be an academic judgment, one which the band itself would understand yet still deny, but the Birthday Party are probably the most important rock group Australia has produced. The Birthday Party have never sold a lot of records, and their full impact may not be felt for some time to come, but already their influence has been enormous, all around the world as well as within Australia.

Surely the number of pale imitators the Birthday Party have spawned, from the Southern Death Cult to the Sacred Cowboys is measure enough of their significance. The Birthday Party have

THE BIRTHDAY PARTY at the Hampton Court Hotel, January 1983, with stand-in drummer Des Hefner. (Pic: Francine Mcdougall)

wrought a change in music which has extended far beyond their own existence, and is still yet to be properly assimilated.

So much ignorant and sensational

garble has been written about the Birthday Party that to say anything more now is to invite criticism. But not if it's neither ignorant nor sensational.

The Birthday Party have left a de-evolutionary trail. Slug-line indeed! Four polite, bushytailed middle-class boys from Caulfield Grammar in Melbourne form a group called the Boys Next Door in 1976, play equally polite punky power-pop. Get artier and artier. It's not until 1980 though, that the group undergoes a musical metamorphosis: Change name to Birthday Party. Move to London. As disillusionment with the contemporary post-punk scene sets in, the Birthday Party become surer of their own worth, and pursue their own obsessions singlemindedly. Totally abandon stilted art-rock predilections. Songs become simpler, sparser. The Birthday Party arrive at a contemporary music that is unashamedly rock (at a time when rock was a dirty word) yet more vital than just about any other music being made. The Birthday Party could never be called primitives because they are too knowing. They are pretentious in the extreme (not necessarily a bad thing, since it can lead to greater things), but they are not contrived. They are always inconsistent (which may or may not be a hallmark of greatness), but when the Birthday Party connect it is with an awesome vengeance. Their rock is crucial because it accepts its own mythology; the Birthday Party re-validate rock. Rock can no longer be so straightforward, it is encumbered with too much past, its implications push beyond the obvious and the immediate. The Birthday Party realise this; their greatness is that they embrace as much so-called 'negativity' as they do 'positivism', as much 'bad' as 'good'. The Birthday Party come not to entertain but to taunt. Their mangled, violent melange may be symptomatic of our apocalyptic times, though they would deny that. Their concerns are inward, timeless and classical. Talk about exorcising the demons — that's what the Birthday Party do for rock, and for themselves. But I wonder if it's not lost on an audience . . .

With every statement the Birthday Party have surpassed themselves. *Prayers On Fire* was a coming-of-age, their baptism; 'Release The Bats' may have been more deliberately trash, but it was more coherent and immensely commercial. *Junkyard* went further in its arrogance, but *The Bad Seed* was better,

it distilled the best elements from *Junkyard* and then expanded upon them. Between *Junkyard* and *The Bad Seed* the Birthday Party sacked drummer Phil Calvert; guitarist Mick Harvey moved to drums, but it was never a particularly stable situation. After recording *The Bad Seed*, Laughing Clown Jeffrey Wegener sat in for Harvey on some Dutch dates, and then when the Birthday Party toured Australia in mid-1983 Harvey refused to come. The group returned to England and then went to Germany to record what would be an epitaph, falling apart amidst walk-outs and squabbling, a sordid, sad end.

Late in 1983, Nick Cave performed in America as part of the Immaculate Consumptive with friends Marc Almond, Lydia Lunch and Clint Ruin. Tracy Pew and Mick Harvey returned to Australia. Rowland Howard remained in London and may or may not manage to get together his long-promised 'super-group' These Immortal Souls. Then Nick Cave too returned to Australia and assembled a group, including Harvey and Pew, as well as Barry Adamson and Hugo Race, called Nick Cave: Man Or Myth, which played a series of gigs and proved that the fire that burnt in the Birthday Party is far from extinguished.

This interview with Rowland Howard and Nick Cave was held in their room at the Barclay Hotel, Kings Cross, at the time of the Birthday Party's 1983 Australian tour.

After living in London for some time, you moved to Berlin, but it wasn't long before you left there. Why was that?
ROWLAND: I think Mick and I felt it first. I left because, for a start, there's the language barrier, and it was just so hard getting basic things, things to read, to watch TV, go to the movies, things like that.
Was it a positive experience though?
ROWLAND: Oh yeah. I don't think *Bad Seed* would've been the same record had it been made in London. We had to get out of London.
Since then you've been on the move continuously, and Nick you often said how you liked being homeless — it gives you a precariousness that helps your creation — but what effect do you think all that touring has on you?
NICK: Well, physically, I'm sure it's taken many years off my life.
ROWLAND: It's really important to me,

because there's not many groups capable of it.
NICK: I think there is some danger in having the opportunity to go any place you like at any time, you're continuously faced with this avalanche of input, where after a while you start to pass things off as uninteresting. And the obvious conclusion to that is that you could eventually become very jaded.

I think I would have reached the same conclusions about things if I had just stayed in Australia, on philosophical questions, but I think the travelling around has helped develop, or speed up, the process, the actual form of its presentation.
The whole thing about the form of the songs, the travelling around, continuous working or something, just the basic flow of ideas is quite fast, and so the kind of basic progression of songwriting is quite fast. I think the simpler everything begats [*laughter*]... gets, the harder the whole thing becomes.
What sort of new influences have you absorbed?
ROWLAND: You just see things every-where, in newspapers, or an image that gets locked into your subconscious and then comes out in a song.

I find it very hard to listen to most music, because it doesn't do anything for me emotionally. The only thing that influences the Birthday Party is the people who are writing the songs.
NICK: The point is that there are certain groups and people we would consider to be great working in music, but all the things they're doing, in the same way as us, are so personal, that's why they're great, so obviously you just don't get influenced. I mean, you could super-ficially plagiarise Mark E. Smith if you wanted to, but I think it would be fairly pointless, because his style and his imagery is entirely his own, and it would stick out like a sore thumb.
ROWLAND: The point is, if you have any real understanding of people like that, then the way in which they would influence you is to learn how to express yourself as personally as possible.
Considering the structure of the Birthday Party in personal terms, how do you work together now?
ROWLAND: It's more a case, I've come to realize, that the Birthday Party has become, in the last two years, more of a vehicle for Nick than anyone else. And that doesn't bother me. Basically, the songs that I write and the songs that

Nick and the group write are two different things.

The way we write songs in the Birthday Party has evolved to a state where we arrive at a bassline or something like that, which is why Tracy plays so repetitively, the basslines are the basis of the songs. Ninety-nine per cent of the time I'm playing what I invent.

When Nick writes songs, he often has only a very abstract idea of what they're going to be like, he needs someone to translate it, and I think we all work really well together.

How personal is your material, Nick?
NICK: Totally that way. I don't really write very much about the situation I'm in today, and kind of disguise it by using characters and a different situation, but I don't write anything I have no feelings for. All of it directly relates to me, but I think also there's a certain discipline involved in writing where you do write so it is entertaining and interesting — and interesting for me too.

Do you think The Birthday Party, your music, is radical?
NICK: I wouldn't . . .
ROWLAND: I mean, as far as I'm concerned, in a sense there are no rock bands left. I really think one thing our group has done has made it patently obvious that so few people are aware or recognise what rock music is meant to be. They've just completely forgotten. I think what we're doing, so few other people are doing.
NICK: I think the extremities of our group have been pursued before us.
ROWLAND: And also, we're not primarily concerned with being radical.
NICK: I think what being radical is, is opening up for other people to follow, surging forth and this type of thing, which I don't think we do. I think what we're doing, just by existing, is making an example of ourselves as one group in history, among the few there are, who display exactly what they are themselves, and have worked out a truly honest, personalised embodiment, through their music, of themselves. I think the bulk of groups rely on what has gone before, the history of rock music, which I don't think our group does.
ROWLAND: Using a certain sequence of notes evokes a certain feel, and you are exploiting that, there are things in our songs that hark back to history, like to a blues-run or something like that, so it is

in a way a real cliché, but you use things like that. I know what Nick means when he says we don't owe much to music history, because we're using things in a different way, and putting them in a different context.
NICK: What I mean is that we don't need music history to qualify what we're doing. We can stand, I think we're successful because even if there was no rock history we could still be relevant because we're expressing our person-ality, which is the basic thing, the whole essence of art is to do that, the art should embody its creator. So in a way we're age-old, but at the same time we're rare, because there's very few artists who do that, particularly in the rock world.

How do you regard Junkyard now?
ROWLAND: I was never really happy with it. In the actual process of recording we tried various experiments, and I think they failed, so the point we were trying to get across . . . I think, basically, *Bad Seed* is a lot more focused.

When we kicked out Phil everything fell into place really quickly. Like, I think Mick is far more capable of expressing himself on the drums than on the guitar.

The idea was, after doing *Junkyard*, we found it really hard to strip down, even though we'd only lost one other instrument. It's a really big jump. We had doubts whether we could pull off being a four-piece.

How did you react immediately to the four-piece line-up?
ROWLAND: Well, personally, it gave me a lot more room, I think I play less than I used to, but what I do has a far greater effect. For ages we'd been wanting to make things a lot sparser and starker, so that, like, every instrument was doing something that was totally necessary, no-one was playing unless it was dynamic. It was really hard to achieve that in a five-piece, with everyone fighting to get their point across sort of thing.

You've also often claimed you find your music funny, that the humour in it is essential. Does that still hold?
NICK: I think there's as much humour, or at least the humour remains in the presentation, but perhaps not so much in the lyrics themselves.
Would you describe it as black humour?
ROWLAND: Well, it's very dry.
NICK: I suppose it's a black humour, but the intention is that it's to take the

importance away from the lyrics so that they become secondary, I mean a second realisation of the Birthday Party.

What's actually there does mean something that is very serious. Whereas the unfortunate thing about a lot of groups who deal honestly with serious sorts of things is that it's always in the foreground. The first thing about Joy Division is that they are talking about very serious things, and I don't think that's really effective. I mean, with Joy Division, there's no reaching beyond their external image, into anything else, but with us I think there's far more layers; for a start the whole thing is glossed over with a layer of humour. It's like something that seems really funny, but has an unsettling effect on you, and you realise that it isn't really funny after all.
ROWLAND: Something like Joy Division, as far as I'm concerned, is just totally unreal, because any sort of situation at all, however serious, is always self-contradictory. There's so many things involved [that] it's never so straightforward.
Which is undoubtedly why you are so often misinterpreted.
ROWLAND: Well, I think the reason the reaction is so varied is that every song has several possible interpretations, and people can pick up on what they consider to be the most important aspect of the song. I just think that contradictions are so necessary. There are so many emotions. People just don't talk about them, in love songs, all they ever talk about is the purest, the most idealistic . . .
NICK: . . . and commercial . . .
ROWLAND: . . . yes, commercialised. There are so many other emotions that go hand in hand with love — jealousy, anger, disgust, and some nice things too. That's what I think we do, I think we show all the joys, and all the petty things, the ugly side as well.
Yeah, it does seem to me that most of your songs are fundamentally love songs. Would you agree that love is a central Birthday Party theme?
NICK: It worries me that every song I write seems to be about love, I mean it's not only central, we just harp on it continuously, and the fact that people don't understand that that's our primary concern shows that either we're not expressing ourselves properly, or that they don't feel the same things that we do about it, or that they're . . . just . . .

thick.

ROWLAND: They've just basically been conditioned. A lot of people just pick up on the aspect of the song that could possibly be interpreted as outrageous.

NICK: Which is the sensational, the violent aspect.

But that aspect is very apparent.

ROWLAND: What I think is amazing is that people think the Birthday Party write songs with the intention of shocking. If we really wanted to be outrageous or violent or whatever, our songs would just be complete failures, because in most of the songs the violence itself is only alluded to, nothing is overt.

NICK: If we wanted to be outrageous, it would be a lot easier than being the way we are. We could be like the Dead Kennedys, and get banned all the time.

ROWLAND: Or even like Alice Cooper, the violence is playacted.

NICK: The thing that mustn't be forgotten is that when we actually write a song, lyrics, the thought of how it's going to be interpreted is the furthest thing from our minds. You just sit down and write a song you're happy with, and you learn it, and play it, and then the consequences of the song become apparent to you. Also, in that respect, we feel no responsibility as to what effect we will have on the audience. This is another point, and that is that there should be no censorship by us, in that we shouldn't do particular things because they might create an adverse reaction, which is something we're criticised for, deliberately inciting audiences.

But at a Birthday Party gig there is always a very real tension, an electricity, in the air.

ROWLAND: Well, I mean, it's really felt, if we're playing well we become totally involved.

NICK: I think, if I was a member of the audience, one of the things I would find most exciting about the Birthday Party when they play live is the fact that it is a kind of dangerous show, without wishing to use too dangerous a word, but that the show can go in any particular way. I think in London people started to kind of come along, no longer to see if we were going to throw ourselves around, but to see if we were going to have any tantrums on stage, or what was going to be the quirk in the show, who would walk off.

But doesn't that add to the drama anyway?

ROWLAND: We always try to cut the stops to as few as possible, because personally it detracts from my pleasure, because you build up personal momentum, and then it's lost, and the idea is to throw yourself into it.

NICK: I think, because we are presenting ourselves as honestly as possible, new areas of performance are being displayed, which doesn't happen with other groups, and, y'know, a good show no longer relies solely on us playing well, or . . . it relies on just how — I find this a bit hard to explain . . . just how strongly our emotions or our situation will be put across. And if it comes down to a show that's just riddled with technical problems, with bad temper, then that can be as kind of poignant and . . . educational, as committed, as any other performance which is a powerful, confident, strong performance.

ROWLAND: I mean, for a start, often the state — I hate to keep talking about this . . . the state we're in is a state most people will never experience, so totally involved in something that you forget, literally, what you're doing. I mean, you're stripped of any selfconsciousness or whatever, and so your personality is being presented in the extreme, and it's a really strong thing. You very rarely see people on stage like that. So it is, I suppose, larger than life, except that it can't possibly be.

NICK: When you're placed in such an extreme atmosphere there's so much focus upon you I think it's a matter of pulling out the innermost, inner personality you may have, wearing that in exchange for your day-to-day . . . exterior.

ROWLAND: Basically, the aspect you see of most people is an incredibly unreal aspect, the one that contains all the conditioning, that they've been bought up with, and basically it bears very little relation to the real spirit of the person.

But the imagery you use — of religion, violence, sex, death — most people wouldn't think of as very realistic.

NICK: I think the things I write about are quite natural for me to write about. I'm talking about just fairly ordinary feelings. One case in point that's always used and may as well be used again is '6-Inch Gold Blade', which talks about murdering a woman, but I mean it's basically a song about jealousy, and . . .

It does have phallic implications, though . . .

NICK: Well, yeah, um, yeah, but that's just the art of writing, expressing a number of things at one time. It's also supposed to express a certain . . . total hatred, and a desire . . . It's just a good diagram why love and death can be joined together so easily, and gracefully, in one song. I mean, some people perhaps have more sensitive views on certain things than other people, I don't know, but to dwell on only one extremity of desire, you can't help but equate it with death anyway, without going up some blind alley. For me, it's a perfectly normal mode of thought. I don't think it's eccentric in any way.

How much do you think you mirror what's around you?

NICK: I think that's perhaps where we miss out . . . I don't think the Birthday Party reflect very well the social climate at the moment, I think there are other groups who do that much better.

ROWLAND: Any kind of politics in our songs, social or otherwise, is sort of incidental in a sense that what we're talking about is basically the effects of certain things upon ourselves.

So where does the Birthday Party's slug-line lead now?

ROWLAND: I don't ever stop to think about the direction we're going in. It's governed by so much, the songs . . .

NICK: You just don't . . . They're things you have to think up answers for for interviewers, but you don't really think about it yourself.

Ever since I started playing seriously in this group, I've become less and less naive, less and less innocent about what we're doing. In the early stages, the Boys Next Door was just a totally intuitive and innocent thing, but I don't think it was terribly good either. These days, nearly every aspect of the group has been talked about, externalised in some way. I mean, the last thing I want to do before we go on stage is an interview, because it's intellectualising something you have to make intuitive in the end, and it all boils down to a process of shaking off all knowledge, in a sense, of what you're doing — fuck, I wish I could find the words — all the effect it's going to have. It has to be a raw emotional experience, and that becomes more and more difficult all the time.

C.W., reprinted from *THE NEXT THING.*

SEVERING OLD TIES

I used to be an advocate of the "electro" revolution in rock, but somewhere along the way I became disenchanted. It's developed a reliance on all the same old values — that is, essentially, the song — only the instrumentation has changed. For all the talk of unlimited possibilities, electropop is characterised by an unwavering hiss-pop sound. Not that that's necessarily bad — but the bitter taste of broken promises lingers on.

Perhaps the whole notion of experimentation was just plain naive anyway. After all, what could anyone do that "serious" composers like Stockhausen and Cage and even Reilly hadn't done already? But that argument is academic, really, and it doesn't alter the fact that Kraftwerk, for instance, made some great records in the Seventies — who cares if they were innovative or not? — and the initial wave of electro-punk also produced some excellent music. Hip-hop probably allows electronics freer rein than any other music these days, but if there's one group that continues to fly the flag for challenging electronic music it is Severed Heads.

Severed Heads, to use my own well-worn phrase, make aural-collage music with tape recorders, drum programming, sequencers, turntables, television and just about anything else they can get their hands on. It is identifiable as 'music' even to the thicker skinned thanks to the Heads' fondness for disguised yet very discernable rhythms, repetitive to the point of relentlessness, and even the odd melodic touch.

A two-man operation comprising Tom

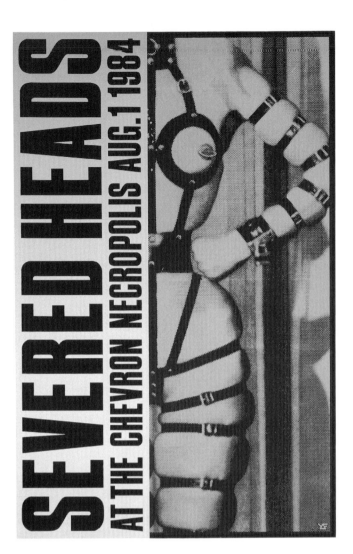

Above: Poster by John Foy.

Right: After returning to Australia and disbanding Hugo Klang, OLLIE OLSEN formed the Orchestra of Skin & Bone.

In an act of self-reflection, he also produced the music for Richard Lowenstein's film *Dogs in Space*, a true story about Ears' vocalist Sam Sejavka (played by Michael Hutchence of INXS) in the recent past of Melbourne's little bands scene, in which Ollie himself had played a pivotal role. (Pic: Ronin Films)

Ellard and Garry Bradbury, Severed Heads seem unencumbered by great ambition, so their development has been natural and logical. Tucked safely away in a bedroom studio at Balmoral Beach in Sydney, the Heads recorded *Since the Accident*, with special guests Simon Insectocutor (guitar) and Stephen Jones (videotape, videosynthesizers), during 1982 and 1983, and it was released originally in the U.K. on Ink Records in early 1984 and now sees release here on Virgin, Ink's parent label.

It's Severed Heads' strength that their sonic explorations are not meandering or aimless, but go straight for the jugular. Their imagery is predictably demonic, death-obsessed, violent and nihilistic, and though this shtick has certainly been devalued it still makes for good theatre.

Once past the opening cut, a sort of switching-the-dial-to-find-the-right-channel number which has become a virtual cliché, *Since The Accident* is an incisive album of abrasive and claustrophobic atmosphere. The songs are built around a grinding rhythm, itself constructed of amassed tape loops. Some songs — like "Gashing the Old Mae West," "Golden Boy" and the choral mutant closer "Brassiere, In Rome" — are little more than that, and are less impressive. More successful are songs which establish a broader soundscape, with chiming sequencer lines, Fripp-ertronic guitar and even occasionally a human voice, which creates the opportunity — and space — for a song to develop. "A Million Angels" is almost pretty, as is "Exploring the Secrets of Treating Deaf Mutes," which recalls the Dead Travel Fast. "Godsong" doesn't live up to its title's promise, while "Dead Eyes Open" is a humorously morbid little tale that might almost be pop and is certainly snappy and Kraftwerkesque.

Since The Accident is the best album of its genre since Laughing Hands' *Dog Photos*. And you know what else? You can play it any speed and it still makes sense. A little twisted maybe, but then it was like that to begin with.

C.W., reprinted from *ROLLING STONE*.

SCATTERED ORDER

P L U S

F A M O U S

ANNANDALE HOTEL FRIDAY 29 JULY

NEW LP ■ C O M F O R T ■ PLUS COMPILATION 81-87 OUT NOW
VOLITION THROUGH CBS

Right: PETER MILTON WALSH left the Laughing Clowns and resurrected the Apartments, and after an unsung single for Hot Records, "All You Wanted" (produced by the Mentals' Peter O'Doherty), he headed for the refuge of exile in the UK, where he recorded the album *The Evening Visits...* for Rough Trade.

Below: Back in Australia, Chris Bailey assembled yet another new incarnation of THE SAINTS. This one included former Birthday Party bassist Tracy Pew, and delivered the stone classic single "Ghost Ships."

NO FUN

Above: Brett Myers broke up the End after winning the Strawberry Hills Band Competition and joined forces with veteran Ron Peno, ex of the Hellcats, to form DIED PRETTY, "the first loud, slow band." (Pic: Francine McDougall)

The Sunnyboys are a group who had success — or near-success, at least — thrust upon them at an early age, and although it's to their credit that they've refused to be boxed in by expectations of eternal adolescence, the question is: how successfully have they evolved?

To answer that question requires a reassessment of just what the Sunnyboys had to offer in the first place, and what that boils down to is this: Jeremy Oxley had a way with simple words and a simple tune, and the group was able to knock his songs out with the requisite amount of energy. But even though their demeanour was ostensibly tough, essentially they were an easy-going, relaxed kind of group, setting neither themselves nor their audience any task too demanding. If the Sunnyboys were to progress, it would be very much one day at a time. Following their successful debut album, the second LP, *Individuals*, was a well-intentioned failure. As a taster for *Get Some Fun*, their third album, the single "Show Me Some Discipline," a perhaps surprising hit last year, did have a sort of brutish appeal.

The Sunnyboys have submitted to the Big Overseas Production Job syndrome in making *Get Some Fun*, going to England to record it with non-renowned producer Nick Garvey (late of the singularly dull Motors). Now, I may only be listening to a pre-release tape, but there doesn't seem to be anything here that Lobby Loyde couldn't have done.

It is, in fact, a misleadingly-titled album. If the Sunnyboys were bright-eyed and bushy-tailed in their youth, *Get Some Fun* suggests they have grown into sullen young adults. Their growth has most definitely been stunted. But the worst part is that the suspicions you might have had about the intent of "Show Me Some Discipline" are in some ways confirmed — *Get Some Fun* often approaches the sort of misogyny of, say, the Rolling Stones' *Black and Blue*, and that can't fail to leave a bad taste in your mouth.

But perhaps *Get Some Fun*'s worst crime is simply that it's not really very much fun at all — it doesn't excite, nothing reaches out, it sags under its own weight. There don't seem to be any new influences at work, and this might partially explain the band's predicament. The Sunnyboys are a two dimensional group. Drums follow bass follows guitars follows vocals along a narrow, barely wavering line. Sure, some decent melodies rise towards the top, but they're dragged down again by ham-fisted instrumentation, not to mention harmonies so close as so be unnecessary. This is dense, air-tight music that allows no room to breathe.

I wanted to like this album. I really did. The Sunnyboys have let me down. They have gotten so far off the track I only hope it's not impossible for them to find their way back.

C.W., reprinted from *ROLLING STONE*.

Right: SUNNYBOYS (Pic: Francine McDougall)

Below: After Ian Rilen broke up Sardine, he re-formed X with Steve Lucas and drummer Steve Caifeiro. But just as the band was getting out of the blocks, Caifeiro died. He was replaced by former *** *** drummer, teen prodigy Kathy Green, with whom the band cut the classic *At Home With You* album. (Pic: Liz Reed)

The BEASTS of BOURBON

"bury the bottle"

FRI JUNE 29 TRADE UNION

Above: The Southern Cross/Strawberry Hills Hotel in Sydney's Surrey Hills became a centre of the scene alongside the nearby Trade Union Club, showcasing a predominantly swamp rock sound with such fixture bands as the Scientists, the Hoodoo Gurus, the Johnnys and the neophyte Tex Deadly and the Dum-Dums.

THE BEASTS OF BOURBON began life as a fun covers band comprising members of all the above outfits, and at the very least went on to make a star apparent out of Tex Perkins.

Left: Poster by John Foy.

Below left: Roddy Ray'da (centre) is the Richard Hell of Australian rock, forming bands and then leaving them almost before they've begun: When Boris Sudjovik left Roddy's original Perth band the Rockets to join the Scientists, Roddy headed to Sydney and joined forces with fellow Sandgroper/former Victim Dave Faulkner to form Le Hoodoo Gurus. Leaving the Gurus after one single, he formed cowpunk band THE JOHNNYS — which he would leave in 1984, also after one single.

BACK TO THE FUTURE

Revisionist is not a term that crops up very often in rock & roll criticism, but it's one that might accurately describe the Hoodoo Gurus' approach. The Gurus are a group that don't so much pick over rock & roll's bones as feast on its prime cuts. They stand back from rock history, reassess it and rechannel it. Even Stuart Coupe, rock commentator for *Dolly* magazine and the Gurus' manager, pinpoints the group as "a curious mixture of rockabilly, Merseybeat, psychedelia, glitter, punk and straight pop."

But what elevates the Hoodoo Gurus above the level of mere pastiche is songwriter Dave Faulkner's individualistic talent and the group's own strong character. There is spirit, sympathy, humour and consistency in the way James Baker (drums), Clyde Bramley (bass) and Brad Shepherd (guitar) render Faulkner's eclectic songs.

Stoneage Romeos is an archetypical debut album. While it presents a clear, concise picture of the Gurus, it is somewhat splayed, and while it's muscular and coherent, it's neither searing nor really inspired. Mainly it serves as an appetizer for a second album.

The delicious pop-art sleeve and the title itself suggest primitivism, but the Gurus are too knowing for that: thankfully, then, their acquired trash aesthetic doesn't degenerate into camp. Take the Hoodoo Gurus at face value — a good-time, rabble-rousing pop group (who certainly don't take themselves too seriously) — and you will enjoy them, guilt-free.

Stoneage Romeos includes the Gurus' three singles to date, "Leilani," "Tojo" and "My Girl." "Leilani" is a great, Gary Glitter-esque stomp, and this re-recording probably surpasses the Phantom original. "Tojo" is less impressive, but "My Girl" was a deserved hit, a pretty song in the true sense of the word.

The album opens with "(Let's All) Turn On," in which the Gurus state their case quite clearly: "Shake Some Action, Psychotic Reaction, No Satisfaction/That's what I like, that's what I like/Blitzkrieg Bop, do the Jailhouse Rock, stop stop At the Hop, do the Blue Jean Bop/ That's what I like, that's what I like . . . Let's all turn on." Elsewhere the Gurus pay further homage to the Flamin' Groovies ("I Want You Back"), the Cramps ("Dig It Up," a live version of which featured on 2JJJ's *Live At The Wireless*) and the New York Dolls ("I Was A Kamikaze Pilot").

Dave Faulkner is indeed a songsmith in the grand tin-pan alley tradition, but his material is unmistakably characterized by its wry wit and narrative qualities, and at his best — with songs like "(Let's All) Turn On," "Death Ship" and especially "Zanzibar" — he's approaching a style less homogenous and more unique.

Stoneage Romeos is an auspicious debut album that promises a great deal more from the Hoodoo Gurus. Get it for your little sister and listen to it yourself.

C.W., reprinted from *ROLLING STONE*.

Above: CRIME AND THE CITY SOLUTION lay in wait until the Birthday Party broke up. Frontman extraordinaire Simon Bonney was then able to usurp most of the band to back him in a reborn Crime, who, nearly ten years after their formation and now based in London, released their first recording in 1985. (Pic: courtesy Bronwyn Adams)

Left: One of the freshest blasts of sound to hit the inner city in 1983 came from a new outfit who couldn't have started further from the inner city. WARUMPI BAND, from Papunya, a couple of hours west of Alice Springs, were an Aboriginal settlement band and they changed the face of black Australian music. (Pic: Frank Lidner)

Right: Many people are still awaiting the reunion of Ed Kuepper and Chris Bailey under the SAINTS banner, but it actually happened in 1985, albeit very briefly and without fanfare, when Kuepper played bass in the line-up Bailey put together to tour Australia that year. The pair went their separate ways again afterwards.

Above: After the Go-Betweens and Triffids had legitimised acoustic guitars in a post-punk context, the LIGHTHOUSE KEEPERS picked up as if where the Particles left off. Arriving with a splash in Sydney from Canberra in 1983, the Keepers boasted the unmistakable voice of Juliette Ward and a positively strange but great songwriter in Greg Appel.

Left: When the classic "Cattle & Cane" failed to make any impression on a broader Australian audience, the GO-BETWEENS returned to the UK, got dumped by Rough Trade, got picked up by Sire, released another great album (*Spring Hill Fair*) in 1984, then got dumped by Sire. (Pic: Sheila Rock)

Below: "Punk's not dead" was the cry from all the stupid bands in studs, Doc Martens and mohawks, but the true spirit of punk coursed through the veins of a band like Sydney's CRAVEN FOPS, whose anarchic enthusiasm could never succeed in the increasingly careerist 1980s. (Pic: Carey Swan)

Above: Nick Cave did more than survive the death of the Birthday Party: he survived a US tour with "The Immaculate Consumptive"; he has survived his self-made mythology; and he has also survived his own terrible Southern Gothic spawn. He delivered his debut solo album, From Her to Eternity, in 1984. (Pic: courtesy Possum Records)

Above left: On the back of their surprise hit debut album, the Hoodoo Gurus sacked drummer James Baker, replaced him with Mark Kingsmill (like guitarist Brad Shepherd, a former Hitman), and set their sights on the US, the first Australian indie band to do so since the sadly unsuccessful Lipstick Killers. (Pic: courtesy Stuart Coupe)

Centre left: With the wreckage of the Laughing Clowns left behind him, Ed Kuepper embarked on a solo career, launched with the back-to-basics guitar rock of the album *Electrical Storm*. He subsequently also formed a side band as a riposte to Chris Bailey's ongoing Saints lineups, which he called the Aints. (Pic: courtesy Hot Records)

Below left: When a former model and an ex-girlfriend of Bon Scott teamed up with a former Thought Criminal and former News-man, they became Do Re Mi, who after a couple of EPs for Green Records joined major label Virgin and in the winter of 1985 delivered the unlikely Top 5 hit, "Man Overboard." (Pic: courtesy Virgin Records)

LAUGHING HANDS

Adhesive

THE BIRTHDAY PARTY
with the FABULOUS MARQUISES
FRI 6th CELL BLOCK BYQ
EAST SYDNEY TECH Taylors So
WILD WEST + the SLUGFUCKERS
SAT 7th BAYVIEW TAVERN
GLADESVILLE

SINGLE OUT NOW
MARKED MAN
PRIMATE CALLING

Go-Betweens
Scarpa Flow
SAT SEPT. 12
Seaview Hotel

HUNTERS

COLLECTORS

X ASPIRATIONS
1st Album OUT NOW!

SHY IMPOSTORS
FLAMING HANDS
PADDINGTON GREEN
THURS 12TH JUNE

THE GO-BETWEENS

thursday 9 brownies   friday 10 marquee
thursday 16 bayview tavern

HIROSHIMA CHAIR
AND
THE SEVERED HEADS

FREE AT
EXILES BOOKSHOP
OXFORD ST - Friday 7th
6pm-8pm SHARP

VESSELS

MAKERS OF THE DEAD TRAVEL FAST

SARDINE v

URFACING

SOME MUSIC

latrobe
union gallery

THUR	2
FRI	3
SAT	4
SUN	5
MON	6
TUES	7
WED	8
THUR	9

2 PER
FRI.2
SAT.2
NUCLEUS

LAUGHING CLOWNS

STAGEDOOR   Fri 24ᵀᴴ Aug
METROPOLE   Sun 26ᵀᴴ Aug
CIVIC HOTEL Wed 29ᵀᴴ Aug
RAGS   Fri 31ˢᵀ Aug

INTRODUCING
RYTHMYX CHYNIX
THIS IS A RECORD
No Vowels
No Bowels
GUITARS
SAXOPHONE CELLO FISH ORGAN ETC

LAUGHING CLOWNS
(LAST APPEARANCE IN 1980)
Birthday party
-LIVE TO AIR-
GO-BETWEENS
FIRST SHOW
PARIS THEATRE
FRI. 28th NOV. 7:30 PM

Splen
SYST
DEAD T

FRI 5
BRO

MACHINATIONS

SUNNYBOYS

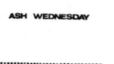

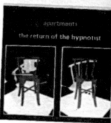

RECORDS/ CASSETTES

This is a selective discography. The criteria for inclusion, given the 1976-1985 timeframe, are based on the same subjective assessments that inspired the book itself. It is not a discography of the Australian independent music of the period. Rather, it charts the outpouring of music that took place in the wake of the Saints and Radio Birdman, who blazed a trail not just with their music but by self-releasing their first records, something virtually unheard of for an Australian band before 1977.

This phenomenon was driven by the DIY ethic, but it allowed for crossing over. Which is why such a discography could never be strictly indie. Otherwise, to begin with, it would have to exclude everything by the Saints after "(I'm) Stranded."

In the main, though, the multi-national major labels in Australia remained terrified of anything that wasn't pub rock until the son-of-punk grunge era of the mid-1990s. The development of punk and post-punk music was fostered by independent labels, whether at home or abroad (a whole generation of acts was forced into UK exile). By the early 80s, sustainable indie labels like Missing Link, Phantom, Au-Go-Go, M Squared, Gap, Doublethink/Green, Hot, Rampant, Greasy Pop, Method, Waterfront, Citadel and others had established regional bases and were building the foundations of an alternative that led all the way to the eventual opening-up of the 1990s.

Many of these recordings — especially singles from the early days — were only ever issued in pressings of a few hundred, and were collector's items even before the first edition of this book was published in 1981. After the dawn of the CD age in the late 1980s, many of them were compiled and/or reissued. Such reissues, legitimate or otherwise, are outside the scope of this discography, which lists only the original/most Australian form of release.

A.E.I.O.U. *(Melbourne)*
10/'80: "Brainwashed" single (AuGoGo, ANDA-11)

APARTMENTS *(Brisbane)*
10/'79: *Return of the Hypnotist* EP (Able Label, ABOO5)
11/'84: "All You Wanted" single (Hot, HOT717)
1985: *The Evening Visits* LP (Rough Trade UK, ROUGH88)

ASPHIXIATION *(Melbourne)*
(See also: →↑→)
2/'81: "L'amour D'Acrostique" 12" single (Missing Link, PRE-1)
12/'81: *What is This Thing Called Disco?* LP (Asphixiation, ONO-001)

ASSASSINS *(Adelaide)*
2/'83: "Assassination" single (Greasy Pop, GPR100)

A.T. WELLS *(Lismore)*
1984: "Maybelline" single (EMI Custom, 13453)

BABEEZ *(Melbourne)*
(See also: NEWS)
11/'77: *Nobody Wants Me* EP (MA7191)

JAMES BAKER *(Perth)*
1985: "Born to be Punched" single (Red Eye, RED1)

BARONS *(Sydney)*
11/'79: *Greatest Hits* EP (Doublethink, DTDT5)
11/'80: "Paint It Black" (track on *Growing Pains*)

BEASTS OF BOURBON *(Sydney)*
7/'84: "Psycho" single (Green, BTS1256)
7/'84: *The Axeman's Jazz* LP (Green, BT7032)

BELLE DU SOIR *(Sydney)*
8/'81: EP (M Squared, M2011)

BIRTHDAY PARTY *(Melbourne)*
(See also: BOYS NEXT DOOR)
7/'80: "Mr. Clarinet" single (Missing Link, MLS-18)

8/'80: "Friend Catcher" single (4AD, AD12)
11/'80: *The Birthday Party* LP (Missing Link, LINK-7)
6/'81: *Prayers on Fire* LP (Missing Link, LINK-8)
6/'81: "Nick The Stripper" 12" single (Missing Link, MSD-479)
8/'81: "Release the Bats" 7" & 12" single (Missing Link, MISS37)
2/'82: *Drunk on the Pope's Blood* mini-LP (Missing Link, ING006)
7/'82: *Junkyard* LP (Missing Link, LINK21)
3/'83: *The Bad Seed* EP (4AD, BAD301)
11/'83: *Mutiny* EP (Mute, 12 MUTE 29)

BLACK CHROME *(Adelaide)*
7/'78: "Australia's God" single (Tomorrow)

BODYSNATCHERS *(Brisbane)*
11/'79: "(I'm) Frantic" single (Savage Music, SM-3)

BOHDAN X *(Melbourne)*
7/'78: "Time To Age" single (Tomorrow, MA-7203)
10/'83: *Fear Of Flying* mini-LP (Rumur, RUME001)

BOX OF FISH *(Sydney)*
11/'83: "Sex Cat Killer" single (Method, MR10)
7/'84: *Slap 'Em Around the Gills* mini-LP (Method, MET003)

BOYS NEXT DOOR *(Melbourne)*
3/'78: "These Boots Are Made for Walking/Masturbation Generation/Boy Hero" (tracks on *Lethal Weapons*)
3/'78: "These Boots Are Made for Walking" single (Suicide, 103140)
5/'79: *Door Door* LP (Mushroom, L36931)
5/'79: "Shivers" single (Mushroom, K7492)
11/'79: "Scatterbrain" single side (Crystal Ballroom, CBR-1)
12/'79: *Hee Haw* 12" EP (Missing Link, MLEP-3)
2/'80: "Happy Birthday" single (Missing Link, MLS-16)

BRING PHILIP *(Sydney)*
1983: *Endoscopy* 12" EP (Major, MRC001)
1984: "Comforts" single (Major, MRC002)

CATCHCRY *(Sydney)*
1983: "Blueprint #9" single (Catch 22)

NICK CAVE *(Berlin)*
6/'84: *From Her to Eternity* LP (Mute, STUMM 17)
5/'84: "In the Ghetto" single (Mute, MUTE 032)
7/'85: *The Firstborn is Dead* mini-LP (Mute, STUMM 21)

CELIBATE RIFLES *(Sydney)*
3/'82: *But Jacques, the Fish* EP (Hot, HOT702)
5/'83: *Sideroxylon* LP (Hot, HOT1001)
10/'83: "Pretty Pictures" single (Hot, HOT704)
12/'83: "Merry Xmas Blues" single (Hot, HOT706)
4/'84: "Wild Desire" single (Hot, HOT711)
5/'84: *Celibate Rifles* (aka *Five Languages*) LP (Hot, HOT 1007)
11/'84: "Sometimes" single (Hot, HOT718)

CHAMPAGNE EDGE *(Melbourne)*
5/'81: EP (AuGoGo, ANDA13)

DAVID CHESWORTH *(Melbourne)*
8/'79: *50 Synthesizer Greats* LP (MA-12131)
7/'81: *Layer On Layer* LP (Innocent, NON-5)

CHOCOLATE GRINDERS *(Melbourne)*
8/'81: "People With Leukemia" single (Innocent, NON-6)

CHOSEN FEW *(Melbourne)*
9/'78: *The Joke's On Us* EP

CLIENTS *(Melbourne)*
5/'81: "Something In The Air" single (Broken Records, BR-1001)

CLIMBING FRAME *(Sydney)*
1984: *Love Music* mini-LP (Bedroom Recordings)

CLUB OF ROME *(Canberra)*
1983: "Jesus Wouldn't Like It" single (Club Of Rome, COR001)

CORPSE GRINDERS *(Melbourne)*
1984: *Corpse Grinders* mini-LP (Man-Made, MM003)
1984: "I Eat Babies" single (Man-Made, MM005)

1984: "I Go Crazy"
(track on *Asleep at the Wheel*)

CRAVEN FOPS (Sydney)
6/'85: "When a Whiskey Buys a
Whiskey" 12" (Bulb, BULB001)

CREDITS (Brisbane)
10/'79: "It's You" single
(Thunder Productions, FV-001)

CRIME & CITY SOLUTION
(London)
6/'85: *The Dangling Man* 12" EP
(Mute, ETUM 804)

CUBAN HEELS (Melbourne)
8/'80: "Little Girl" single
(Greville, GR-1)

DAGOES (Adelaide)
5/'80: *Dagoes Sell Soul* EP
(Greasy Pop, DAG-001)
4/'81: "Kid's Got Style" (track on
5MMM's *Adelaide Bands*)
8/'81: *It's You* double single
(Greasy Pop, DAG-002/003)
8/'81: "Ten Years On" single
(Phantom, PH-10)
8/'82: "Daunting" single
(Greasy Pop, DAG-004)
8/'84: "Heartbeat" single
(Greasy Pop, GPR109)

DANCE SET (Melbourne)
7/'81: "Melody Smiles" single
(AuGoGo, ANDA-12)

DAVE & PHIL DUO (Melbourne)
3/'80: *Present Themselves* EP
(Innocent, NON-2)
11/'81: "Studio Time" (track on *The
Signal-To-Noise Set Vol. 2*)

DECLINE OF THE REPTILES
(Sydney)
5/'84: "What I Feel" single
(Waterfront, DAMP10)
9/'85: *The Hammer Speaks* mini-LP
(Waterfront, DAMP18)

DEL WEBB EXPLOSION
(Adelaide)
1983: "Gardening as a Finer Art"
single (Greasy Pop, GPR102)

DIED PRETTY (Sydney)
4/'84: "Out of the Unknown" single
(Citadel, CIT007)
10/'84: "Mirror Blues" single
(Citadel, CIT010)
8/'85: *Next to Nothing* 12" EP
(Citadel, CITEP901)
8/'86: *Free Dirt* LP
(Citadel, CITLP504)

DO-RE-MI (Sydney)
1982: *Standing on Wires* 12" EP
(Green, LRM680)
1/'83: *The Waiting Room* 12" EP
(Green, LRM117)
7/'85: "Man Overboard" single
(Virgin, VOZ00312)
9/'85: *Domestic Harmony* LP
(Virgin, VOZ2001)

DORIAN GREY (Melbourne)
6/'82: "Emperor's New Clothes"
single (AuGoGo, ANDA19)

DRESDEN WAR CRIMES
(Melbourne)
1981: cassette (Yarra Beat)

EARS (Melbourne)
6/'80: "Leap For Lunch" single
(MA-7343)
5/'81: "Scarecrow" single
(Missing Link, MISS-26)

10/'81: "Perennial Boogie/One Light"
(tracks on *From Belgrave With
Love*)

ELECTRIC FANS (Sydney)
1980: "Run, Ray, Run" EP
(EMI Custom, 13062)

END (Brisbane)
1983: "My Confession" single
(13199)
1983: *The End,* cassette (Hot, END1)

EQUAL LOCAL (Melbourne)
9/'81: "Madagascar" 12" single
(Missing Link, MSD519)
1982: "12 Ways to Go" 12" single
(Missing Link, POWT0067)

ESSENDON AIRPORT
(Melbourne)
3/'80: *Sonic Investigations* EP
(Innocent, NON-1)
7/'80: "Talking to Cleopatra" single
(Innocent, NON-3)
1982: *Palimpsest* LP
(Innocent, NON-13)

E.S.T. (Sydney)
12/'80: "Yvonne is Out Again"
(track on *Growing Pains*)
12/'80: "Just Not True" single
(M Squared, M2002)

FABULOUS MARQUISES
(Melbourne)
7/'80: "Honeymoons" single
(Unforgettable Music, UMS-3)
10/'81: "Heart To My Hands" (track
on *From Belgrave With Love*)

FAST CARS (Sydney)
6/'81: "Saturday's Girl" single
(Method, MR-4)
11/'81: *Annual* EP (Method, MR-5)
1983: *Fast Cars,* cassette
(Hot, FAST1)
6/'84: "Love Child" single
(Method, MR-15)

FERAL DINOSAURS (Melbourne)
1985: *You've All Got a Home to Go
To* mini-LP (Major, MRLP004)

FLAMING HANDS (Sydney)
9/'80: "I Belong To Nobody" single
(Phantom, PH-3)
5/'81: "Wake Up Screaming" single
(Phantom, PH-8)
3/'82: "It's Just That I Miss You"
single (Phantom, PH-14)
10/'83: "Cast My Love" 12" single
(Big Time, BTE1001)
3/'84: "The Edge" single
(Big Time, BTS1175)
8/'84: "Breakdown and Cry" single
(Big Time, BTS1272)
10/'84: *Flaming Hands* LP
(Big Time, BT7025)

FOUR GODS (Brisbane)
9/'81: "Enchanted House" single
(Able Label, AB006)

JAMES FREUD (Melbourne)
3/'80: "Modern Girl" single
(Mushroom, K7863)
7/'80: *Breaking Silence* LP
(Mushroom, L37309)
12/'80: "Enemy Lines" single
(Mushroom, K8097)
3/'83: "Automatic Crazy" single
(Mushroom, K8236)

FUN THINGS (Brisbane)
5/'80: *Fun Things* EP
(Machine Music, PRS-2783)

FRONTIER SCOUTS (Sydney)
1982: "When Daddy Blows His Top"
single (AuGoGo, ANDA28)
1984: *Museum Collection* mini-LP
(AuGoGo, ANDA34)

FUNGUS BRAINS (Melbourne)
1983: *Ron Pisto's Real World* LP
(Max)

GO-BETWEENS (Brisbane)
9/'78: "Lee Remick" single
(Able Label, ABOO1)
9/'79: "People Say" single
(Able Label, ABOO4)
11/'80: "I Need Two Heads" single
(Postcard, 80-4)
9/'81: "Your Turn, My Turn" single
(Missing Link, MISS-29)
11/'81: *Send Me A Lullaby* LP
(Missing Link, ING005)
3/'82: "Hammer the Hammer" single
(Missing Link, MISS33)
5/'83: *Before Hollywood* LP
(Stunn, STUN508)
5/'83: "Cattle & Cane" single
(Rough Trade, RT124)
11/'83: "Man O' Sand to Girl O'
Sea" single (Rough Trade, RT144)
8/'84: "Part Company" single
(Sire UK, W9211)
9/'84: *Spring Hill Fair* LP
(Sire, 25179)
11/'84: "Bachelor Kisses" single
(Sire, 729156)

GROOVEYARD (Adelaide)
1983: "Avalanche of Love" single
(Green, BTS1246)

GROUND ZERO (Perth)
9/'80: "Double Meaning" EP
(White Rider, WEEP-2)
7/'81: "Oceans" EP side
(SMX-57836)

HELTER SKELTER (Sydney)
3/'84 "Make Believe" single
(Hot, HOT708)

HIROSHIMA CHAIR (Sydney)
11/'81: LP side
(Dogfood Productions 4)

HITMEN (Sydney)
11/'78: "Under The Boardwalk"
single (RCA, 103131)
9/'79: "Didn't Tell The Man" single
(WEA, 100095)
4/'80: "I Want You" single
(WEA, 100129)
7/'81: *Hitmen* LP (WEA, 600097)
7/'81: "I Don't Mind" single
(WEA, 100169)
4/'82: "Everybody Knows" single
(RCA, 103982)
11/'82: "Bwana Devil" single
(RCA, 104097)
11/'82: *It Is What It Is* LP
(RCA, VPL 10403)
11/'84: *Tora Tora D.T.K.* LP
(ABC, L38240)

HONEYMOON IN GREEN
(Melbourne)
1983: "Acrobatic in Love" single
(Mad-On-Mercy, 13451)

HOODOO GURUS (Sydney)
10/'82: "Leilani" single
(Phantom, PH-15)
6/'83: "Tojo" single
(Big Time, BTS984)
10/'83: "My Girl" single
(Big Time, BTS1077)
3/'84: *Stoneage Romeos* LP
(Big Time, BT7018)

HOWLING COMMANDOES
(Sydney)
7/'84: "90 Days" 12" single
(Waterfront, DAMP6)

HUGO KLANG (London)
1982: "Beat Up The Old Shack"
single (Prince Melon)
1982: "Wheel of Fat" single
(AuGoGo, ANDA24)

HUMANS (Brisbane)
12/'79: "Teen Idol" single
(PRS-2677)

HUNTERS & COLLECTORS
(Melbourne)
11/'81: "World of Stone" 12" single
(White Label, X1307)
7/'82: *Hunters & Collectors* mini-
LP+12" (White Label, L42002)
7/'82: "Talking to a Stranger" single
(White Label, K8754)
12/'82: *Payload* 12" EP
(White Label, X14002)
8/'83: *Judas Sheep* 12" EP
(White Label, X12032)
9/'83: *The Fireman's Curse* LP
(White Label, L38066)
11/'83: "Sway" single
(White Label, K9261)
7/'84: *Jaws of Life* LP
(White Label, L38222)
8/'84: "The Slab" single
(White Label, K9444)
11/'84: "Throw Your Arms Around
Me" single (White Label, K9539)

IDIOM FLESH (Sydney)
1984: *Inheritance* mini-LP (Rama)

IDIOT SAVANT (Sydney)
7/'84: *Idiot Savant* 12" EP
(Icon, IR0001)

INSERTS (Melbourne)
6/'80: "Amateur Hour" single (V-001)

INTERNATIONAL EXILES
(Melbourne)
6/'80: "Miniskirts In Moscow" single
side (MA-7371)
10/'80: "Let's Be Sophisticated"
single (Missing Link, MISS 20)

INTROVERTS (Sydney)
7/'83: "Girl on Page 3" single
(Method, MR11)

JETSONNES (Melbourne)
6/'80: "Newspaper" single side
(MA-7371)

J.F.K. & THE CUBAN CRISIS
(Brisbane)
3/'82: "Am I a Pagan?" single (Two
Possibilities)
12/'82: *Careless Talk* EP
(Waterfront, DAMP1)
5/'84: "Ballad of Jackie O" EP
(Waterfront, DAMP5)
9/'84: *End of the Affair* LP
(Waterfront, DAMP7)

JOHNNYS (Sydney)
10/'83: "I Think You're Cute" single
(Regular)
11/'84: "My Buzzsaw Baby" single
(Green, POWO240)
11/'84: *The Johnnys* 12" EP (Green)
11/'85: "Injun Joe" single
(Mushroom)

JUMP VISION (Sydney)
3/'80: "Can't Get Used To You"
single (Basilisk, BAS-004)

JUST URBAIN (Brisbane)

11/'79: *Burning, Part Two* EP (Shake Music, SM1)

4/'80: *Everybody Loves Just Urbain* EP (Shake, SM4)

1980: *Final Program* EP (Shake, SM04)

KELPIES (Sydney)

11/'82: "Take Me Away" single (Phantom, PH-17)

KICKS (Brisbane)

1980: "Return of the Action Men" single (Shake, 13248)

KIKX (Melbourne)

5/'80: "Nova Express" single (MA-7344)

KINGSWOODS (Brisbane)

1982: "Purdy Vacant" single (Green, BTS994)

KLERKS (Sydney)

1983: "I Need A Pardon" single (Vi-Nil, VR002)

ED KUEPPER (Sydney)

10/'85: *Electrical Storm* LP (Hot, HOT1020)

LA FEMME (Melbourne)

6/'79: "Chelsea Kids" single (Missing Link, MLS-5)

11/'80: "I Don't Wanna Go Home" single (Seven, MS-401)

11/'80: *La Femme* LP (Missing Link, MCF351)

11/'81: "Looking for a Laugh" single (Space, 13201)

LAST WORDS (Sydney)

3/'78: "Animal World" single (Remand, RRCS2439)

2/'79: "Animal World" single (Wizard, ZS-196)

10/'79: "Animal World" single (Rough Trade UK, RT-022)

1/'80: "Today's Kidz" single (Remand 2, UK only)

8/'80: *The Last Words* LP (Armageddon, ARM-2)

8/'80: "Top Secret" single (Armageddon, A-S-002)

LAUGHING CLOWNS (Sydney)

5/'80: *Laughing Clowns* mini-LP, (Missing Link, MCB-001)

1/'81: "Sometimes the Fire Dance" single (Prince Melon, PM-01)

3/'81: *Laughing Clowns 3* mini-LP (Prince Melon, PM-05)

7/'81: *Reign Of Terror/Throne Of Blood* LP (Prince Melon, PM-2000)

3/'82: *Mr. Uddich-Schmuddich Goes to Town* LP (Prince Melon, PM5000)

3/'82: "Mad Flies" single (Prince Melon, PM020)

7/'83: "Everything that Flies" 12" single (Prince Melon, PM03012)

3/'84: *Eternally Yours* 12" single (Hot, HOT12001)

4/'84: *Law of Nature* LP (Hot, HOT1004)

11/'84: *History of Rock'n'Roll, Vol.1* LP (Hot, HOT1010)

6/'85: *Ghosts of an Ideal Wife* LP (Hot, HOT1013)

2/'85: "Just Because I Like" single (Hot, HOT719)

LAUGHING HANDS (Melbourne)

6/'80: *Ledge* LP (Adhesive 1)

1/'81: *Dog Photos* LP (Adhesive 2)

1981: "Vibrate/Scatter/Picture/ Splinter" cassette (Adhesive)

LEFTOVERS (Brisbane)

6/'79: "Cigarettes And Alcohol" single (Punji Stick , PRS-2624)

LIGHTHOUSE KEEPERS (Canberra)

1983: "Gargoyle" single (Guthugga Pipeline, GPR001)

'83: *Exploding Lighthouse Keepers* mini-LP (Guthugga Pipeline, GPR004)

11/'84: *Tales of the Unexpected* LP (Hot, HOT1011)

11/'84: "Ocean Liner" single (Hot, HOT720)

8/'85: "Ode to Nothing" single (Hot, HOT 724)

LIME SPIDERS (Sydney)

6/'83: "25th Hour" double single (Green, BTS972)

3/'84: "Slave Girl" single (Citadel, CIT008)

LIMP (Sydney)

5/'81: "Marked Man" single (Primate, PM-03)

11/'81: "Pony Club" (track on *A Selection*)

LIPSTICK KILLERS (Sydney)

11/'79: "Hindu Gods (Of Love)" single (Lost In Space, PRS-2661)

1984: "Sockman" single (Vi-Nil, VLK001)

1984: *Mesmeriser* LP (Citadel, CITLP501)

LITTLE MURDERS (Melbourne)

11/'79: "Things Will Be Different" single (AuGoGo, ANDA-3)

4/'80: "High School" single (AuGoGo, ANDA-6)

7/'81: "She Lets Me Know" single (AuGoGo, ANDA-14)

LOVE & SQUALOR (Sydney)

1985: "Swap" single (PRS-13858)

LOVS E BLUR (Brisbane)

12/'84: "In My Head" single

MACHINATIONS (Sydney)

9/'81: "Average Inadequacy" single (Phantom, PH-12)

11/'81: "Arabia" 12" EP (Phantom, PH-13)

3/'82: "Average Inadequacy" single (White Label, K8581)

3/'83: "Jack" single (White Label, K8928)

6/'83: "Pressure Sway" 12" single (White Label, X12026)

4/'83: *Esteem* LP (White Label, L37946)

10/'83: "Jumping the Gap" 12" single (White Label, X13128)

MADROOM (Sydney)

7/'82: *Cruelty of Beauty* 12" EP (Talk-of-the-Author, YPRX1963)

1984: *"I am for an art..."* LP (Dog, DOG001)

(MAKERS OF) THE DEAD TRAVEL FAST (Sydney)

11/'80: "The Dead Travel Fast" (track on *Growing Pains*)

1/'81: "Tael of a Saeghors" single (M Squared, M2004)

4/'81: *The Vessels* LP (M Squared, M2005)

11/'81: "Urchin" (track on *A Selection*)

2/'82: "Why Don't We Wake?" single (M Squared, M2015)

1983: *Zoom M* LP (M Squared, M2022)

MANIKINS (Perth)

11/'78: "I Never Thought I'd Find Someone Who Could Be So Kind" single (PRS-2708)

1979: *Live Locally*, cassette

8/'80: "Premonition" single (SMX-46969)

10/'80: "Love At Second Sight" single (SMX-55051)

MARCHING GIRLS (Melbourne)

5/'80: "True Love" single (AuGoGo, ANDA-8)

KAREN MARKS (Melbourne)

4/'81: "Cold Cafe" single (Astor, 7324)

METRONOMES (Melbourne)

2/'80: "Saturday Night" single (Cleopatra, CSP 2203)

9/'80: "A Circuit Like Me" single (Cleopatra, CSP-2205)

10/'81: *Multiple Choice* LP (Cleopatra, CLP-210)

MICROFILM (Melbourne)

7/'80: "Centrefold" single (Unforgettable, MCC4/UMS 2)

10/'81: "Summerhouse" (track on *From Belgrave With Love*)

MINUTEMAN (Sydney)

9/'82: "Voodoo Slaves" single (Citadel, CIT001)

MODELS (Melbourne)

11/'79: "Early Morning Brain" single side (Crystal Ballroom, CBR-1)

8/'80: "Owe You Nothing" single (MA-7356)

11/'80: "Two People Per Sqare Kilometre" 12" EP (Mushroom, RR1)

11/'80: *Alphabetacharliedelta...* LP (Mushroom, L37495)

8/'81: *Cut Lunch* mini-LP (Mushroom, L20001)

10/'81: *Local &/Or General* LP (Mushroom, L37637)

11/'81: "Local &/Or General" single (Mushroom, K8489)

8/'82: "On" single (Mushroom, K8815)

9/'83: "I Hear Motion" single (Mushroom, K9187)

10/'83: *Pleasure of Your Company* LP (Mushroom, L38065)

MOODISTS (Melbourne)

9/'81: "Where The Trees Walk Downhill" single (AuGoGo, ANDA15)

10/'81: "Gone Dead" single (AuGoGo, ANDA18)

1/'83: *Engine Shudder* mini-LP (AuGoGo, ANDA26)

6/'82: "Runaway" 7" & 12" single (Red Flame, RFB39/-12)

4/'84: *Thirsty's Calling* LP (Red Flame, RFA39)

9/'84: "Enough Legs to Live On" single (Red Flame, RFB41)

3/'85: *Double Life* mini-LP (Red Flame, RFM44)

8/'85: "Justice and Money Too" 12" single (Creation, CRE022T)

10/'85: "Take the Red Carpet Out of Town" single (Time/Abstract, 12MOT)

MOVING PARTS (Sydney)

2/'80: "Chevy" EP (EMI Custom, PRS 2711)

9/80: "Living China Doll" single (Alternative, K8028)

MYSTERY OF SIXES (Brisbane)

1982: "Mystery Of Sixes" single (EMI Custom, 13359)

1983: *Something Mechanical* EP (Sundown, SUN0045)

NASTY NIGEL (Adelaide)

12/'79: "Jonestown Suicide" single (PRS-2708)

NEGATIVE REACTION (Sydney)

11/'81: "Land Of Surrender" (track on *A Selection*)

11/'81: *Negative Reaction* LP (Dogfood Productions 3)

NERVOUS SYSTEM (Sydney)

12/'81: *Last Avenue* EP (PRS-13195)

NEVER NEVER BAND (Geelong)

12/'80: "It Doesn't Mean A Thing" single (Never Never Music)

NEW CHRISTS (Sydney)

8/'81: "Face A New God" single (Green, LRS-076)

4/'84: "Like a Curse" single (Citadel, BTS1218)

1985: "Born Out of Time" single (Citadel, CIT017)

NEW RACE (Sydney)

9/'82: *The First and the Last* LP (WEA, 600120)

4/'83: "Crying Sun" single (Citadel, CIT002)

NEWS (Melbourne)

5/'78: "Dirty Lies" single

2/'79: *Dirty Secrets* double single

4/'80: "That Girl" single (Missing Link, MLS-14)

N-LETS (Woollongong)

K-Set, cassette (2-Tapes)

"Let's-N" cassette single (2-Tapes)

Sussex Success, cassette (2-Tapes)

At St Peter's/Australian Heritage, cassette (2-Tapes)

Indoors/Outdoors, cassette (2-Tapes)

I Shall Respect Them, cassette (2-Tapes)

Radio Play, cassette (2-Tapes)

Yeaauh, cassette (2-Tapes)

NO ACTRESSES (Perth)

6/'81: "Entertainment" EP side (SMX-57835)

NO-DANCE (Sydney)

3/'84: *Carnival of Souls* EP (Hot, HOT709)

NOT DROWNING, WAVING (Melbourne)

4/'84: "Moving Around" single (Rampant, RR007)

1/'85: *Another Pond* LP (Rampant, RR010)

NUMBERS (Brisbane)

(See also RIPTIDES)

9/'78: *Sunset Strip* EP (Able Label, ABOO3)

NUVO BLOC (Adelaide)

11/'80: "Atomic Fiction" single (EMI Custom, 13022)

ORCHESTRA OF SKIN & BONE (Melbourne)

1985: *Orchestra of Skin & Bone* LP (Major, MR LP003)

OTHER VOICES (Brisbane)

1983: "World War III" single (Sundown, SUN0035)

1/'85: "She Walks Down" single (Waterfront, DAMP12)

PARAMETERS (Brisbane)
9/'84: "Pig City" single

PARTICLES (Sydney)
4/'80: Colour-In EP
(Certain Music, FRS 2768)
1980: Advanced Colouring EP
(Remington, 13179)
1983: I Luv Trumpet EP
(Waterfront, DAMP2)

PASSENGERS (Sydney)
4/'80: "Face With No Name" single
(Phantom, PH1)

PEL MEL (Newcastle)
2/'81: "No Word From China" single
(Primate, PM-02)
11/'81: "Click Click" (track on
A Selection)
12/'81: "Head Above Water" single
(Gap, SAP702)
11/'82: "Blind Lead the Blind" single
(Gap)
12/'82: Out of Reason LP
(Gap, GAPLP2001)
6/'83: "Shoes Should Fit" single
(Gap, GAP101)
9/'83: "Pandemonium" single (Gap)
10/'83: Persuasion LP
(Gap, GAPLP2002)

**PEOPLE WITH CHAIRS UP
THEIR NOSES** (Melbourne)
1982: "Road to Egg" single side
(AuGoGo, ANDA21)

ANGIE PEPPER (Sydney)
5/'84: "Frozen World" single
(Citadel, CIT003)

PLANTS (Sydney)
1981: Dark Sky Exhibitionists EP

PLAYS WITH MARIONETTES
(Melbourne)
1982: "Witchenkopf" single side,
(AuGoGo, ANDA21)

POLES (Brisbane)
4/'81: "Over And Beyond And
Through" single (PRS-13068)

POP GUN MEN (Melbourne)
2/'80: "Behind Dark Glasses" single
(PRS-2749)

POPULAR MECHANICS
(Sydney)
12/'79: From Here To Obscurity EP
(Doublethink, OTDT4)
2/'81: "You Get The Picture" single
(Basilisk, BAZ-003)

PRESS (Sydney)
10/'79: Fodder For The Critics LP
(Laser, VXLI-4187)
10/'79: "Alcoholic" single
(Laser, 103446)

PRIMITIVE CALCULATORS
(Melbourne)
2/'80: "Do That Dance" single
(Slow Drama, FRS2746)
1982: Primitive Calculators LP
(Slow Drama, PC-1)

PROD (Sydney)
6/'81: Contents One EP
(M Squared, M2007)

PROGRESSION CULT (Sydney)
1982: New Blood EP (Method, MR6)

PROLES (Melbourne)
1/'80: "Police" single (SF-328)

PSYCHO SURGEONS (Sydney)
9/'78: "Horizontal Action" single
(Wallaby Beat, PRS-2551)

PUBLIC EXECUTION (Brisbane)
1982: "Methadone Slave" single
(Sundown, SUN0032)

QUICK AND THE DEAD (Perth)
5/'81: "Child Molester" EP

QUINTREX BOP (Canberra)
5/'80: "Judith"
(track on Canberra Calling)
12/'80: Effigies EP (13005)

RADIO BIRDMAN (Sydney)
10/'76: Burn My Eye EP
(Trafalgar, ME-109)
6/'77: "New Race" single
(Trafalgar, TRS-11)
10/'77: Radios Appear LP
(Trafalgar, TRL-1001)
1977: "Burned My Eye"
(track on Long Live The Evolution,
JJ-AA9042)
2/'78: Radios Appear (overseas
version) LP
(Trafalgar/WEA, TRL-102)
5/'78: "Aloha Steve And Danno"
single (Trafalgar/WEA, TRS-12)
8/'78: "What Gives?" single
(Sire UK, 6078 617)
3/81: Living Eyes LP (WEA, 600085)
5/'81: "Alone In the Endzone" single
(WEA, 100160)
10/'82: Soldiers of Rock'n'Roll LP
(WEA, YEAHUP-1)

RAZAR (Brisbane)
9/'78: "Task Force" single
(Able Label, ABOO2)
1979: "Shutdown Countdown" EP
(EMI Custom, PRS-2645)

REJEX (Sydney)
12/'79: "Niagra Baby" single
(Doublethink, DTDT3)

RELATIVES (Melbourne)
6/'79: "Picasso" EP
(Red Ash, RAP-001)
12/'79: Uncle Theo Comes To Visit
EP (Red Ash, RAP-002)

RHYTHMX CHYMX (Sydney)
7/'80: No Vowels, No Bowels LP
side (Terse, YPRX-1 706)

RIPTIDES (Brisbane)
(See also NUMBERS)
7/'79: Sunset Strip EP
(Able Label, AB-004, reissue)
2/'80: "Tomorrow's Tears" single
(Flat Records, FLAT-1)
11/'81: Swept Away mini-LP
(Regular, L20004)
11/'81: "OnlyTime" single
(Regular, K8341)
9/'82: "Hearts & Flowers" single
(Regular, RRSP716)
7/'83: The Last Wave LP
(Regular, RRLP1207)

ROCKETS (Perth)
4/'80: "Mean Mistress" single
(White Rider, WAS-1)

ROCKMELONS (Sydney)
1984: "Time Out" single
(Phantom, PH-19)

ROCKS (Sydney)
5/'78: You're So Boring EP
(Point Blank, PBR-101)

RON RUDE (Melbourne)
8/'79: The Borders Of Disgrace LP
(Rudesound. RUD-001)
6/'80: "Piano Piano" single
(Unforgettable Music, UMS1)
3/'81: The Vorpal Blade LP
(Unforgettable Music, RUD-002)

SACRED COWBOYS
(Melbourne)
11/'82: "Nothing Grows in Texas"
single (White Label, K8927))
7/'83: "Bangkok" single (SC 001)
12/'83: Sacred Cowboys mini-LP
(White Label, L20030)
1984: We Love You . . . Of Course
We Do! LP (Man Made, MM006)

SAINTS (Brisbane)
9/'76: "(I'm) Stranded" single
(Fatal, MA-7158)
2/'77: "(I'm) Stranded" single
(EMI, 11346)
2/'77: Stranded LP (EMI, EMC-2570)
5/'77: "Erotic Neurotic" single
(EMI, 11438)
7/'77: "This Perfect Day" 12" single
(Harvest UK, HAR-5130)
10/'77: 1-2-3-4 EP (Harvest, 5137)
2/'78: "Know Your Product" single
(Harvest, 11673)
5/'78: Eternally Yours LP
(Harvest, SHSP-4078)
1978: "Demolition Girl"
(track on Hope & Anchor Front
Row Festival)
10/'78: Prehistoric Sounds LP
(Harvest, SHSP-4094)
11/'78: "Security" single
(Harvest, 11795)
4/'80: Paralytic Tonight, Dublin
Tomorrow 12" EP (Lost, PRS-2773)
11/'80: "Always" single
(Larrikin, RISS-003)
2/'81: Monkey Puzzle LP
(Lost, YPRX1806)
4/'81: "Let's Pretend" single
(Lost, 13093)
7/'82: Casablanca LP (Lost, YPRX1968)
7/'84: "Ghost Ships" single
(RCA, 104254)
7/'84: A Little Madness to Be Free LP
(RCA, VPL10437)

SAME (Sydney)
2/'82: The Same EP
(M Squared, M2014)

SARDINE (Sydney)
10/'81: "Sabotage" single
(EMI Custom, PRS-13206)
3/'82: "Sabotage" single
(White Label, K-8582)
6/'83: I Hate You mini-LP
(Phantom, PH-18)

SCAPA FLOW (Sydney)
3/'81: "Endless Sleep" single
(AuGoGo, ANDA-4)
5/'81: "At Home And Abroad" single
(G.O.G., SCPFLW-1)
1982: Now And Forever EP
(G.O.G., SCPFLW-2)

SCATTERED ORDER (Sydney)
11/'80: "Bent Up"
(track on Growing Pains)
6/'81: Screaming Trees EP
(M Squared, M2008)
11/'81: "I'm Not Whole"
(track on A Selection)
1982: Prat Culture 12" EP
(M Squared, M2020)
10/'83: I Feel So Relaxed with You
EP (M Squared, M2025)
3/'84: A Dancing Foot and a Praying
Knee Don't Belong on the Same
Leg LP (Volition, VOLT1)
9/'85: Career of the Silly Thing LP
(Volition, VOLT2)
9/'85: "Escape Via Cessnock" single
(Volition, VOLT4)

SCIENTISTS (Perth)
3/'79: "Frantic Romantic" single
(D.N.A., SMX-46960)
3/'80: Scientists EP (White Rider,
WEEP-1)
8/'81: The Pink Album LP (HAVE-1)
12/'82: "Happy Hour" single
(AuGoGo, ANDA25)
10/'83: "Ghost Train" single
(AuGoGo, ANDA31)
9/'83: Blood Red River mini-LP
(AuGoGo, ANDA27)
12/'83: "We Had Love" single
(AuGoGo, ANDA29)
9/'84: This Heart Doesn't Run on
Blood mini-LP (AuGoGo, ANDA32)
6/'85: "Atom Bomb Baby" single
(AuGoGo, ANDA35)
6/'85: Atom Bomb Baby mini-LP
(AuGoGo, ANDA37)
6/'85: Heading for a Trauma LP
(AuGoGo, ANDA39)

SCREAMING BELIEVERS
(Adelaide)
1982: Show Me Your Money EP
(Empty Dogma)
2/'84: "My Eyes" single
(Greasy Pop, GPR104)

SEEMS TWICE (Sydney)
2/'80: Non-Plussed EP
(Doublethink, DTDT12)

SCRAP MUSEUM (Melbourne)
1984: "Say Die" single (Rampant)

SCREAMING TRIBESMEN
(Brisbane)
1982: Screaming Tribesmen EP
(EMI Custom, 13349)
10/'83: "Igloo" single (Citadel,
CIT004)
11/'84: "A Stand Alone" single
(Citadel, CIT009)

SEEMS TWICE
1980: Live, cassette (2-Tapes)

SEKRET SEKRET (Sydney)
3/'80: "Charity" single
(Happy Town Sounds, PRS-2801)
2/'81: "New King Jack" single
(Basilisk, BAZ-002)
6/'84: "Girl with a White Stick"
single (Waterfront, DAMP8)
10/'84: "Just to Love You" single
(Waterfront, DAMP13)

SERIOUS YOUNG INSECTS
(Melbourne)
8/'81: "Trouble Understanding
Words" single
(Native Tongue, ES-654)
5/'82: "Be Patient" single
(Native Tongue, ES-730)
9/'82: "Faraway Places" single
(Native Tongue, ES-784)
6/'82: House Breaking LP
(Epic, ELPS 4294)

SEVERED HEADS (Sydney)
7/'80: Ear Bitten LP side
(Terse, YPRX-1706)
1980: Side 2, cassette (Terse 5)
11/'81: Clean LP (Dogfood
Productions, 1-YPRX1860)
11/81: "Eat Roland"
(track on A Selection)
1984: Since the Accident LP (Red
Flame, RFA32)
1984: "Dead Eyes Opened" 12"
single (Ink, INK122)
11/'85: Stretcher LP
(Volition, VOLT3)

LETHAL WEAPONS

HITMEN

RADIO BIRDMAN

RADIOS APPEAR

DOG PHOTOS

THE THOUGHT CRIMINALS

Speed.. Madness.. Flying Saucers...

Two People Per Sq Km

M O D E L S

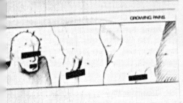

Door, Door

VESSELS

THE SAINTS

Eternally Yours

JAMES FREUD

Breaking Silence

PRIMITIVE CALCULATORS

STUART – guitar, vocals   DAVID – bass
DENISE – keyboards   FRANK – drums, vocals
I can tell   do the icepick   signals
stains   mud in my eye   beat goes on
lullaby do that dance I can't stop it
bake in the sun   shout

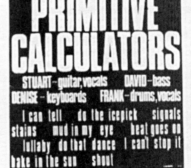

TACTICS
TACTICS
TACTICS
TACTICS
TACTICS
TACTICS
TACTICS
TACTICS
TACTICS
TACTICS
TACTICS
TACTICS
TACTICS

ron rude   the borders of disgrace

THE BIRTHDAY PARTY
PRAYERS ON FIRE

THE SHARKS (Brisbane)
1979: "Freud" single
(EMI Custom, PRS-2713)

SHEIKS (Sydney)
1979: *The Sheiks* EP (Slack, LOCAL4)
1980: "New York" single
(Standard, SINGLE1)

SHY IMPOSTORS (Sydney)
2/'81: "At The Barrier" single
(Phanton, PH-6)

SICK THINGS (Melbourne)
1985: "Committed to Suicide"
single (Max Cass)

SINGLES (Sydney)
7/'80: "Stay" single
(Doublethink, DTDT 11)
2/'81: "Someone That I Knew"
single (Basilisk, BAZ-001)

SKUNKS (Adelaide)
7/'82: *Scratch 'n' Sniff* EP
(RRCS3183)

SLUGFUCKERS (Sydney)
10/'79: "Deaf Disco" single
(Instant Classic, PRS-2678)
11/'79: *Live At Budokan* EP
(Instant Classic, PRS-2698)
9/'81: *Transformational Salt* LP
(Dogfood Productions 2)
1981: *Live*, cassette (2-Tapes)

CLINT SMALL (Melbourne)
9/'81: "Crack In The Wall" single
(AuGoGo, ANDA-2)
3/'80: "On The Fourth Floor" single
(AuGoGo, ANDA-5)

SOCIAL COMMENT (Sydney)
11/'80: "Five O'Clock Fever" single
(Listen Music, LMS-001)

SPIES (Melbourne)
3/'80: "Rat Spat Back" EP
(Normal Records, NRS-1)

SPIKES (Adelaide)
12/'83: "She's Melting" single
(Greasy Pop, GPR103)
6/'85: "Bloody Mess" EP
(Greasy Pop, GPR112)
7/'85: *6 Sharp Cuts* mini-LP
(Greasy Pop, BTB908)

SPITFIRES (Adelaide)
1983: "Rumble in Jungle" single
(Rivet, K9094)
1983: *I Was a Teenage Teenager* LP
(Rivet, L20025)

SPK (Sydney)
4/'79: *Germanik* EP
(Side Effect, PRS 2617)
11/'79: *Mekano* EP
(Side Effect, PRS-2655)
6/'80: "Slogun" single
(Industrial, IR-0011)
1981: *Information Overload Unit* LP
(Side Effektsm SER 01)
7/'81: "See Saw" single
(M Squared, M2009)
1982: *Leichenschrei* LP
(Side Effekts, SER 02)
1983: "Dekompositiones" 12"
(Side Effekts. SER 03)
3/'84: "Metal Dance" 12" (WEA)
1984: "Junk Funk" 12"
(WEA, 0249244)
1/'85: *Machine Age Voodoo* LP
(WEA, 2405151)

SPUTNICKS (Adelaide)
11/'79: "Our Boys" single (324)

SUICIDE SQUAD (Sydney)
1/'80: "I Hate School" single
(Doublethink, DTDT7)

SUNDAY PAINTERS
(Woollongong)
2/'80: "Like A Reptile" single
(Terminal, TER-001)
5/'81: "In My Dreams" single
(Terminal, TER-002)
12/'81: "Please Kill Me" single
(Terminal, TER-003)
1981: *Three Kinds of Escapism* EP
(Terminal, TER-004)
1982: *Something to Do* LP
(Terminal, TER-005)
1983: *4th Annual Report* LP
(Terminal, TER007)

SUNNYBOYS (Sydney)
12/'80: "Love to Rule" EP
(Phantom, PH-1)
7/'81: "Happy Man" single
(Mushroom, K8335)
7/'81: "Happy Birthday" Live EP
(SMX-57856)
9/'81: *Sunnyboys* LP
(Mushroom, L37696)
11/'81: "Alone with You" single
(Mushroom, K8476)
5/'82: *Individuals* LP
(Mushroom, L37836)
5/'82: "You Need a Friend" single
(Mushroom, K8683)
8/'82: "This is Real" single
(Mushroom, K8832)
6/'83: "Show Me Some Discipline"
single (Mushroom, K9142)
3/'84: "Love in a Box" single
(Mushroom, K9363)
4/'84: *Get Some Fun* LP
(Mushroom, RML53129)
5/'84: "Comes as No Surprise"
single (Mushroom, K9422)
11/'84: *Real Live* LP
(Mushroom, L38259)

SUPER-K (Sydney)
1983: "Recurring Nightmare" single
(Green, LRS 694)

SURFSIDE 6 (Sydney)
4/'80: "Cool In The Tube" single
(Phantom, PH-2)
8/'81: "(Can't You See) The Sign"
single (Phantom, PH-9)

SURVIVORS (Brisbane)
1/'78: "Baby Come Back" single
(Real, RR100)

SWELL GUYS (Brisbane)
9/'80: "Smack In The Head" EP
(Flat Records, FLAT2)

SYNTHETIC DREAM (Melbourne)
12/'81: "Fee Fy" single (Innocent)

SYSTEMATICS (Sydney)
1/'80: "Pulp Baby" single
(Doublethink, DTDT8)
11/'80: "Midnight On Balancing
Day" (track on *Growing Pains*)
11/'80: *Rural* mini-LP
(M Squared, M2001)
1980: *Rural Side 3*, cassette
(M Squared, M200C1)
11/'81: "Die For My House"
(track on *A Selection*)
1982: "My Life in the Field of Cows"
single (M Squared, M2012)

TABLEWAITERS (Sydney)
11/'81: "Between The Lines" single

TACTICS (Canberra)
9/'79: *Long Weekend* EP
(Folding Chair, PRS-2653)

7/'80: "Hole In My Life" single (Doublethink, DTDT9)

2/'81: *My Houdini* LP (Green, LRG-064)

4/'81: "Second Language" single (Green, LRS-072)

11/'81: "Gold Watch" single (Green, LRS-619)

11/'81: *Glebe* LP (Green, LRG-094)

8/'82: *The Bones Of Barry Harrison* LP (Larrikin, LRF1134)

7/'85: "Fatman" single (Waterfront, DAMP19)

1985: "Coat-Tails" single (Folding Chair, PRS13835)

TANGLED SHOELACES
(Brisbane)

1983: *Tangled Shoelaces* 12" EP (M Squared, M2023)

TEENAGE RADIO STARS
(Melbourne)

3/'78: "Wanna Be Ya Baby/Learned Ones" (tracks on *Lethal Weapons*)

4/'78: "Wanna Be Ya Baby" single (Suicide, 103139)

DENIZ TEK *(Sydney)*

5/'84: "100 Fools" single (Citadel, CIT003)

TERMINAL TWIST *(Adelaide)*

7/'79: "Common Knowledge" EP (PRS-2630)

THIS FIVE MINUTES *(Brisbane)*

6/'83: "How" single (Cubbyhouse, RRCS3216)

THOUGHT CRIMINALS
(Sydney)

6/'78: "Hilton Bomber" EP (Doublethink, DTDT1)

7/'79: *Food For Thoughtcrimes* EP (Doublethink, DTDT2)

8/'80: "Land of the Living Room" single (PRS 13000)

8/'80: *Speed, Madness, Flying Saucers* LP (Doublethink, DTDT6)

8/'80: "Edge Of Time" single (Doublethink, DTDT10)

10/'81: *You Only Think Twice* LP (Green, LRG-082)

TINY TOWN *(Brisbane)*

1984: "Drop By Drop" single (Elastic, EM001)

1984: "Living Out of Living" single (Elastic, EM002)

1985: *Little Tin God* LP (Elastic, EM004)

TOY WATCHES *(Brisbane)*

1980: "Too Long" single (Peanut Republic, PRR001)

TRANS 262 *(Sydney)*

1981: "Don't Hold Me Down" EP (EMI Custom, 13174)

TRIFFIDS *(Perth)*

6/'78: *Triffids 1st,* cassette

10/'78: *Triffids 2nd,* cassette

3/'79: *Triffids 3rd,* cassette

9/'79: *Triffids 4th,* cassette

5/'80: *Tape 5,* cassette

1981: *Triffids Sixth,* cassette

7/'81: "Stand Up" single (Shake Some Action/WAIT, SG MX-57828)

8/'81: *Reverie* EP (Resonant, REZ 011)

10/'82: "Spanish Blue" single (No Records, 13314)

4/'83: *Bad Timing and Other Stories* EP (White Label, K9003)

1983: *Dungeon Tape* cassette (self-released)

11/'83: *Treeless Plain* LP (Hot, HOT1003)

2/'84: "Beautiful Waste" single (Hot, HOT707)

7/'84: *Raining Pleasure* mini-LP (Hot, MINIHOT1)

10/'84: *Lawson Square Infirmary* mini-LP (Hot, MINIHOT2)

2/'85: *Field of Glass* 12" EP (Hot, HOT12007)

TUFF MONKS *(Melbourne)*

1982: "After the Fireworks" single (AuGoGo, ANDA22)

TU LASSOO *(Sydney)*

4/'84: "Hi-De-Hi" single (Oossalut)

TWO WAY GARDEN
(Melbourne)

7/'79: *Overnight* EP (AuGoGo, ANDA-001)

U-BOMBS *(Adelaide)*

1/'79: "Give Me A Medal" single (Radio Active, PRS-2584)

UNITS *(Adelaide)*

2/'81: "Baby, You Flirt" single (Brainbuster, BUST-001)

UPS & DOWNS *(Brisbane)*

1985: "Living Inside My Head" single (Basketcase, PRS13677)

1985: "The Perfect Crime" single (Basketcase, PRS13773)

THE UPSETS *(Brisbane)*

1981: "Back to Afghanistan" single (EMI Custom, PRS-2899)

UPSIDE-DOWN HOUSE
(Sydney)

1982: *Mauve Xylophone* mini-LP (MX Records, UDH001)

VACANT LOT *(Canberra)*

1981: *Living Underground* EP (Doublethink, 13055)

VAMPIRE LOVERS *(Brisbane)*

1983: "Buzzsaw Popstar" EP (Sundown, SUN0078)

7/'84: "Sweetheart's Blown Mindless" single (Rubber, 13598)

VICTIMS *(Perth)*

3/'78: "Television Addict" single (SMX-46813)

9/'78: *Victims* EP (SMX-46871)

VISITORS *(Sydney)*

9/'80: *Visitors* 12" EP (Phantom, PH-4)

VOIGT/465 *(Sydney)*

2/'79: "A Secret West" single (U.W.E., E593)

10/'79: *Slights Unspoken* LP (B.U.W.E., L4673)

WARUMPI BAND *(Papunya)*

3/'84: "Jailanguru Pakarnu" single (Hot, HOT703)

WEDDINGS, PARTIES, ANYTHING *(Melbourne)*

1985: *Weddings, Parties, Anything* EP (Suffering Tram)

ASH WEDNESDAY *(Melbourne)*

7/'80: "Love By Numbers" single (MA-7351)

WET TAXIS *(Sydney)*

1980: *Taxidermy,* cassette (Terse 8)

5/'84: "C'mon" single (Hot, HOT712)

WHIRLYWIRLD *(Melbourne)*

6/'79: "Window To The World" EP (Missing Link, MLS-3)

2/'80: *Whirlyworld* 12" EP + 7" (Missing Link, ML EP-4)

WILDLIFE DOCUMENTARIES
(Sydney)

6/'82: *Wildlife Documentaries* EP (M Squared, M2017)

WILD WEST *(Sydney)*

4/'81: *Beat The Drought* EP (SMX-55193)

11/'81: "Pelican" (track on *A Selection*)

WORLD WAR XXIV *(Sydney)*

2/'83: "Azaria" single (Eyebrow, 13445)

X *(Sydney)*

1/'80: *X-Aspirations* LP (International Electronics, YPRX-1 645)

1/'80: "I Don't Wanna Go Out" single (PRS-2721)

11/'84: "Mother" single (13639)

10/'85: *At Home With You* LP (Major, MR LP002)

XERO *(Brisbane)*

1982: *Lust in the Dust* 12" EP (M Squared, M2019)

X-RAY-Z *(Melbourne)*

1977: "Poor Image" single (Mushroom)

3/'78: "Three Glorious Years/ Valium" (tracks on *Lethal Weapons*)

YA-YA CHORAL *(Sydney)*

7/'82: "Such a Dutchman" single (M Squared, M2018)

5/'83: *What's a Quaver?* LP (M Squared, M2021)

YOUNG DOCTEURS *(Canberra)*

11/'79: "Bronze Portrait" single (Dull, PRS-2709)

5/'80: "Broken Man" (track on *Canberra Calling*)

YOUNG IDENTITIES *(Brisbane)*

11/'79: "Positive Thinking" EP (Shake Music, SM-2)

4/'80: *New Trends* EP (Shake Music, SM-5)

YOUNG MODERN *(Adelaide)*

10/'78: "She's Got The Money" single (Top Gear)

12/'79: *Play Faster* LP (Local Label 5)

Z-CARS *(Melbourne)*

8/'80: "Is There Someone Out There?" single (AuGoGo, ANDA-9)

ZORROS *(Melbourne)*

10/'81: "Too Young" single (AuGoGo, ANDA-16)

→↑ *(Melbourne)*

5/'79: *Venetian Rendezvous* EP

10/'79: *Nice Noise* EP

12/'79: "Pop Art" single side (Crystal Ballroom, MLC-102)

2/'80: "Only Quantity Counts" single

11/'80: *Caprice* EP (Innocent, NON-4)

10/'81: *Spaces* LP (Innocent, NON-9)

1982: *No Dance* LP (Present, PRE004)

1983: *Soundtracks* LP (Present, PRE003)

COMPILATIONS

1978: *LIVE AT THE MARRYATVILLE*, cassette, incl. Accountants; U-Bombs; Dagoes

3/'78: *LETHAL WEAPONS* LP (Suicide, VXL14072), incl. Boys Next Door; Jab; Negatives; Survivors; Teenage Radio Stars; Wasted Daze; X-Ray-Z

1979: *INNER SANCTUM* LP (Missing Link, MLP3), incl. Bleeding Hearts; Sports; Millionaires; Victims; Pelaco Brothers; Dave Warner's From the Suburbs; News; Young Modern; Relaxed Mechanics; Thorburn; Belair Bandits; Norman Gunston

1979: *PERTH PUNK*, cassette (Shake Some Action), incl. Rockets; Enemy Sounds; Dugites; Victims; Cheap Nasties; Manikins; Blankettes; Orphans; Scientists; Blok Music; Triffids

2/'80: *THE LITTLE BANDS EP* (PRS-2765), incl. Morpions; Ronnie and the Rhythm Boys; Take; Too Fat To Fit Through The Door

5/'80: *CANBERRA CALLING* EP (Dull Events, PRS-2814), incl. Naturals; No Concept; Quintrex Bop; Young Docteurs

11/'80: *GROWING PAINS* mini-LP (M Squared, M2003), incl. Barons; EST; Height/Dismay; (Makers Of) The Dead Travel Fast; Pleasant Pheasants; Scattered Order; Systematics

12/'80: *TERSE SAMPLE* EP (Terse, TRS-002), incl. Agent Orange; Mindless Delta Children; Rhoborhythmaticons; Wet Taxis

1980: *MELBOURNE LITTLE BANDS*, double cassette (2-Tapes), incl. Alan Bamford Experience; Nookies; Jim Buck; Use No Hooks; Pastel Bats; Persons Brothers; Stuttgarters; Oraton Bags; Spontaneous Combustion; Present; Company I Keep; Bags Of Personality; So Tuff; Boys Next Door; I Feel Good

1980: *MYSTERIOUS KITCHENS*, cassette (Terse 4), incl. In Church; Pissy Relay Switch; Holiday Fun; Axe Murderers; Lamington Lady; Nobodies; 2 Man Submarine; Mr + Mrs No-Smoking Sign; Wet Taxis; Rhino Rhino; Japanese Gene Kelly; Burt Blanka; Mindless Delta Children

1980: *MORE SONGS THAT WILL NEVER BE RELEASED*, cassette (M Squared, M200C2), incl. Scattered Order; Jonathan Dunshea; Systematics; EST; Pleasant Peasants; ACRA; Prod; East End Butchers; (Makers Of) The Dead Travel Fast; Height/Dismay

4/'81: *5MMM'S COMPILATION OF ADELAIDE BANDS* LP (5MMMusic, MMM-001), incl. Bad Poets; Brats; Dagoes; Desperate Measures; Haves; Jumpers; Natasha Koodraser; Lounge; Manics; Nuvo Bloc; Street Corner Jack; Systems Go; Ungrateful Children

1981: *SOUND OF SYDNEY* LP (Method, MET001), incl. Products; Personnel; Fast Cars; Allniters;

Girlfriends; Spy V. Spy; Progression Cult; Division 4; Skolars; Moving Parts

10/'81: *FROM BELGRAVE WITH LOVE* LP (Cleopatra, ING-006), incl. Daily Planet; Ears; Fabulous Marquises; Liza Gerard; Vicki Hayes; Lachelle; Microfilm; Microtech; Steve Vanguard; Video Pirates

11/'81: *THE SIGNAL TO NOISE SET, VOL. 1* LP (Cleopatra, CLP-206), incl. David Chesworth; Cybotron; Ian MacFarlane; Metronomes; Ash Wednesday; TTT

11/'81: *THE SIGNAL TO NOISE SET, VOL. 2* LP (Cleopatra, CLP-207), incl. Dave & Phil Duo; Liza Gerard; Primitive Calculators; Tolley & Dare; Whirlywirld

11/'81: *A SELECTION* LP (M Squared, M2010), incl. Aural Indifference; Limp; (Makers Of) The Dead Travel Fast; Negative Reaction; Pal Mel; Scattered Order; Severed Heads; Slug-fuckers; Solipsik; Splendid Mess; Systematics; Tame O'Mearas; Wild West

12/'81: *NEW MUSIC, 1978/79* LP (Innocent, NON-7), incl. Ernie Althoff; David Chesworth; John Crawford; Dave & Phil Duo; Graeme Davis; Essendon Airport; IDA; Ron Nagarka; Plastic Platypus; David Tolley; Paul Turner; Chris Wyatt

12/'81: *NEW MUSIC, 1980* LP (Innocent), incl. Ad Hoc; Warren Burt; David Chesworth; Dave & Phil Duo; Essendon Airport; KGB; Laughing Hands; LIME; Lunatic Fringe; Mere C Pollard; Threeo; Chris Wyatt

1981: *ONE STOP SHOPPING*, triple cassette (Terse 9), incl. Agent Orange; Alan Bamford Experience; Ernie Althoff; Art Throbs; Bathroom Beans; Bleeding Arseholes; David Chesworth; Graeme Davis; Disneyland; East End Butchers; Essendon Airport; Electric Shock Treatment; Graeme Gerrard; Holiday Fun; Incredibly Strange Creatures Who Stopped Living And Became Mixed Up Zombies; Institute Of Dronal Anarchy; Invisible Boys; Invisible Music; 2 Johnnies; JP Sartre Band; Junk Logic; Klu; Laughing Hands; Lazlo Toth; Limp; Lunatic Fringe; Mesh; Mice Against God; Mindless Delta Children; Multiplicative Inverse; Music4; N-Lets; Negative Reaction; Nervous System; Oroton Boys; Painkillers; Pastel Bats; Persons Brothers; Pissy Relay Switches; Rhythmyx Chymx; Saxophone Caper; Scattered Order; Paul Schutze; Severed Heads; Shane Is Dead; Slugfuckers; Somersaulting Coincidences; Stuttgarters; Sunday Painters; Swinging Hogs; Sydney Quads; Systematics; Tame O'Mearas; Teese An Tattersall; Peter Thin; →↑←; Paul Turner; Use No Hooks; Wet Taxis; Wild West; ZGlutz; Zzzzzzzzz

1982: *PATHS OF PAIN TO JEWELS OF GLORY* LP (Phantom, PHANTOM 100). incl. Sunnyboys; Passengers; Shy Impostors; Surfside 6; Visitors; Flaming Hands; Machinations; Cockroaches; Kelpies; Hoodoo Gurus; Dagoes

1982: *NO SIN LIKE DANCING* LP (Slow Drama), incl. Alan Bamford Musical Experience; Kim Beissel; Boswell/Boyce/Beissel; Hoy Family Swingers; Incredibly Strange Creatives...; Irreplaceables; J.P. Sartre Band; Junk Logic; Klu; Leapfrogs; Lunatic Fringe; Marcus & Frank; Oroton Bags; Pink Bats; Primitive Calculators; Somersaulting Consciences; Soporifics; Stick To Your Guns; Stuttgarters; Thrush & the Cunts; Use No Hooks

1982: *AFTER THE BALL*, cassette (Cleopatra), incl. Game; Ears; Go Guys; Kaos; Dresden War Crimes

1982: *WILL IT NEVER END?* cassette, (Rampant, RR003), incl. GlamStars; Dee Rays; Kaos

1982: *MELBOURNE SAMPLER #1*, cassette (Rampant, RR004), incl. Scrap Museum; Curse; Fungus Brains; Wild Dog Rodeo; Teen Beat; David Chesworth; Second Glance; People with Chairs Up Their Noses; GlamStars; Temple Dance; Maverick's Blood; Sing Sing; New Five; Mother's Nightmare; Tester Housing; Flying Zulus; Impossibles

3/'83: *CASTRAK*, cassette (released with *Ratsack* #3), incl. Other Voices; Xero; Dumbshow; My Three Sons; Tex Deadly and the Dum-Dums; Pork; Dobie Gillis Experience; JFK and the Cuban Crisis

1983: *FLOWERS FROM THE DUSTBIN* LP (Aberrant 1), incl. Kelpies; Positive Hatred; Queen Anne's Revenge; WWXXIV; Vellocette; Box Of Fish; What?!!

10/'83: *LIVE AT THE WIRELESS* LP (2JJJ, L38084), incl. Private Lives; Particles; Samuri Trash; Go-Betweens; Triffids; Second Language; Do-Re-Mi; DropBears; Soggy Porridge; Hoodoo Gurus; Idiom Flesh

1983: *RARE TRAX FROM THE ARCHIVES*, cassette (Missing Link), incl. Birthday Party; Go-Betweens; Riptides; Ears; News; International Exiles; Torn Ox Bodies; Peter Lillie

6/'84: *DISTANT VIOLINS CASSETTE #1*, cassette released with *Distant Violins* #12, incl. Tiny Town; Triffids; Great Unwashed; Pictish Blood; Particles; Frontier Scouts; Damn Heck; These Future Kings; Newie

1984: *SOUND OF SYDNEY, VOLUME 2* LP (Method, L38263), incl. Rigid With Desire; Snorkels; Leftovers; Johnnys; Fiction Romance; Trench Gashes; Hoi Polloi; Jaguars; Skolars; Soggy Porridge

1984: *ON THE WATERFRONT* EP (Waterfront, DAMP4), incl. Particles, JFK and the Cuban Crisis, Ups & Downs, Lonely Hearts

1984: *EAT YOUR HEAD* 2x12" (Greville, GR-4), incl. Civil Dissident, Vicious Circle, Murder Murder Suicide, End Result, Scum, Royal Flush, I Spit On Your Gravy, Charred Remains, Bodies, Permanent Damage, Mad Flowers

1984: *NOT SO HUMDRUM* LP (Aberrant 2), incl. Rocks; Suicide Squad; Exserts; Vigil-Anti; Happy Hate Me Nots; Wrong Kind Of Stoneage; Itchy Rat

1984: *ASLEEP AT THE WHEEL* LP (AuGoGo, ANDA33), incl. Huxton Creepers; Corpse Grinders; Painters & Dockers; Crushed Buzzards; Lynching Party; Feral Dinosaurs; Tombstone Hands; Harem Scarem; Spring Plains; Olympic Sideburns; Andy Caltex; Bum Steers

1984: *STRAWBERRY HILLS BAND COMPETITION* LP (Green, SHRON1), incl. Temper Temper; Tu Lassoo; Vagary; Zulu Rattle; Leaping fences; Trench Gashes; Bally Train; Passing Strangers

1984: *THIS IS HOT* LP (Hot, WORRIED1), incl. Gondwanaland Project; Angie Pepper; Celibate Rifles; Tuff Monks; Screaming Believers; Triffids; Birthday Party; Soggy Porridge; Plays With Marionettes; Lighthouse Keepers; Bring Philip; Screaming Tribesmen; Scientists; Laughing Clowns

1984: *QUEENSLAND IN QUARANTINE*, cassette, incl. Pork; Dance Theatre; Ups & Downs; Tim Gruchy; Eugene and the Egg; Gatekeepers; Lovs e Blur; This 5 Minutes; Presidents 11; Tangled Shoelaces; Matt Mawson; Pictish Blood; Different Cartoons; Linda & Harley; Colours; Furious Turtles; Vacant Rooms; Strange Glory; Tiny Town; Persia; Sister Christmas; Suzette

1984: *LEAVING HOME FOR A PARTY ON THE ROOF*, cassette, incl. Gatekeepers; Dog-E-Style; Tex Deadly and the Dum-Dums; Crib Sex; Kicks; Tapeloops; Pits; Runabella; Roger T. Band; Pictish Blood; Xero; Pork; Infidels; I; New Improved Testament; Tony

5/'85: *TROUSERS IN ACTION* EP (Aberrant, ACT1), incl. Positive Hatred; Suicide Squad; Box Of Fish; Vigil-Anti-Mitchell Gang

1985: *ON THE WATERFRONT VOL. 2* EP (Waterfront, DAMP21), incl. Eastern Dark, Happy Hate Me Nots, Itchy Rat, Tactics

1985: *AT THE FUHRER'S REQUEST* LP (Rubber, RR01), incl. Leftovers; Just Urbain; Public Execution; Mystery Of Sixes; Young Identities; Kicks; Razar; Vampire Lovers; Strange Glory; Vacant Rooms; Dementia 13; End

BIBLIOGRAPHY

***ROLLING STONE*,** Sydney-based national monthly, 1972–

***RAM*,** Sydney-based national fortnightly, 1974–

***PLASTERED PRESS*,** Melbourne fanzine, 1 issue, 1977

***SUICIDE ALLEY*,** Brisbane fanzine, 1 issue, 1977

***PULP*,** Melbourne/Brisbane fanzine, 4 issues, 1977

***SPURT*,** Sydney fanzine, 7 issues, 1977-79

***ALIVE 'N' PUMPING*,** Melbourne fanzine, 1 issue, 1977

***THE RAT*,** Brisbane fanzine, 3 issues, 1977-78

***SELF-ABUSE*,** Sydney fanzine, 3 issues, 1977-78

***REMOTE CONTROL*,** Perth fanzine, 1 issue, 1977

***STREET FEVER*,** Adelaide fanzine, 1 issue, 1977

***AUTOPSY*,** Sydney fanzine, 1978

***ROADRUNNER*,** Adelaide-based national monthly, 1978–1982

***CHOKE*,** Sydney fanzine, 3 issues, 1979

***ROAD TRAFFIC CONTROL*,** Adelaide fanzine, 2 issues, 1979–80

***D.N.A.*,** Adelaide fanzine, 1979 onwards...

***NICE IMAGES*,** Brisbane fanzine, 2 issues, 1979

***ATTACK*,** Adelaide fanzine, 2 issues, 1979-80

***AUSTRALIAN 'NEW WAVE' FAMILY TREE*,** poster drawn by Clinton Walker, 1980

***THE NORTH FITZROY BEAT*,** Melbourne paper, one-off, 1980

***NEW MUSIC*,** Melbourne zine, 1980-81

***PANIC*,** Adelaide fanzine, 5 issues, 1980

***BACKSTAGE*,** Brisbane magazine, 3 issues, 1980

***RIPCHORD*,** Canberra magazine, 3 issues, 1980

***THE NEW MUSIC*,** book by Stuart Coupe and Glenn A. Baker (Bay Books, 1980)

***SMASH IT UP*,** Adelaide fanzine, 3 issues to 1981

***X-CHANGE*,** Brisbane fanzine, 3 issues to 1981

***WOMBAT TURD*,** Adelaide fanzine, 1981–

***VOX*,** Melbourne-based national monthly, 1981–1982

***STEREOTYPED*,** Adelaide fanzine, 1981

***ARCHANGEL*,** Adelaide fanzine, 4 issues, 1981

***FAST FORWARD*,** Melbourne-based cassette magazine, bi-monthly, 1980–1983

***ON THE STREET*,** Sydney free street paper, 1981 onwards...

***VIRGIN PRESS*,** Melbourne-based national magazine, 21 issues, 1981–1983

***DISTANT VIOLINS*,** Melbourne fanzine, 1982–

***THE NEW ROCK 'N' ROLL*,** book by Stuart Coupe and Glenn A. Baker (Omnibus, 1983)

***B-SIDE*,** Sydney fanzine, 1983–

***TENSION*,** Melbourne-based national magazine, 1983–

***TROUSERS IN ACTION*,** Sydney fanzine, 1983–

***REGRESSION*,** Melbourne fanzine, 1983–1984

***STILETTO*,** Sydney-based national bi-monthly, 1983–

***STUFF*,** Melbourne journal, 5 issues in 1983

***MADE BY →↑←, 1977-1982*,** book by →↑← (1983)

***THE NEXT THING*,** book edited by Clinton Walker (Kangaroo Press, Sydney, 1984)

***BIG AUSTRALIAN ROCK BOOK*,** edited by Ed St. John (Megabooks, Sydney, 1985)

INDEX

Crowd scene, SIDE FX, Darlinghurst
1980 (Pic: Peter Nelson)